Visions of Presence in Modern American Poetry

NATHAN A. SCOTT, JR.

Visions of Presence in Modern American Poetry

The Johns Hopkins University Press

Baltimore and London

© 1993 The Johns Hopkins University Press
All rights reserved
Printed in the United States of America on acid-free paper

The Johns Hopkins University Press
2715 North Charles Street
Baltimore, Maryland 21218-4319
The Johns Hopkins Press Ltd., London

Library of Congress Cataloging-in-Publication Data
Scott, Nathan A.
Visions of presence in modern American poetry / Nathan A. Scott.
p.   cm.
Includes bibliographical references and index.
ISBN 0-8018-4537-8
1. American poetry—20th century—History and criticism.
I. Title.
PS323.5.S34   1993
811'.509—dc20   92-27648

A catalog record for this book is available
from the British Library

TO MY GRANDCHILDREN

Nathan A. Scott IV and Douglas Robert Scott

AND

Priscilla, Charlotte, Emmanuel,
and Elizabeth Ashamu

CONTENTS

Visions of Presence in Modern American Poetry

CHAPTER ONE

Introduction

The current tendency in the academy is to view *presence* as a superstitious illusion. As the lesson is laid down by one line of argument, none of our *signifiers* actually delivers a *signified*, because to turn to a dictionary for the meaning of any particular signifier is only to be referred to alternative signifiers. And, when the meanings of these are in turn checked, we find ourselves again confronted with still other signifiers, and so on ad infinitum. All our signifiers merely bear upon themselves the traces of other signifiers—and thus the very distinction between *le signifiant* and *le signifié* proves in the end to be an utter delusion. For what we dwell amidst is the unending *jeu* (play) of significations whose meanings are always deferred into an ever more distant future. In this version of things, there is nothing at all that can be counted on to "center" language, to limit the "free-play" of the significatory process, or to establish stable referents outside language for spoken and written utterance. Nowhere, in short, is it possible within the terms of this scheme of thought to locate any kind of "presence," any kind of being or reality which is outside the play of signification and on which our thought and language might be taken to be grounded, for outside language there is only *le néant*—which, as Jacques Derrida would warn, is not itself to be taken as presenting any sort of alternative ontological principle, because nothing is, quite simply, nothing.

George Steiner is, of course, doubtless right in suggesting that, *"on its own terms and planes of argument,"* deconstructionist ideology may well be irrefutable,[1] and I have no interest in presenting still another exposition of it for the sake of a polemical purpose, because its real refutation will be found not in some pirouette of dialectic but in the kind of testimony that is offered by autobiography and prose fiction and, most especially, by poetry.

A generation ago (1958) the American philosopher Henry G. Bugbee published a most remarkable book, *The Inward Morning*, which, though it was reissued in 1976, still remains largely (and strangely) unknown. It presents in the form of a daily philosophical journal the record of an exacting project of meditation extending from 26 August 1952 to 5 November 1953, and in the entry for 27 August 1953 he says: "In our experience of things as presences, reality conveys itself and permeates us as a closed electrical circuit in which we are involved with things."[2] Then in the entry for the following day he returns to this theme and says:

> The phenomenological image of the closed circuit is misleading if it tempts us to assign priority to a dead circuit, to be characterized from a standpoint outside of the energized circuit. The closed circuit is meant as ultimate. . . . The subject-object distinction converts the genuine mutual independence of self and other *in the closed circuit* into the separateness of dead poles. Self and other become merely objects for thought, and experience is regarded as something that happens to a subject conditioned in its relation to other objects. To think experientially is to partake in thought of the closed circuit of reality, in which we live and move and have our being.[3]

Now it is precisely "the closed circuit" embracing both "self and other" in which the poetic imagination finds its main ballast. Initially, it has as its most immediate end nothing more ambitious than a vivid realization of what Gerard Manley Hopkins called the "inscape" of things. By this term that he coined, Hopkins meant, it would seem, to indicate not merely an outer reality, not something automatically and inescapably present, but something to be discovered only by a seeing-*into*, by a strict and loving attention to the radical actuality of the things of earth. And this is indeed the end toward which all the rhetoric and dramatic gesture of poetic art are devoted: the whole object of the poet's enterprise is to apprehend and to disclose "the character of particular things in the starkness and strangeness of their being what they are."[4] The poetic world is rooted in the concrete particularity of lived experience; and poetic art, in its deepest aspect, is a way of loving the concrete, the particular, the individual. But, of course, to love is to enter the dimension of what the French Catholic philosopher Gabriel Marcel called *presence:* it is to approach a given reality out of a sense of its having the character of a *Thou*, whether that reality be "Fountains, Meadows, Hills, and Groves" or some "Attic shape . . . with brede / Of marble men and maidens overwrought" or a father who "moved through dooms of love." The intensity of its love for the quiddities and haecceities of experience conditions the poetic imagination, in other words, to view whatever it contemplates as ignited by the capacity for exchange, for reciprocity: it has the dimension of presence.

And, having the dimension of presence, things exist always for the poetic imagination in relationship: the world is a body wherein all things are "members one of another." As Coleridge reminded us in the *Biographia Literaria*, the poet does not characteristically view the things of earth as "essentially fixed and dead" but as "essentially vital": and it would appear that, in his stress on the vital quality of poetic experience, he was intending to speak of the poet's habit of confronting concrete particulars with such intensity that their significances are beheld as flowing from relations in which they stand to still other things consubstantial with themselves. As he says in chapter 14 of the *Biographia*, the poet "diffuses a tone and spirit of unity, that blends, and (as it were) *fuses*, each into each, by that synthetic and magical power, to which we have exclusively appropriated the name of imagination."

Here, for example, is the illustrative instance that Wordsworth offers in the preface to the 1815 edition of his verse. He first quotes from his poem "Resolution and Independence" the following passage:

> As a huge stone sometimes is seen to lie
> Couched on the bald top of an eminence,
> Wonder to all who do the same espy
> By what means it could thither come, and whence,
> So that it seems a thing endued with sense,
> Like a sea-beast crawled forth, which on a shelf
> Of rock or sand reposeth, there to sun himself.
> Such seemed this Man; not all alive or dead,
> Nor all asleep, in his extreme old age.

Then he says:

> In these images, the conferring, the abstracting and the modifying powers of the imagination immediately and mediately acting are all brought into conjunction. The stone is endowed with something of the power of life to approximate it to the sea-beast; and the sea-beast stripped of some of its vital qualities to assimilate it to the stone; which intermediate image is thus treated for the purpose of bringing the original image, that of the stone, to a nearer resemblance to the figure and condition of the aged man; who is divested of so much of the indications of life and motion as to bring him to the point where the two objects unite and coalesce in just comparison.[5]

It is precisely such a coalescence as this within reality which is indeed a chief feature of the world when it is beheld in the terms of poetic vision. True, it is nothing larger than a certain concrete particular that commands upon itself an act of attention, but so intensely, then, is it contemplated that it takes on the luster of a "something more." Wordsworth confronts a decrepit old man with such intensity that he finds himself confronting in the same moment a huge stone "couched on the bald top of an eminence" and a sea-beast "crawled forth to sun himself"—and the stone and the sea-beast and the old man are all one: they unite and coalesce in just comparison. And this is a part of the mystery of *poiesis*, that, when the concrete individual is faced with great intensity, "without losing any of its bright actuality, [it] tends also to be, or at least to suggest overtones of, something more."[6] Taking possession of the world in this way is, of course, very largely dependent on metaphoric modes of apprehension, and the test of a good metaphor is just its capacity to produce coalescence of the heterogeneities of experience and thus to evoke in us awareness of "the flowing wholeness of things"[7] and of what Wordsworth called "unknown modes of being."

It is, indeed, a part of the enduring greatness of Wordsworth that through the arguments of so much of his prose and poetry he succeeded in teaching the Romantic movement—and through it all the modern generations—to see the kind of attestation which poetic experience makes to an infinitude beyond "the light of sense." For what he noticed, with a singular sensitivity and perceptiveness, is that, in finding all the concrete realities of experience to point beyond themselves, the poetic imagination is restlessly driven from "the visionary dreariness" of earth toward "unknown modes of being." The silent ways in which every particular thing, when deeply contemplated, attests to a something more, the fact that everything appears to stand on the threshold of something else—this, as Wordsworth perceived, awakens in us (as he says in book 2 of *The Prelude*) a profound

> sentiment of Being spread
> O'er all that moves and all that seemeth still
> O'er all that, lost beyond the reach of thought
> And human knowledge, to the human eye
> Invisible, yet liveth to the heart.

And it was in this sentiment of Being that he found "a never-failing principle of joy."

But the complete abrogation of meaning that is posited by deconstructionist ideology presents only the extreme instance of how utterly Being, as Heidegger would put it, has been "forgotten" in this late time at the end of the modern age. Remembering Gertrude Stein's sally about the city of Oakland ("There's no there there"), we might say indeed that so thoroughly has Being been forgotten that, no longer having a sense of there being any there, the reigning clerks in our phase of civility have quite lost the capacity for any simple intuition of Being: or, in Steiner's formulation, their confidence that there "is something *in* what we say"[8] has entirely collapsed.

Now in such a time of dearth, if a sense of presence, of some intimacy of relationship with reality, is to be restored to contemporary consciousness, the *retour* that is necessary will be a coming back to poetry. One of the lessons that Jacques Maritain never wearied of reiterating was that "poetry is ontology"[9]—by which, of course, he was not intending to suggest that the operation the poet performs is identical, in its kind or agency, with the operation performed by a metaphysician. For, unlike the philosopher, the poet does not usually deal with *generalizations* about anything at all: his mode of statement, as we say, is a "nondiscursive" mode. He does not discourse, for example, about the mortality of the human creature with the dull earnestness of a young parson: no, Shakespeare simply says:

> Golden lads and girls all must,
> As chimney-sweepers, come to dust.

Nor does he talk about the internal complications of the mind in the labored manner of the academic psychologist: no, Hopkins tells us:

> O the mind, mind has mountains; cliffs of fall
> Frightful, sheer, no-man-fathomed. Hold them cheap
> May who ne'er hung there. Nor does long our small
> Durance deal with that steep or deep.

The poet wants, in other words, to reveal the stark irrevocability of things as they are. As Hugh McCarron remarked long ago in his fine little book *Realization*, "the texture of poetry is of actual things."[10] Homer dealt with the ocean and Wordsworth with the farmland and Gerard Manley Hopkins with "the dearest freshness deep down things." And the poetic imagination is regularly captivated by things, by that which is *other than* the human mind. As H. D. Lewis said in his essay "On Poetic Truth," to which Wallace Stevens was greatly attracted, it is "the wonder and mystery of art" that it proffers "the revelation of something 'wholly other' by which the inexpressible loneliness of thinking is broken and enriched."[11] And it is in this sense that poetry may be said to be a kind of ontology: by making palpable to us the alterity that is ineluctably a part of all the things and creatures of earth, it brings a kind of *katharsis*, the kind of profound relief that is to be had when we succeed in gaining such release from the prison of the mind as enables us simply to contemplate the intractable givenness of the myriad realities that press in upon us.

Yet, though "Mont Blanc" and the *Duino Elegies* and "Little Gidding" speak of a world that moves (in M. Chaning-Pearce's phrase) to "a rhythm which is neither the strophe nor the antistrophe of our mortal music,"[12] "the truth of the independence of things should not," as Bugbee rightly warns,

> lead us to succumb to a sense of isolation and insularity among independent existents. . . . For concretely, experience of the presence of things is also complete intimacy with them, the opposite of estrangement from them and ourselves. The gift of things in their independence is also the gift of ourselves together with them. And here Marcel seems to me very clear and just right: In the experience of presence that estrangement between self and other, that tension between self and other, which supports the representation of the other as over against the self, that estrangement and that tension are dissolved. To be aware of the other as a presence in its independence is an experience of participation in reality with the other, and such experience concretely resists the reduction of the independence of the other [merely] to the terms of objectivity.[13]

I am indebted to my friend the late Philip Wheelwright for having brought to my attention many years ago a seventeenth-century Chinese treatise on the art of painting, *The Mustard Seed Garden Manual*,[14] which propounds a lesson not unlike Bugbee's. In this venerable handbook, the artist is advised so to compose his picture that, if, say, he is painting a man looking at a mountain, the man will appear bent in an attitude of homage and the mountain will itself appear slightly bent, in an attitude of acknowledgment. Or, if a lutist is playing his instrument under the moon, the painter is advised to make it appear that the lutist is listening to the moon and that the moon is listening to him. And the presupposition of this charming aesthetic is Bugbee's, that "we are monads haunted by communion,"[15] that we stand in a relation of reciprocity with the world, and that things will not take on the glow and splendor of presence until, refusing to be put off by their "in-itselfness," we approach them in a spirit of solicitousness and *cortesia*.

All things, of course, remain "silent" for as long as they are approached merely as things to be "attacked" in the manner of a technological project, and, as Martin Heidegger often argued in the later phase of his career, they do not begin to "hail" us, to "salute" us, until they themselves are first "hailed." What is required, as Heidegger urged, is that we undertake to learn the discipline of "letting be." "We usually talk of 'letting be,'" he says, "when . . . we stand off from some undertaking we have planned. 'We let it be' means: not touching it again, not having anything more to do with it. 'Letting be' here has the negative sense of disregarding something, renouncing something, of indifference and even neglect." But, as he insists, in his lexicon "the 'letting-be' of what-is . . . does not . . . refer to indifference and neglect, but to the very opposite of them,"[16] because to let what-is *be* what it is is to confront it with such a piety as entails a grateful acquiescence in that plenitude of reality to which the particular existent belongs. And, indeed, it is only when we have learned again the discipline of "letting-be" that we shall achieve that condition which he calls "releasement toward things,"[17] which is nothing other than an attitude of simple enthrallment before the various givens of the earth—in their dimension of *presence*. Then it is that "thinking thanks": *Das denken dankt*. Then it is—by way of "the letting-be of beings"—that we "pay heed to" and "hail" the concrete actualities of the world.

Heidegger, however, with a remarkable humility was careful to concede that philosophic inquiry may not, finally, be the most adequate way of probing the deep places of life. Indeed, the prospect of giving offense to his philosophic colleagues did not keep him from declaring that, before the truly elemental realities of existence, philosophy must at last give way to poetry. Or, as he says in the collection of his essays entitled *Holzwege (Paths in the Forest)*, any really fundamental or meditative act of thinking is *Dichten* (poetizing).[18] For *der Dichter* (the poet) is, in Heidegger's view, far more than *der Denker* (the thinker) an adept in the art of "paying heed" to the things of earth. True, the poet is also an adept in the art of supervising language, but his literary craftsmanship is wholly dedicated to the disclosure of the things and creatures of this world in their sheer specificity, "in the starkness and strangeness of their being what they are." And this is why he declared that "truth is at work"[19] in poetry: truth is at work because poetic art, by inviting an attitude of enthrallment before the various concrete givens that surround us, prepares us to be laid hold of by that wherewith these things are inwardly constituted and enabled to be what they are—which is none other than Being itself. It is, in short, the poetic imagination that so grasps and renders things as to convey to us the wondrous bouquet of presence. And, as evidence of this, I undertake in the following pages to exhibit the kind of recuperative percipience that may be offered by a line of modern American poetry to a time of dearth in which the idea of presence has been so greatly darkened that the very term is often by way of being converted into a simple pejorative.

In the preface to his little book *Three Philosophical Poets* (which was first published in 1910), Santayana says, in explaining why he selected his particular trio of Lucretius and Dante and Goethe: "My excuse for writing about them . . . is merely the human excuse which every new poet has for writing about the spring. They have attracted me; they have moved me to reflection; they have revealed to me certain aspects of nature and philosophy which I am prompted by mere sincerity to express, if anybody seems interested or willing to listen."[20] And it is such a testimony that I might also make. Beyond the writers whom I have chosen to discuss, I should like to have prepared for this book essays on Josephine Jacobsen and Robert Hayden, on May Swenson and Amy Clampitt, on Charles Wright and Rita Dove, on Michael Harper and still other American poets of the present and the recent past. But I could not venture to present anything even approaching so encyclopedic a conspectus as, say, the 1980 edition of Richard Howard's *Alone with America*, and thus I settled on the nine figures with whom over many years I have found myself most deeply involved. There may be some, of course, who will question the propriety of my taking Auden to be a part of the American canon, but to them I would simply reply that the accidents of history arranged a kind of swap between Great Britain and the United States that entailed Britain's getting Eliot and the States getting Auden—which would seem to have been a fair exchange; and the phase of Auden's career on which I concentrate is his late phase, which was indisputably an outcome of his long American residence.

And why is it that I scan only an American canon? If asked this question, my first instinct would be simply to say that its poetry is that with which I am most intimately familiar. But, were I to attempt a more measured response, it would involve little more than a careful rehearsal of the principal argument in the brilliant book published in 1965 by the English critic Tony Tanner, *The Reign of Wonder*, which contends that that "way of world-watching" which has chiefly distinguished the American imagination has consistently been an affair of *wonder* at the sheer "presence" of all the remarkable things one finds outside oneself, and of wonder at the "sort of lodgment and anchorage in the world"[21] that one discovers to be available. From Whitman to Gary Snyder and Robert Duncan, from Robert Frost and William Carlos Williams to William Meredith and Peter Davison, and from E. E. Cummings and Hart Crane to the generation of Brad Leithauser, the American poet more often than not has found the chief source of the sublime in the rich density of the quotidian and has felt there to be a sufficient affluence in the world at hand. So our native tradition tends predominantly to yield a poetry of presence that pronounces a severe word of judgment on the received wisdom of our period.

CHAPTER TWO

Wallace Stevens' Route—
Transcendence Downward

*W*e often suppose the name of the modern poet to be Orpheus, because in so many of his characteristic manifestations (from Novalis to Mallarmé and Valéry, and from Blake to Rilke and St.-John Perse) he takes it to be within the power of song to assemble, or reassemble, all the *disjecta membra* of the earth and to build a world that will suffice in a time of dearth. And, in the common view, it is Wallace Stevens, the invincible poet of the Supreme Fiction, who brings the whole Orphic venture to its point of culmination. So generous is the hospitality that this Connoisseur of Chaos offers to a wide variety of divergent perspectives and projects that one can, of course, find some basis in the poetry on which to ground any one of a dozen or so quite different views of his basic tendency. But, undoubtedly, the Stevens of *Harmonium* and *Ideas of Order*, of *The Man with the Blue Guitar* and *Parts of a World* and *Transport to Summer*, may be thought of as the last great heir of the ancient Thracian lyrist who, when he touched his frail golden lyre, brought, as it were, "the disparate halves / Of things [that] were waiting in a betrothal"[1] unto marriage.

The long meditation recorded by his poetry—the meditation extending, say, from "Sunday Morning" (1915) to the great work of his last years in *The Auroras of Autumn* (1950) and *The Rock* (1954)—is one whose enabling principle derives from a deep sense of ours being indeed a time of dearth, for this poet takes it for granted that we have seen "the gods dispelled in mid-air and dissolve like clouds"—"as if they had never inhabited the earth."[2] True, when he wrote these words, in the essay "Two or Three Ideas," he was speaking of "the ancient and the foreign gods" (*OP*, 259), but, as he says in one of his "Adagia," "The death of one god is the death of all" (*OP*, 191). And his recurrent testimony about collapse in the Courts of Heaven is most principally intended to make reference to the death of the *ens realissimum*, the *deus faber*, of old Christendom, for, in his sense of things, this divine Pantocrator, this immaterial Person behind the myriad phenomena of existence, has been so laid to rest that it is now only "the last fading smile of a cosmic Cheshire Cat."[3]

Like Nietzsche, whose influence may have been less marginal than is commonly supposed,[4] Stevens does not present any systematic argument in support of his conviction that God is dead: it is rather a matter to be reported simply as a datum of immediate experience, of the experience of one who is like "the listener, who listens in the snow, / And, nothing himself, beholds / Nothing that is not there and the nothing that is" (*CP*, 10). As he says in his "Conversation with Three Women of New England," "The author of man's canons is man, / Not some outer patron" (*OP*, 134). He conceives himself to dwell in an "island solitude, unsponsored." And this "introspective voyager" concludes, therefore, that something *else* "must take the place / Of empty heaven and its hymns" (*CP*, 167).

So, given the basic drift of Stevens' thought and feeling, the little tableau that we meet in his early masterpiece "Sunday Morning" is not at all surprising. As a certain lady one Sabbath morning sits on her sunny porch over her late coffee and oranges, it occurs to her to reflect on how the "pungent fruit" and the "comforts of the sun" and the green cockatoo that adorns her rug "mingle to dissipate / The holy hush of ancient sacrifice" (*CP*, 66–67). Indeed, she asks herself if these—the "pungent fruit and bright, green wings" and "any balm or beauty of the earth"—shall not be "all of paradise that we shall know":

> She says, "I am content when wakened birds,
> Before they fly, test the reality
> Of misty fields, by their sweet questionings;
> But when the birds are gone, and their warm fields
> Return no more, where, then, is paradise?"
> (*CP*, 68)

The Morning Office that she soliloquizes on this Lord's Day is, in other words, a thoroughly pagan rite. Yet, though the day is for her but a *dies solis*, she finds her reverie after breakfast taking her back "to silent Palestine, / Dominion of the blood and sepulchre." But, even so, "the measures destined for her soul" belong to the sensuous world of April's green and swallows' wings and misty fields, and the poem's conclusion is that the "tomb in Palestine" which formed "the grave of Jesus" has no claim upon us ("Why should she give her bounty to the dead?"), that

> We live in an old chaos of the sun,
> Or old dependency of day and night,
> Or island solitude, unsponsored.
>
> (*CP*, 70)

The "dark / Encroachment of that old catastrophe" (*CP*, 67)—presumably, the Passion of Christ—has quite lost its power to disturb: not only is old Jove of "inhuman birth" a god now dead, but also, because the death of one god is the death of all, the entire structure of the Christian *mythos* has given way as well, and thus at eventide, when "casual flocks of pigeons make / Ambiguous undulations as they sink, / Downward to darkness, on extended wings" (*CP*, 70), the heavens from which they descend are empty.

Now the poems by which "Sunday Morning" was surrounded in *Harmonium*, Stevens' book of 1923—such poems as "Le Monocle de Mon Oncle," "The Comedian as the Letter C," "Peter Quince at the Clavier," and "Sea Surface Full of Clouds"—have been much talked about in terms of the extravagant gaudiness of imagery and language which they present. But the elaborate dance that these poems perform round sun and moon and snails and pears and plums is calculated in part to say simply that this is all there is and that it is foolish, therefore, to "persist with anecdotal bliss / To make believe a starry *connaissance*" (*CP*, 13). Indeed, for all the carefully wrought felicities and gorgeous elegance of the poetry making up Stevens' first book, its general ethos is perhaps best instanced by the severe disenchantment of the rarely noticed poem "Palace of the Babies":

> The disbeliever walked the moonlit place,
> Outside of gates of hammered serafin,
> Observing the moon-blotches on the walls.
>
> The yellow rocked across the still façades,
> Or else sat spinning on the pinnacles,
> While he imagined humming sounds and sleep.
>
> The walker in the moonlight walked alone,
> And each blank window of the building balked
> His loneliness and what was in his mind:
>
> If in a shimmering room the babies came,
> Drawn close by dreams of fledgling wing,
> It was because night nursed them in its fold.

Night nursed not him in whose dark mind
The clambering wings of birds of black revolved,
Making harsh tirment of the solitude.

The walker in the moonlight walked alone,
And in his heart his disbelief lay cold.
His broad-brimmed hat came close upon his eyes.
(CP, 77)

But, now, if the whole structure of the *philosophia perennis* and the Christian system has dropped away, what, then, remains for this walker in the moonlight whose solitude makes a harsh torment? The answer that Stevens was to give to this question is, of course, already being hinted at in one of the most famous poems in *Harmonium*, "Anecdote of the Jar":

I placed a jar in Tennessee,
And round it was, upon a hill.
It made the slovenly wilderness
Surround that hill.

The wilderness rose up to it,
And sprawled around, no longer wild.
The jar was round upon the ground
And tall and of a port in air.

It took dominion everywhere.
(CP, 76)

As it stands here amidst this desolate Tennessee landscape, the jar proves itself capable of ordering and subduing its slovenly environment simply by dint of its nature as a work of artifice, for, as such, it substantializes a form round which the formlessness of this wilderness can assemble itself into a scene less formless than that which would appear were the jar not there. The jar is an emblem of the imagination and of its power to take dominion of the world. And it was just in this capacity of the imagination to create out of the sheer fecundity of its own inventiveness new patterns of order that Stevens found a sovereign principle for reckoning with a world from which the gods have been dispelled. As he says in one of the "Adagia," "in the absence of a belief in God, the mind turns to its own creations and examines them . . . for what they reveal, for what they validate and invalidate, for the support that they give" (OP, 186).

Nowhere perhaps does Stevens more beautifully evoke the transforming and creative power of the imagination than in his book of 1935, *Ideas of Order*, in the great poem "The Idea of Order at Key West," where we meet a girl singing by the sea:

It may be that in all her phrases stirred
The grinding water and the gasping wind;
But it was she and not the sea we heard.

For she was the maker of the song she sang.
. . . .
She was the single artificer of the world
In which she sang. And when she sang, the sea,
Whatever self it had, became the self
That was her song, for she was the maker. Then we,
As we beheld her striding there alone,
Knew that there never was a world for her
Except the one she sang and, singing, made.
. . . .
Oh! Blessed rage for order . . .
(CP, 129–30)

And the triumphalist imperialism that belongs to the "doctrine" of the imagination expressed in the Key West poem is being sounded again and again in many of Stevens' most frequently cited poems—in, for example, "Tea at the Palaz of Hoon," "To the One of Fictive Music," and "Sea Surface Full of Clouds" in *Harmonium*, in many of the poems in *Ideas of Order*, in "The Man with the Blue Guitar" (1937), in "Connoisseur of Chaos" and "Of Modern Poetry" and "Mrs. Alfred Uruguay" in *Parts of a World* (1942), and, of course, in "Notes toward a Supreme Fiction," which was written in the first months of 1942 and which presents his fullest statement in this vein. Moreover, many of the essays gathered in *The Necessary Angel* and in Milton J. Bates's edition of the *Opus Posthumous* are also striking that Coleridgean note which figures so prominently in Stevens' testimony, that it is the imagination which "struggles to idealize and to unify" and that it is "essentially *vital*, even as all objects (*as* objects) are essentially fixed and dead."[5] Indeed, says the poet of "Final Soliloquy of the Interior Paramour," "The world imagined is the ultimate good":

We say God and the imagination are one . . .
How high that highest candle lights the dark.

Out of this same light, out of the central mind,
We make a dwelling in the evening air,
In which being there together is enough.
(CP, 524)

But not even in the world as it is *post mortem Dei* may the imagination arrogate to itself any sort of absolute autonomy, for, unless it holds itself accountable to what Stevens calls "reality," it will inevitably come to represent a principle of frivolity, of caprice, of irresponsible vagary. And Stevens' "reality" in much of the work of his early and middle period is essentially the universe being plotted in Santayana's *Scepticism and Animal Faith* and *Realms of Being*. The aboriginal otherness that the imagination faces is simply the order of nature, what Santayana called "the realm of matter"; and it often appears to Stevens to be something as opaque and impenetrable as it seemed from Santayana's standpoint.

The imagination—which is, says Stevens, his term for "the sum of our faculties"[6]—wants to "step barefoot into reality" (*CP*, 423), but reality proves to be our "inescapable and ever-present difficulty and inamorata" (*OP*, 256). The poet—"meaning by the poet," he says, "any man of imagination"[7]—hopes to find ways of so taking hold of the world that we may find ourselves "Within the very object that we seek, / Participants of its being" (*CP*, 463). But the things and creatures of earth are fugitive and evanescent, as we are being reminded, for example, in one of his early poems, "Earthy Anecdote," where a little tale is told about a herd of bucks clattering across an Oklahoma landscape while being chased by something called a firecat—presumably, the poem's emblem of the imagination. The bucks—Stevens' image of things "earthy"—swerve in "a swift, circular line / To the right," or they swerve in "a swift, circular line / To the left" (*CP*, 3), depending on the direction in which they are prodded by the bristling firecat, but their galloping does not cease. At last, says the "Anecdote," the firecat closes his bright eyes and goes to sleep, and the poem invites us to suppose that the bucks continue on in their headlong, clattering flight across the plains: the firecat's rage for order notwithstanding, they cannot be stilled, in the way that the flux of existence must somehow be arrested if the imagination is to win that immediacy of contact with reality for which it yearns. "The squirming facts exceed the squamous mind" (*CP*, 215), as many of his focal poems are often remarking with dismay.

But the facts surpass the grasping power of the imagination not only because of the restless dynamism that keeps reality forever in transit, forever in motion. As the poem "Someone Puts a Pineapple Together" (*NA*, 83–87) poignantly reminds us, their elusiveness is also occasioned by "the irreducible X" (*NA*, 83) in the *Ding an sich*, which remains forever hidden: the absolute noumenality of things is not endowed with a candor that permits any sort of easy apprehension of "The angel at the center of the rind" (*NA*, 83), when we confront a pineapple on a table.

The poet wants, of course, to render things in their pristine transparency, and this, says Stevens, must involve a certain process of "decreation" (*NA*, 174–75). The term is one that he borrows from Simone Weil, who says that decreation is "to make something created pass into the uncreated."[8] And her point is that "decreation" defines the discipline whereby the creature nullifies itself in order that it may enter into the eternal life offered by the divine Creator. But Stevens appropriates the term for his own purposes and makes it stand for that whole effort to "see the very thing and nothing else," and to "see it with the hottest fire of sight." "Burn everything not part of it to ash" (CP, 373), he says. Or, as he phrases it in another formulation, you must

> Throw away the lights, the definitions,
> And say of what you see in the dark

> That it is this or that it is that,
> But do not use the rotted names.
> (CP, 183)

And the process whereby we dispose of "the rotted names" in order to reach things in their "pure reality, untouched / By trope or deviation" (CP, 471), he calls "decreation."

The counsel being offered to a young poet ("ephebe") in the opening lines of "Notes toward a Supreme Fiction" suggests something of what Stevens takes the discipline of decreation to entail. In the headnote presiding over the first section of the tripartite structure of the poem he states that *"It Must Be Abstract."* And then he says:

> Begin, ephebe, by perceiving the idea
> Of this invention, this invented world,
> The inconceivable idea of the sun.

> You must become an ignorant man again
> And see the sun again with an ignorant eye
> And see it clearly in the idea of it.
> (CP, 380)

Now Stevens' language here is curious indeed, for one might well suppose that, if the young poet is really to see the sun, he would want to concentrate his attention not on the "idea of the sun," not on any sort of "abstraction," but on the sun itself. And the inattentive reader of the poem might well conclude with the English critic A. Alvarez that Stevens' "method is the exact reverse of the slogan William Carlos Williams uses in his epic *Paterson*," that "instead of Williams' axiom, 'No ideas but in things,' Stevens . . . [is proposing] 'No things but in ideas.' "[9] But so to interpret his meaning is quite radically to misinterpret it. As Joseph Riddel wisely says in this connection, "there are abstractions and abstractions":[10] some are different from others—and, for Stevens, the abstractive process involves not the contraction of reality into some notional, theoretic construct but, rather, its disimprisonment from within all such constructs. The poet must abstract the sun from all the old "rotten names" for the sun, from all the old mythologies of the sun, from all the clichés of science and religion: from all this the sun must be "abstracted," if it is to be simply beheld in its naked celestial glory. And then, as Stevens wants to say, when it is so beheld, it will be seen "in the idea of it"—not, that is, in the Platonic sense of idea as general or ideal form but in the archaic sense of the term as (in the O.E.D.'s definition) "the original of which something else is a copy." As he once remarked in a letter (28 October 1942) to his friend Henry Church, "If you take the varnish and dirt of generations off a picture, you see it in its first idea. If you think about the world without its varnish and dirt, you are a thinker of the first idea."[11] And it is such a thinker that he would have a young poet aim to be, for, thinking in this way, he will be able to do what it is the poet's principal obligation to do: he will perform the act of decreation, facing *this* or *that* in its "first idea," everything else having been burned to ash.

Yet Stevens finds it difficult to rest even in the "idea" of the sun, and it sometimes appears that his sense of the "idea," of what Henry James called the "direct impression," is of something not much different from Santayana's "essence." For Santayana, of course, the great world by which we are surrounded, a world of a well-nigh infinite variety of things and creatures, must simply be *postulated* as a matter of "animal faith," because, Lockean that he was, he could not be persuaded that, given the ultimate inaccessibility of this world in its primitive quiddity, we have actually at hand anything more than *our* apprehensions of things—which cannot in the nature of the case be in any way absolutely authenticated as to their factuality. And these apprehensions he called "essences." Essences do not "exist": they in their totality are what the mind, after its encounter with "matter," *posits*, as a kind of rough chart or map of the world—which, happily, turns out generally to afford a reliable basis for the conduct of life.

Strictly considered, the essence is only a postulate of the imagination, as it reaches out toward "the realm of matter," and Santayana envisages no possibility of our transcending what the phenomenologists call the dimension of "intentionality." Which would seem the kind of impasse that occasions in Stevens a very profound disquiet. For his "idea" strikes him often as being nothing other than what Santayana took his "essence" to be: it is simply *our* apprehension of this and that, so that the disillusion of that agnostic "walker in the moonlight ("Palace of the Babies") appears only

the last illusion,
Reality as a thing seen by the mind,

Not that which is but that which is apprehended,
A mirror, a lake of reflections in a room,
A glassy ocean lying at the door.
(*CP*, 468)

In short, as he is so to be found remarking again and again, we seem tragically fated to fail in our effort to grasp "Not the symbol but that for which the symbol stands, / The vivid thing in the air that never changes, / Though the air change" (*CP*, 238).

Indeed, the encystment of the mind within its own concepts and categories does at times appear so unbreakable that Stevens is occasionally, as it would seem, at the point of regarding "reality" as but an epiphenomenon of the mind itself—as when, for example, he tells us that the imagination is "the one reality / In this imagined world" (*CP*, 25). As he says in one of the "Adagia," "There is nothing in life except what one thinks of it" (*OP*, 188), and the kind of primitive idealism expressed in this word forms a note that he recurrently strikes. "We live in the mind" (*OP*, 190—and thus the world that is built by the imagination is "indistinguishable from the world in which we live, or," as he says he ought to put it, "from the world in which we shall come to live, since what makes the poet the potent figure that he is . . . is that he creates the world to which we turn incessantly and without knowing it and that he gives to life the supreme fictions without which we are unable to conceive of it" (*NA*, 31). "Reality . . . [is] a thing seen by the mind, / Not that which is but that which is apprehended" (*CP*, 468)—and so on and so on. "Imagination is the only genius" (*OP*, 204).

But the fullest weight of Stevens' testimony inescapably conveys the impression that his most central and *final* sense of things is not of our being locked up within our own brainpan but of the mind's having to confront and reckon with that which is *totaliter aliter*, which is wholly other, than itself. As he said in a letter to Bernard Heringman (20 March 1951), "Sometimes I believe most in the imagination for a long time and then, without reasoning about it, turn to reality and believe in that and that alone. But both of these things project themselves endlessly and I want them to do just that" (*L*, 710). And, in the end, he seems never to be able quite to persuade himself that "the mind in the act of finding / What will suffice" (*CP*, 239) need only explore its own interiority, because "the imagination [always finds itself] pressing back against the pressure of reality" (*NA*, 36). In, for example, the late poem "Saint John and the

Back-Ache," the Back-Ache's contention that "The mind is the terriblest force in the world" prompts in Saint John a riposte that is brief and brusque: "The world is presence . . . / Presence is not mind" (*CP*, 436). So, veiled though the essential nature of things seems to be, Stevens, like Santayana, nevertheless stubbornly posits—by something like a kind of "animal faith"—the eternal perdurance of the rock of reality. It is

> The starting point of the human and the end,
> That in which space itself is contained, the gate
> To the enclosure, day, the things illumined
>
> By day, night and that which night illumines,
> Night and its midnight-minting fragrances. . . .
>   (*CP*, 528)

"The real will from its crude compoundings come," however, only as we "hear / The luminous melody of proper sound" (*CP*, 404): "man is the intelligence of his soil" (*CP*, 27), and reality "untuned by the imagination is not enough: the green day must be played by a blue guitar."[12] True, "'Things as they are / Are changed upon the blue guitar.'" Yet they must not be so changed that, finally, the musician (or the poet) fails to play "'A tune upon the blue guitar / Of things exactly as they are'" (*CP*, 165).

Stevens desires a constant commerce between the imagination and reality. But he does not expect this to be anything swift and easy, given that tragic principle deeply inwrought into the nature of things which is an affair of nothing less than a fundamental "maladjustment between the imagination and reality" (*NA*, 33). He often wants to think of "the imagination and reality as equals" (*NA*, 27), but the mind in its search for the real finds itself over and again frustrated by a strange perversity in things that leads them to withdraw so deeply into their own otherness as to make the bridging of the chasm between them and the human spirit appear something that "could occupy a school of rabbis for the next few generations" (*L*, 435). Reality confers no cheap grace, and so elusive, so inaccessible indeed, does it prove to be that Stevens concludes at last that the rigors of the quest for "what will suffice" can be borne only by him whom in "Notes toward a Supreme Fiction" he calls "major man."

The major man is a "figure of capable imagination" (*CP*, 249), one

> who has had the time to think enough,
> The central man, the human globe, responsive
> As a mirror with a voice, the man of glass
> Who in a million diamonds sums us up.

> He is the transparence of the place in which
> He is and in his poems we find peace.
>
> (*CP*, 250–51)

As we are told in canto 9 of "Examination of the Hero in a Time of War," the central man or the major man

> seems
> To stand taller than a person stands, has
> A wider brow, large and less human
> Eyes and bruted ears: the man-like body
> Of a primitive. He walks with a defter
> And lither stride. His arms are heavy
> And his breast is greatness. All his speeches
> Are prodigies in longer phrases.
> His thoughts begotten at clear sources,
> Apparently in air, fall from him
> Like chantering from an abundant
> Poet, as if he thought gladly, being
> Compelled thereto by an innate music.
>
> (*CP*, 277)

It is

> As if, as if, as if the disparate halves
> Of things were waiting in a betrothal known
> To none, awaiting espousal to the sound
>
> Of right joining, a music of ideas, the burning
> And breeding and bearing birth of harmony,
> The final relation, the marriage of the rest.
>
> (*CP*, 464–65)

And the major man is the priest who solemnizes this marriage, who brings to pass this mysterious conjunction of reality and the imagination.

Yet, though he seems to stand taller than most of us, the major man is not to be regarded as any *simple* analogue of Nietzsche's *Übermensch*, for, as Stevens says in canto 5 of the "Examination,"

> The common man is the common hero.
> The common hero is the hero.
>
> (*CP*, 275)

This is to say that the central man is not a "heroic" figure. He is "Without panache, without cockade": he is "With all his attributes no god but man"

(*CP,* 185–86), one indeed who in his external ordinariness is something like Kierkegaard's "knight of faith"—a chap who of a given afternoon

> may be seated in
> A café. There may be a dish of country cheese
> And a pineapple on the table. It must be so.
> (*CP,* 335)

Major men, in other words, are not world-historical figures who alter the course of the kinds of events reported in our daily newspapers: the central man is, rather,

> The pensive man . . . He sees that eagle float
> For which the intricate Alps are a single nest.
> (*CP,* 216)

His pensiveness, to be sure, is, paradoxically, a kind of ignorance, for he knows that, in order to see the sun "in the idea of it,"

> You must become an ignorant man again
> And see the sun again with an ignorant eye.
> (*CP,* 380)

The special kind of ignorance he cultivates is not that of the "anti-master-man, [the] floribund ascetic," who (as Stevens says in "Landscape with Boat") would reach the center of reality by brushing away the thunder and the clouds, "by rejecting what he saw / And denying what he heard," by choosing

> not to live, to walk in the dark,
> To be projected by one void into
> Another.
> (*CP,* 242)

No, the major man knows that all the things of earth may be parts of "the heraldic center of the world" (*CP,* 172)—

> the irregular turquoise, part, the perceptible blue
> Grown denser, part, the eye so touched, so played
> Upon by clouds, the ear so magnified
> By thunder, parts, and all these things together,
> Parts, and more things, parts. . . .
> (*CP,* 242)

So he does not elect any *via negativa:* his is rather the Way of Affirmation, and, through—let us use Whitehead's term—his "prehensions" of things, he seeks, in relation to his fellows, "to make his imagination theirs," to make it "become the light in the minds of others. His role, in short, is to help people to live their lives" (*NA*, 29).

The major man—whose image in the poetry of Stevens is but one of the conceits wherewith he proposes to talk about the imagination—the major man is, of course, an adept in the art of decreation. His principal concern, indeed, is to cast aside the old "rotted names" and to try to see everything in its "first idea": he is committed to that "difficultest rigor [which] is forthwith / On the image of what we see, to catch from that / Irrational moment its unreasoning" (*CP*, 398). And the morality, the ethic, the *ascêsis*, to which the major man is dedicated forms one of the leading themes of "Notes toward a Supreme Fiction," the great poem of 1942 whose long first section is devoted to what Stevens calls "abstraction," which is his term for that whole process whereby all the old rotted names and conventional schemes of interpretation are so "bracketed" (by something like the Husserlian *epoché*) that their "ravishments of truth, so fatal to / The truth itself" (*CP*, 381), are rendered inefficacious. Then it is, after the poetic imagination performs the phenomenological reduction (or "abstraction"), after it puts aside all those concepts and sentiments that are the result of routinized modes of thought and perception—then it is that at last it begins to discover the "candor" in things, the munificence with which they show themselves forth as what they irrevocably and most essentially are, and

> the candor of them is the strong exhilaration
> Of what we feel from what we think, of thought
> Beating in the heart, as if blood newly came,
>
> An elixir, an excitation, a pure power.
> The poem, through candor, brings back a power again
> That gives a candid kind to everything.
>
> (*CP*, 382)

It is in the moment of what the Greeks called *aletheia*, in the moment of revelation, when the candor in things leads them to unveil themselves, that we find ourselves savoring that "bouquet of being" (*OP*, 109) which reaches us when we begin to notice how, as Hopkins says,

> Each mortal thing does one thing and the same:
> Deals out that being indoors each one dwells;
> Selves—goes itself; *myself* it speaks and spells,
> Crying *What I do is me: for that I came.*[13]

To win the great gift of *aletheia* there must, of course, be a right disposition of the mind and heart, such as the disciplines of decreation and abstraction prepare. But, once this *habitus* has been achieved, we discover (in Hopkins' words) that

> These things, these things were here and but the beholder
> Wanting.[14]

Or, as Stevens says in the "Notes," to have begun to encounter the things of earth in their "first idea" is to realize that

> The clouds preceded us.
>
> There was a muddy centre before we breathed.
> There was a myth before the myth began,
> Venerable and articulate and complete.
>
> From this the poem springs: that we live in a place
> That is not our own and, much more, not ourselves
> And hard it is in spite of blazoned days.
>
> (*CP*, 383)

The aboriginal reality is not the isolate self but a prior otherness with which the self must reckon, "a place / That is not our own," the "muddy centre [that was] before we breathed." True, Stevens appears to postulate an aboriginal Fall, for, as he says, "Adam / In Eden was the father of Descartes / And Eve made air the mirrors of herself" (*CP*, 383). No sooner did man enter the world than he was displacing the "first idea" of this and that by his own concepts and perspectives and categories: he was by way of making the world but a mirror of himself and was thus presuming to dwell, as it were, in a place of the mind. But "The clouds preceded us. / There was a muddy centre before we breathed. . . . we live in a place / That is not our own"—and it is "From this the poem springs," or ought to spring. "The poem refreshes life so that we share, / For a moment, the first idea" (*CP*, 382).

So, in the lesson being laid down for the young poet in the long and difficult opening section of "Notes toward a Supreme Fiction," Stevens wants to say that in a time *post mortem Dei*, however we define the ultimate belief now possible for us, "It Must Be Abstract": it must be calculated, that is, to rescue us from all the superstructures thrown up by the mind between the imagination and the "first idea," in order that efficacy may once again be restored to the primordial bond uniting us with the *milieu ontologique*.

Not only must "It" be abstract," the headnote presiding over the second section of the "Notes" declares, "*It Must Change*." Any ultimate structure of belief must take full account of the impermanencies and mutabilities that are everywhere a part of the ongoing life of the world. And thus the poetic imagination must "move to and fro," must be "a luminous flittering" (*CP*, 396), in all its solicitations of this "universe of inconstancy." So it is no wonder, as the poem remarks, that the great equestrian "statue of the General Du Puy" seems mere "rubbish in the end," for, in its massive bronze fixity, it is something wholly stiff and unpliant and inflexible:

> The right, uplifted foreleg of the horse
> Suggested that, at the final funeral,
> The music halted and the horse stood still.
>
> On Sundays, lawyers in their promenades
> Approached this strongly-heightened effigy
> To study the past, and doctors, having bathed
>
> Themselves with care, sought out the nerveless frame
> Of a suspension, a permanence, so rigid
> That it made the General a bit absurd,
>
> Changed his true flesh to an inhuman bronze.
> There never had been, never could be, such
> A man . . .
>
> (*CP*, 391)

"The great statue of the General Du Puy / Rested immobile"—and precisely for this reason it has the effect not of enlivening the past but of divesting it of any merest semblance of life. And, like Coleridge, Stevens, through all the complex tropes and fables making up the second section of the "Notes," wants to insist that the imagination cannot reckon with this various world by way of "fixities and definites."[15] "*It Must Change.*"

Then, as the headnote of the final section of the poem says, "*It Must Give Pleasure.*" By which Stevens means that the Supreme Fiction—or whatever it is that may suffice in the way of a final structure of belief—should make people happy. But he is immediately at pains to speak of the kind of rejoicing and exultation that will not do; he wants not to endorse the old stylized festivities of traditional religious piety:

> To sing jubilas at exact, accustomed times,
> To be crested and wear the mane of a multitude
> And so, as part, to exult with its great throat,
>
> To speak of joy and to sing of it, borne on
> The shoulders of joyous men, to feel the heart
> That is the common, the bravest fundament,

This is a facile exercise . . .
(CP, 398)

Whereas Stevens, as against this "facile exercise," wants to commend "the difficultest rigor"—which is

forthwith,
On the image of what we see, to catch from that

Irrational moment its unreasoning,
As when the sun comes rising, when the sea
Clears deeply, when the moon hangs on the wall

Of heaven-haven. These are not things transformed.
Yet we are shaken by them as if they were.
We reason about them with a later reason.
(CP, 398–99)

It is, in short, the pleasure consequent upon a naked, "unreasoning" confrontation with the things of earth that will be known by the major man—who in this final section of the poem is imaged forth in the figure of Canon Aspirin.

Although the Canon likes to drink Meursault and to eat "lobster Bombay with mango / Chutney," he is far from being any sort of unthinking hedonist: indeed, he is one who (as Stevens said in a letter to Hi Simons, 29 March 1943) "has explored all the projections of the mind, his own particularly": yet he has won no "sufficing fiction" (L, 445). When we meet him, he has returned to the "sensible ecstasy" of the house of his widowed sister, where she dwells with her two little daughters in what appears a kind of retirement from the world, "rejecting dreams" and demanding of sleep only "the unmuddled self of sleep" (CP, 402). But at midnight, when "normal things had yawned themselves away," there is no unmuddled sleep for the Canon, who remains wakeful and who finds himself facing a nothingness that is "a nakedness, a point, / Beyond which fact could not progress as fact" (CP, 402). Presumably, this nocturnal reverie on "the finality and limitation of fact" (L, 445) is prompted by a depressing sense he has of a certain poverty in his sister's defeatist rejection of all dreams. In any event, as he lies on his bed and thinks of how beyond a point fact as sheer fact takes one nowhere at all, he begins to let his imagination play on fact, on the darkness, on "night's pale illuminations, gold / Beneath, far underneath, the surface of / His eye and audible in the mountain of / His ear":

Straight to the utmost crown of night he flew.
The nothingness was a nakedness, a point

Beyond which thought could not progress as thought.

(*CP*, 403)

The Canon has arrived, then, at two extremities—the point beyond which fact cannot progress as fact and the point beyond which thought cannot progress as thought. Neither reality nor imagination can be sufficient unto itself. And, for a time, in his exasperation he simply

imposes orders as he thinks of them,
As the fox and snake do. It is a brave affair.
Next he builds capitols and in their corridors,

Whiter than wax, sonorous, fame as it is,
He establishes statues of reasonable men.

(*CP*, 403)

He forgets, it seems, that "to impose is not / To discover." But, as Stevens declares,

To discover an order as of
A season, to discover summer and know it,

To discover winter and know it well, to find,
Not to impose, not to have reasoned at all,
Out of nothing to have come on major weather,

It is possible, possible, possible. It must
Be possible . . .

(*CP*, 403–4)

The dialectic of the poem wants, then, to suggest two things at once—that, on the one hand, reality untuned by the imagination's guitar is something barren and unprofitable (because fact as fact can progress only so far and no further); and that, on the other hand, the imagination must not deal so aggressively with reality as simply to impose upon it its own "fictive coverings." What is to be desired is that there should be a true marriage of the one with the other, because only out of this can come any full "discovery" of "the whole, / The Complicate, the amassing harmony." Indeed, it would seem that the Canon is beginning at last to see this, is beginning to see that, choosing not *between* imagination and reality but choosing rather "to include the things / That in each other are included," there will be "an hour / Filled with expressible bliss, in which I have / No need, am happy, forget need's golden hand, / Am satisfied without solacing majesty" (*CP*, 404–5). And thus the poem moves toward its final doxology, about the "thing final in itself and, therefore, good"— the "Fat girl, terrestrial, my summer, my night." But, as we may perhaps gloss Stevens' resolutely opaque lines, the final thing—the fat girl, the terrestrial—is good in part because its "candor" is just enough to permit the imagination to dance round it, "round and round, the merely going round, / Until merely going round is [itself] a final good" (*CP*, 405). "In short," to allow Stevens now his own gloss, "a man with a taste for Meursault, and lobster Bombay, who has a sensible sister and who, for himself, thinks to the very material of his mind, doesn't have much choice about yielding to 'the complicate, the amassing harmony.'" But, then, as he adds in a parenthesis, "How he ever became a Canon is the real problem" (*L*, 445). And, though it may not be anything like *the* problem in what is one of the most difficult poems of the modern period, it does undoubtedly remain a small bafflement (which is in no way clarified by Harold Bloom's energetic fidgetings over it, though his suggestion that the Canon is intended to figure forth a "cure for our headache of unreality" is appealing).[16]

Now it is the beautifully doxological reflections on the final goodness of things predominating in the closing cantos of the "Notes" that look toward the central themes in the rich and inexhaustible poems of Stevens' last years, the poems making up *The Auroras of Autumn* (1950) and *The Rock* (that body of new work forming the last section of *The Collected Poems* of 1954). At the end of a poem "The Ultimate Poem Is Abstract" in *The Auroras of Autumn*, Stevens says:

It would be enough
If we were ever, just once, at the middle, fixed
In This Beautiful World Of Ours and not as now,

Helplessly at the edge, enough to be
Complete, because at the middle, if only in sense,
And in that enormous sense, merely enjoy.
(*CP*, 430)

And this is where the great poems of his final period want to take us—to the middle, to the very center of reality: they want to present nothing less than "The outlines of being and its expressings, the syllables of its law" (*CP*, 424). The poet of *The Auroras* and *The Rock* wants to explore that

huge, high harmony that sounds
A little and a little, suddenly,
By means of a separate sense. It is and it
Is not and, therefore, is.
(*CP*, 440)

What he is struggling toward is "the central poem," and, as he says (in "A Primitive Like an Orb"), the central poem is

> a poem of
> The whole, the essential compact of the parts,
> The roundness that pulls tight the final ring
>
> And that which in an altitude would soar,
> A vis, a principle . . .
> . . . .
> Or else an inherent order active to be
> Itself, a nature to its natives all
> Beneficence, a repose, utmost repose,
> The muscles of a magnet aptly felt. . . .
>   (CP, 442)

This "principle" or "inherent order," this "essential compact of [all] the parts" making up "the whole," is, of course, nothing other than Being itself. And in these late days of our post-Wittgensteinian misery nothing is more likely to strain the patience of the cognoscenti than the very notion of Being—which, as the late English philosopher A. J. Ayer told us more than a generation ago, presents an instance merely of "the way in which a consideration of grammar leads to metaphysics." We are afflicted by "the superstition . . . that, to every word or phrase that can be the grammatical subject of a sentence, there must somewhere be a real entity corresponding."[17] So, because we have in our inherited language the participle *being*, which may also function as a noun, we mistakenly suppose that there is some discriminable entity to which the noun refers. But, as Ayer and numerous other philosophers of his general persuasion would insist, no such entity exists.

Stevens' usages, however, make it fully apparent that it never occurs to him to think of Being as simply one item amongst those belonging to the category of "things." He stands indeed in the line of Aristotle and Aquinas and Kant and all the great strategists of Western metaphysics in taking it for granted that Being is not *a* being but, rather, that informing élan or power, that "dearest freshness deep down things,"[18] that enables all the various particular things of earth to be what their inner entelechies intend them to be. One does not see it as one sees a rose, and it is not *here* or *there*. Yet it is the "insolid billowing of the solid" (OP, 111); it is nothing other than that ontological energy wherewith a bird or a flower or a cloud in the sky is assembled into the given *Gestalt* that it constitutes and made to be what it is—rather than another thing. But, because it is not one thing among other things and because it is nowhere to be encountered simply in its naked isolateness, Stevens often speaks of it apophatically—as when, for example, he tells us, "It is and it / Is not and, therefore, is" (CP, 440), or when he says:

> If
> It was nowhere else, it was there and because
> It was nowhere else, its place had to be supposed,
> Itself had to be supposed, a thing supposed
> In a place supposed . . .
> (CP, 242)

This led the late Randall Jarrell to mutter in irritation that all this was the "spun-sugar" of a "pastry-cook"—or, rather perhaps, something like "G. E. Moore at the spinet."[19] But what Jarrell was very probably quite unaware of is that the language of apophasis forms one of the great classical idioms for discourse about Being—in Dionysius the Areopagite, in Eckhart, in Boehme, in Schelling, and in many others in the Western tradition who unintentionally echo the "Neti, Neti" ("Not this! Not this!") of Hinduism. In any event, though Stevens is not finally an adherent of the via negationis, he keeps a certain reluctance to speak "univocally" about Being, because it is perceptible nowhere in and by itself alone and is, therefore, like "beasts that one never sees, / Moving so that the footfalls are slight and almost nothing" (CP, 337).

At times the course of Stevens' thought seems curiously to have paralleled in some degree that of Heidegger, and, particularly in one respect, to remark the parallel is perhaps to clarify a certain phase of Stevens' poetic procedure that may otherwise appear hopelessly oblique. One turns here not to the later Heidegger, the Heidegger of the Brief über den Humanismus (1947), the Holzwege (1950), Was heisst Denken? (1954), and Gelassenheit (1959)—between whom and the later Stevens there are, to be sure, many fascinating convergences—but to the early Heidegger of Sein und Zeit (Being and Time, 1927), one of whose major presuppositions was that "Being" is accessible only by way of a very strict analysis of the human modes of being. Because that which "assembles" everything that exists does not itself belong to the category of things and is therefore "above" the ordinary categories of reflection, Heidegger reasoned that it needs to be approached not theoretically but existentially, by way of the one creature whose relation to it is that of conscious participant—namely, man himself. Because man, by the inner dynamism of his own nature, is driven to search out the ultimate ground of his existence, Heidegger decided that the appropriate technical term indeed for the distinctively human mode of being is Dasein, which means literally "being-there." "Dasein," as he said, "is an entity for which, in its Being, that Being is an issue."[20] Thus he concluded that our best path into Being-itself is one that leads through those structures of existence that belong to the particular being whose unique vocation it is to be obsessed with the question concerning what it means to *be*. As he laid it down, to do "fundamental ontology" is to seek after not a "transcendental analytic" but an "existential analytic," and such was the undertaking to which he dedicated his brilliantly original book of 1927.

Now it would seem to be some such intuition as this, of the relation of *Dasein* to Being-itself, that underlies Stevens' penchant in many of his poems for imaging forth Being anthropomorphically. True, Being is a "transcendental," is "above" the ordinary categories of reflection, and cannot be properly spoken of univocally: indeed, when it is thought of in relation to the world of particular beings, Being, because it is not *a* being, may seem to require that we consider it to be "that-which-is-not." But the kind of discourse that a poet supervises cannot be wholly an affair of negatives, of "not this" and "not that." Moreover, as we may take Stevens to have reasoned, because Being is inherent in man and may be thought to attain self-consciousness in man alone, it is surely not illicit for the poet to regard his "license" as entitling him to give Being a human form (this being understood to be a purely tropological maneuver). And the preeminent case in point is the beautiful poem in *Transport to Summer* "Chocorua to Its Neighbor," which, in its meditation on the mystery of Being, looks forward to the great statements being made in this vein by many of the last poems.

Mount Chocorua belongs to the chain of the White Mountains in New Hampshire, and she is imagined in the poem as speaking quietly to some neighboring mount. Hers is, of course, a great eminence from the perspective of which the wars between cities far below appear merely "a gesticulation of forms, / A swarming of number over number." But her great elevation is not so lofty that she fails to be deeply stirred by what happened "At the end of night last night," when, as she says,

> a crystal star,
> The crystal-pointed star of morning, rose
> And lit the snow to a light congenial
> To this prodigious shadow, who then came
> In an elemental freedom, sharp and cold.
>
> The feeling of him was the feel of day,
> And of a day as yet unseen, in which
> To see was to be . . .
> (CP, 296–97)

"He was not man, yet he was nothing else," and so huge was he (with "more than muscular shoulders, arms and chest") that, says Chocorua, "Upon my top he breathed the pointed dark." And, as she reports to her neighbor, she heard him say: "'I hear the motions of the spirit and the sound / Of what is secret becomes, for me, a voice / That is my own voice speaking in my ear.'"

"Now," says Chocorua, "I . . . speak of this shadow as / A human thing," but this "eminence," as she suggests, is really "the common self" that potentializes and gives character to all the things and creatures of earth, "So that, where he was, there is an enkindling, where / He is, the air changes and grows fresh to breathe." And thus she speaks of this prodigious presence as "the collective being" of whom captains, cardinals, heroes, mothers, and scholars are but embodiments, "True transfigurers fetched out of the human mountain." So it is that Chocorua's *Benedicite* goes, and, despite all the majesty that she can herself claim, her great hymn in praise of Being ends on a note of utmost humility:

> How singular he was as man, how large,
> If nothing more than that, for the moment, large
> In my presence, the companion of presences
> Greater than mine, of his demanding, head
> And, of human realizings, rugged roy . . .
>
> (*CP*, 302)

Stevens says in his "Adagia" that "A poem is a meteor" (*OP*, 185). Which invites one to think of the arc described by the meteor of "Chocorua" as reaching directly toward "An Ordinary Evening in New Haven," the dominating masterpiece in his book of 1950, *The Auroras of Autumn*. For this is the poem that, perhaps more than any other, fully effectuates the shift in his late poetry from his earlier view of the imagination as the principle of ultimacy to his final view of ultimacy as resident in nothing less than Being itself. As in "Chocorua to Its Neighbor" and "Credences of Summer" (with its great canto 6 on "the rock [that] cannot be broken") in *Transport to Summer*, Stevens in "An Ordinary Evening in New Haven" keeps

> coming back and coming back
> To the real: to the hotel instead of the hymns
> That fall upon it out of the wind. We seek
>
> The poem of pure reality, untouched
> By trope or deviation . . .
>
> (*CP*, 471)

And, of course, at the end Stevens can so resolutely give his suffrage to a reality untouched by trope because of the conviction he had won in working through "Notes toward a Supreme Fiction" that "the whole, / The Complicate, the amassing harmony," solicits and sanctions a true marriage between reality and the imagination, such a marriage indeed as allows the poetry of the imagination to be at last "Part of the res itself and not about it" (*CP*, 473).

"An Ordinary Evening in New Haven" in its first version (a sequence of eleven rather than of the thirty-one cantos constituting the final version) was prepared in fulfillment of a commission Stevens had been given to prepare a poem commemorating the one thousandth meeting of the Connecticut Academy of Arts and Sciences (4 November 1949), and in due course he read the new work before that gathering. While it was in preparation he, in a letter (3 May 1949) to Bernard Heringman, spoke of the project and of his "interest . . . [in trying] to get as close to the ordinary, the commonplace and the ugly as it is possible for a poet to get. It is not," he said, "a question of grim reality but of plain reality" (*L*, 636). And it is indeed "The eye's plain version" of things, what he calls "The vulgate of experience" (*CP*, 465), that the poem wants to render.

Stevens begins a little self-mockingly:

> The eye's plain version is a thing apart,
> The vulgate of experience. Of this,
> A few words, an and yet, and yet, and yet—
>
> As part of the never-ending meditation.
> >   (*CP*, 465)

The poem is being written in his seventieth year, and, being filled with age, he is wryly acknowledging that he has an old man's inclination toward garrulity, that with him "a few words" were likely to be an affair of yakking on and on, with one "and yet" following another, and it being followed by still another. And, for all its richness, his discourse here does indeed prove to be very much like this, the poem seeming, despite its thirty-one long cantos, never really to want to come to an end. It is wonderfully sinuous and wrought with the craft of a master, but it is the poem of an old man, one for whom "the wind whimpers oldly of old age / In the western night" (*CP*, 477).

So it is not surprising that the evening of which Stevens writes is one in the autumn, when the cycle of the seasons is just at the point of winding down into the death of winter. The town and the weather are "a casual litter" of whirling leaves and mud and squirrels huddled together "in tree-caves," and drenching everything is "the repugnant rain" that constantly "falls with a ramshackle sound" (*CP,* 475). The scene is one of bleakness and dilapidation. "The wind has blown the silence of summer away"—and "The last leaf that is going to fall has fallen":

> The barrenness that appears is an exposing.
> It is not part of what is absent, a halt
> For farewells, a sad hanging on for remembrances.
>
> It is a coming on and a coming forth.
> (*CP,* 487)

It is a "plain version" of things that the poem presents, but it is a savage kind of plainness—as Stevens says, "the last plainness of a man who has fought / Against illusion" (*CP,* 467).

Yet he calls the dark, wind-swept streets of the town "metaphysical streets," because it is just amidst their dilapidated ordinariness that we, when thinking deeply, may realize that they do not in any final sense imprison us, that we do most truly reside

> In a permanence composed of impermanence,
> In a faithfulness as against the lunar light,
>
> So that morning and evening are like promises kept,
> So that the approaching sun and its arrival,
> Its evening feast and the following festival,
>
> This faithfulness of reality, this mode,
> This tendance and venerable holding-in
> Make gay the hallucinations in surfaces.
> (*CP,* 472)

And thus, given this "faithfulness of reality," given the steadfastness and graciousness of that uncreated power of Being which gathers all things into themselves, the poet—"Professor Eucalyptus of New Haven," scholar of the ordinary and the commonplace—as he sits in his hotel room, does not expect to find God "in the rainy cloud" but, rather,

> seeks him
> In New Haven with an eye that does not look
>
> Beyond the object. He sits in his room, beside
> The window, close to the ramshackle spout in which
> The rain falls with a ramshackle sound. He seeks
>
> God in the object itself, without much choice.
> (*CP,* 475)

Professor Eucalyptus says:

> "The search
> For reality is as momentous as
> The search for god." It is the philosopher's search

> For an interior made exterior
> And the poet's search for the same exterior made
> Interior . . .
>
> (*CP*, 481)

"After the leaves have fallen, we return / To a plain sense of things" (*CP*, 502)—and "a plain sense of things" seeks

> Nothing beyond reality. Within it,

> Everything, the spirit's alchemicana
> Included, the spirit that goes roundabout
> And through included, not merely the visible,

> The solid, but the movable, the moment,
> The coming on of feasts and the habits of saints,
> The pattern of the heavens and high, night air.
>
> (*CP*, 471–72)

The "poem of pure reality" wants to define "a fresh spiritual"—which concerns nothing other than the "essential integrity" of "The actual landscape with its actual horns / Of baker and butcher blowing" (*CP*, 474, 475).

As "An Ordinary Evening in New Haven" slowly and reluctantly moves toward its close Stevens says in canto 28:

> This endlessly elaborating poem
> Displays the theory of poetry,
> As the life of poetry. A more severe,

> More harassing master would extemporize
> Subtler, more urgent proof that the theory
> Of poetry is the theory of life,

> As it is, in the intricate evasions of as,
> In things seen and unseen, created from nothingness,
> The heavens, the hells, the worlds, the longed-for lands.
>
> (*CP*, 486)

But, indeed, he is nothing if not a severe and harassing master, and the whole intention of his work in its final phase is to persuade us that the theory of poetry is the theory of life. Stevens wants, of course, to propose that we think of the poet as (in Heidegger's phrase) a "shepherd of Being," but, more basically even, he (like Heidegger)[21] wants us to think of man as a "shepherd of Being," the poet therefore offering only an ideal *exemplum* of the quintessentially human vocation. It is in this way that his theory of poetry is also his theory of life.

True, the poet is most immediately distinguished by his adeptness in the art of supervising the word, but, when he rightly understands the poetic office, his most fundamental purpose is so to supervise the word as to show forth the things and creatures of earth "in the starkness and strangeness of their being what they are."[22] He teaches us how to revel in their particularity, in their *presence*, in the marvelous inner cohesion whereby they manage to be what they are, rather than something else. And thus, by inviting an attitude of enthrallment before the various concrete realities of the world, he prepares us to be laid hold of by that wherewith these things are inwardly constituted and enabled to be what they are—which is none other than Being itself. The great gift, in other words, that he confers is what Wordsworth in book 2 of *The Prelude* calls "the sentiment of Being."

Now, in inviting us to offer a kind of *Amen* to the various finite realities that make up the earth because they are themselves instinct with Being, Stevens is attributing to Being the character of holiness. For him, Being is, indeed, the primary focus of a radically religious faith. And, here, we are bound to be put in mind of two words that he addressed to Sister M. Bernetta Quinn—the one in a letter (7 April 1948) that said, "Your mind is too much like my own for it to seem to be an evasion on my part to say merely that I do seek a centre and expect to go on seeking it" (L, 584); and the other in a Christmas letter (21 December 1951), which said, "I am not an atheist although I do not believe to-day in the same God in whom I believed when I was a boy" (L, 735). But, of course, conventional opinion amongst Stevens' interpreters represents a great disinclination to take him at his word when he forswears any sort of allegiance to atheism. How, it will be asked, can any other position be attributed to one who proclaimed so imperatively the death of all the gods and who, now that "the phantoms are gone," conceived himself to be a "shaken realist" committed to "the imagination's new beginning" (CP, 320)? Or, if it be granted that the position expressed in the poetry of his final period is in some sort religious, it will then be asked how this *mystique* of Being can be considered anything other than a kind of pantheism.

These are difficult questions, and questions it is well-nigh impossible to answer to the satisfaction of the kind of *simplicitas* about religious discriminations which usually belongs to the literary community. For, there, it is the common tendency to suppose either that the term "God" refers to *a* being such as archaic mythology represented as "dwelling" at the summit of a mountain or somewhere in the skies, or that it refers to that metaphysical entity conceived by classical theism to be a person "dwelling" incorporeally beyond the world. And, accordingly, it is assumed that to refuse, as Stevens most assuredly does, "the gods" of ancient mythology and the God-thing of traditional theism is to embrace what amounts to atheism. Indeed, Heidegger himself, who reinstated the doctrine of Being more powerfully than any other philosopher of the modern period, seems to have been so convinced of the term "God" ineradicably carrying the implication of *a* being over and above the world that he was always careful to insist on the impropriety of equating "Being" with "God,"[23] for he knew that even to appear to be postulating *a* being "above" or "beyond" the world that is studied by empirical science is to violate the grammar of modern intelligence to a degree intolerable by the people of our age.

But, though the categories of classical theism (insofar as they posit *a* supreme being above or beyond the world) may no longer represent a negotiable currency, it remains the case today as much as ever before that the religious imagination finds itself wanting to regard the world as charged with "a kind of total grandeur at the end" (*CP*, 510) and as tabernacling grace and glory. True, it may not any longer feel it to be possible to articulate such a vision by making reference to some exalted supernatural Person—the divine Pantocrator—whose "existence" and whose interventions in the world have the effect of validating or sanctifying the significant realities of nature and history. Yet it may, by a decision of faith, choose to regard as essentially trustworthy, as indeed holy and gracious, that mysterious *dynamis* that simply lets all the particular beings of earth *be*. This would seem precisely the kind of vision at work in the late poetry of Stevens, where all its "edgings and inchings" appear calculated at the end to speak of the "final goodness" of things. And, of course, when, in an attitude of faith, we regard as *holy* the Incomparable that "lets-be" all the things and creatures of this world, then Being itself begins to take on something of the status assigned by traditional theism to "God." Such a God, to be sure, is not "the same God in whom [Stevens] believed when [he] was a boy," though he was surely justified, nevertheless, in asserting to Sister M. Bernetta Quinn that "I am not an atheist." Traditional atheism has undoubtedly directed its polemic at a different God, but to give one's suffrage to such a God as Stevens appears to have embraced is not to assert that *a* particular being dwells in some invisible realm above or beyond the phenomenal world. It is, rather, to declare, as a matter of radical faith, that Being itself is steadfast, reliable, gracious, and deserves our trust: it is to say that the Wholly Other, the uncreated Rock of reality, is *for* us, not against us.

Still, it will be asked if the equation of Being with God does not present what is at bottom only another version of pantheist theosophy—and, as it will be further asked, disbelievingly, is *this* what Stevens is up to? Such a question, however, will be prompted by a very great misunderstanding, for Being, as it is envisaged by Stevens, is no more the sum or the totality of all beings than it is *a* particular being *in addition to* all the other beings that make up our world. Being is, rather, that *transcendens* which, as the enabling condition of everything that exists, is "wholly other" than and distinct from all particular beings, even in their totality. And nowhere in Stevens' poetry is there to be found the merest hint of any sort of pantheistic mysticism.

In one of his "Adagia" he says that "The poet is the priest of the invisible" (*OP*, 195). But he does not, of course, conceive the "invisible" of which he speaks to be any sort of sheer blankness, and to recall the late poem "Of Mere Being" is to feel, indeed, that, had he taken thought, it is of this that he would perhaps have wanted to say that the poet is a priest—mere Being (which is, to be sure, itself invisible). This is the poem:

> The palm at the end of the mind,
> Beyond the last thought, rises
> In the bronze distance,
>
> A gold-feathered bird
> Sings in the palm, without human meaning,
> Without human feeling, a foreign song.
>
> You know then that it is not the reason
> That makes us happy or unhappy.
> The bird sings. Its feathers shine.
>
> The palm stands on the edge of space.
> The wind moves slowly in the branches.
> The bird's fire-fangled feathers dangle down.
>
> (*OP*, 141)

Here, then, are the tree and the bird—which simply sings because it is its nature to sing; it is "without why," without "care"; it does not fret about the enabling conditions of its existence, and, with its fire-fangled feathers dangling down, it sings for the sake of nothing other than its song. Dylan Thomas says that "The force that through the green fuse drives the flower / Drives my green age. . . . / The force that drives the water through the rocks / Drives my red blood."[24] And, in its innocent openness to this "force," the bird stands for Stevens as something like a sacrament of the mystery of Being—"mere Being," which is that

> life brighter than this present splendor,
> Brighter, perfected and distant away,
> Not to be reached but to be known,
> Not an attainment of the will
> But something illogically received.
>
> (*OP*, 128)

So, despite all the testimony to the contrary that comes from many of his principal interpreters, Stevens is a profoundly religious poet. But he exemplifies a kind of sensibility for which the direction of transcendence is not upward but downward. The transcendentality of Being is apprehended as given in and with and under the immanent. For Stevens, the universe is not a two-storied affair, with the realm of the divine above nature and history, to be reached by way of some *scala sacra* leading up beyond the phenomenal world into the timelessness of eternity. On the contrary: the sense of reality controlling his theory of poetry and his own poetic utterance tells him that we dwell in *one* world, not at a point of juncture between two worlds. And thus he finds the transcendent in the most intimate neighborhood of our experience: he finds it (in Teilhard de Chardin's phrasing) to be the "within" of all things, "shining forth from the depths of every event, every element."[25] He finds grace not overhead but in the world,[26] in (as Meister Eckhart would say) the *Is-ness* of everything that exists—in "The actual landscape with its actual horns / Of baker and butcher blowing."

This "inquisitor of structures" (*CP*, 510) does, then, through his "poem of pure reality," through his "Whole Harmonium,"[27] define what is indeed "a fresh spiritual"—which speaks of "that nobility which is our spiritual height and depth. . . . Nothing could be more evasive and inaccessible. . . . But there it is. . . . If it is defined, it will be fixed and it must not be fixed. . . . To fix it is to put an end to it" (*NA*, 33–34). So he does indeed find, as he says in his great tribute to Santayana ("To an Old Philosopher in Rome"),

> a kind of total grandeur at the end,
> With every visible thing enlarged and yet
> No more than a bed, a chair and moving nuns,
> The immensest theatre, the pillared porch,
> The book and candle in your ambered room.
>
> (*CP*, 510)

His ultimate apostrophe is to "mere Being," "the human end in the spirit's greatest reach" (*CP*, 508).

It was within the terms of such a vision of the world as this that Wallace Stevens, lawyer and vice-president of the Hartford Accident and Indemnity Company, dwelt poetically in Connecticut from the spring of 1916 until his death in the summer of 1955. "He dwelt in Connecticut," says Frank Kermode, "as Santayana dwelt in the head of the world, as if it were origin as well as threshold."[28]

CHAPTER THREE

W. H. Auden's Way: Toward the City— from the "Suburb of Dissent"

I heard Orpheus sing; I was not quite as moved as they say.
—AUDEN, "Memorial for the City"

. . . my name
Stands for my historical share of care
For a lying self-made city. . . .
—AUDEN, "Prime"

And where should we find shelter
For joy or mere content
When little was left standing
But the suburb of dissent.
—AUDEN, "To Reinhold and Ursula Niebuhr"

*A*midst the various darkly oracular pronouncements making up the lectures of the late R. P. Blackmur at the Library of Congress in the winter of 1956—*Anni Mirabiles, 1921–1925: Reason in the Madness of Letters*—there are occasional passages whose pithiness and cogency reflect the special kind of brilliance that marked this gifted critic's finest moments. And, amongst these passages, one of the most suggestive is that which invites us to think of Rainer Maria Rilke in relation to Robert Herrick and Emily Dickinson, for the three, says Blackmur, "are nuptial poets." "Herrick marries the created world, Dickinson marries herself, Rilke creates within himself something to marry which will—which does—marry and thereby rival the real world."[1] Rilke makes, that is, what Wallace Stevens (in his "Esthétique du Mal") calls a "new beginning." For, given the emptiness of the heavens above and the abandonment by the gods of man's earthly abode, the fearsome task to which he felt the poet elected was that of rescuing the world from the absolute transitoriness and chaos by which, apart from the poet's ministries, it must at last be overwhelmed. And this redeeming work (*Herz-Werk*—"heart-work"—as he called it) was conceived most essentially to involve not any effort to transfigure dinginess and mediocrity, so that the actual world might be newly renovated, but rather such a liberation altogether of things (*die Dinge*) from their hopelessly inert facticity as would permit them to find a new home in the inwardness of the heart. Since the Holy Spirit has disappeared and the region of our habitancy is no longer a place of grace and glory, the things and creatures of earth must be offered the one asylum that now remains—namely, that inland sanctuary remote from the exposed frontiers of the world which is provided within, by the creative largesse of the human spirit itself.

What we must do, as Rilke said in a now famous letter to his Polish translator, is "to impress this fragile, transient earth so deeply, sufferingly, and passionately upon our hearts that its essence shall rise up again, 'invisible,' within us. *We are the bees of the Invisible.*"[2] As the Seventh Duino Elegy says—"Nowhere . . . will be world but within." And to answer the earth's beseechings, that its *disjecta membra* be gathered into the inwardness of the heart, is to fulfill Rilke's definition of the poet's principal office. "How other future worlds will ripen to God I do not know, but for us art is the way"[3]—and, for him, the way of art was the way of the Angel, the way of Orpheus, the way of world-building. So the poet of the *Duino Elegies* and the *Sonnets to Orpheus* does in truth show himself to be one creating "within himself something to marry which will—which does—marry and thereby rival the real world."

Indeed, it is precisely the austerity of Rilke's commitment to his angelism, to his *religio poetae,* that makes him one of the primary saints of modern literature. For the lordly assurance with which he took it for granted that metaphysical anarchy requires the poet to be his own legislator leads us to accord him a central place in that strain of modern writers who ask to be regarded as having been at bottom "theologians of the poetic imagination."[4] The tradition reaches back to Mallarmé and farther still to Rimbaud, and possibly even to Hölderlin and Leopardi; and, after Valéry (and perhaps Juan Ramón Jiménez), it is Wallace Stevens who is the last master of this line—the great dandiacal artificer of "supreme fictions" who was claimed, above all else, by what he called the "mystical theology" of poetry.[5] This "passionately niggling nightingale," in the vast and beautiful palace for the mind which his art creates, brings the whole modern venture in absolute poetry to its absolute climax. For he asserts more radically than any of his predecessors that, given that poverty of our condition consequent upon the emptying of the heavens, the only unified realm of experience in which we may now dwell, the one *world* remaining, is the world of poetry—which, in our own late time, is "indistinguishable from the world in which we live."[6] "The final belief is to believe in a fiction, which you know to be a fiction, there being nothing else."[7] And thus the poet is the "necessary angel of earth,"[8] because it is he ("the priest of the invisible")[9] who "gives to life the supreme fictions without which we are unable to conceive of it"[10] and who, in teaching us how to perceive ("as far as nothingness permits")[11] the mysterious coruscations of Being, clears a space for the human endeavor. The poet of *Four Quartets* says (in "East Coker"), "The poetry does not matter," but the poet of *Harmonium* and *Ideas of Order* and *Transport to Summer* wants to say that nothing else matters but the poetry, wants to say indeed with Rilke (in the third sonnet of the first Orpheus cycle) that Song *is* existence ("Gesang ist Dasein"); and it is the extraordinary eloquence with which he makes this testimony—in some of the most beautiful and moving poems of the modern period—that prompts us to think of Stevens as the last great examplar of that heroic attempt in literature of the past hundred years to locate anew "the heraldic center of the world" or, given (as it may be) the irreparable fracture of that center, to build a new center and, by doing so, to save us.

Now there is perhaps no major poet of the twentieth century who stands in so resolute an opposition as does W. H. Auden to that Orphic line in modern poetry which Stevens may be regarded as having brought to a kind of conclusion. As he said in an essay of the late 1940s, "How glad I am that the silliest remark ever made about poets, 'the unacknowledged legislators of the world,' was made by a poet whose work I detest."[12] And it was with a similar severity that, over the last thirty years of his career, Auden regularly rejected, again and again in his essays and reviews, the attempt of the Orphic-Romantic movement to offer poetry "as a guide to life" and to establish "a new nonsupernatural Catholicism."[13]

It may of course be taken for granted that Auden, very early on, in his undergraduate years at Oxford in the late 1920s, was captivated—like most young men then aiming at a poetic vocation—by that whole view of poetry which Eliot was enforcing upon the literary world of the time. Although the specialities of stress and idiom characteristic of Auden's *Poems* (1930) are in no simple way derivative from the poet of "The Love Song of J. Alfred Prufrock," the basic style of procedure represented by that early book clearly indicates that he, too, conceived the Wordsworthian formula—about "emotion recollected in tranquillity"—to be "an inexact formula"[14] and that he, like *il miglior fabbro* of *The Waste Land*, was by way of assuming the poet to be not any sort of *vates sacer*, but rather a kind of technician who manufactures an artifact of words and sounds. Nor do we find it difficult to imagine that the young Oxonian brooding on how "In sanatoriums they laugh less and less / Less certain of cure" (Poem XVI), was ready, in quite the same way as Eliot, to respond to Matthew Arnold's word about poetry being "at bottom a criticism of life." "At bottom: that is a great way down; the bottom is the bottom"—which "few ever see."[15]

One also suspects that Auden's never having been charmed by the Orphic vision of the poetic enterprise was a result of his literary conscience having been early formed by the kinds of lessons being laid down in those brisk manifestoes of T. E. Hulme which Herbert Read collected and published in 1924 under the title *Speculations*. Stephen Spender reports that, in their undergraduate days at Oxford, Auden was in the habit of flatly informing him and others whom he admitted to his rooms at Christ Church that a poem's subject is "only the peg on which to hang the poetry" and that the poet is merely one like a chemist who mixes "his poems out of words whilst remaining detached from his own feelings." And this young man, whose preference was for a "monosyllabic, clipped, clear-cut, icy poetry,"[16] was undoubtedly one who had been very greatly swayed by Hulme's declarations against the "spilt religion" of "romanticism," against that damp, high-falutin' sort of poetry that is always "flying up into the eternal gases" and talking about "the infinite," that is always "moaning or whining about something or other" and refusing to be a small, hard, dry statement.[17] Indeed, for all the shifts of emphasis in theme that belong to Auden's literary pronouncements spanning a public career of more than forty years, what is constantly to be remarked is this insistence that the poet is "a pedestrian taking you over the ground"[18] of the quotidian, and he always wanted utterly to refuse the kind of magniloquence which says that, when every other compass has failed, it is on poetry that we must rely for the charting of a route into some brave new world.

Auden's predilection would seem never to have been one for supposing that the duty of a poem is to create a world *ex nihilo* or any sort of heterocosmic alternative to the *actual* universe: its duty was, rather, always for him that of bearing "witness to the truth,"[19] and the Johnsonian refrain consistently made by his testimony (in the verse as well as in his essays) speaks of poetic art as "a mirror held up to nature"— a mirror wherein we remain in the neighborhood (as Caliban calls it in *The Sea and the Mirror*) of "the Grandly Average Place from which at odd hours the expresses leave seriously and sombrely for Somewhere,"[20] and

> . . . where Euclid's geometry
> And Newton's mechanics would account for our experience,
> And the kitchen table exists because I scrub it.[21]

Yet, despite his disbelief in anything like *la poésie pure*, Auden's insistence on the great gulf dividing "the poetical" and "the existential" was unremitting and was expressed always with a very blunt kind of pungency. For, as he conceived the matter, the "old innocent game of playing God with words"[22] "makes nothing happen"[23]—at least nothing truly serious, because poetry "does not of itself move what is serious, the will."[24] "Poetizing" is, indeed, simply a game—a difficult game no doubt but a game nevertheless, a form of play whose essential frivolity stands at a great distance from anything genuinely serious, because the gulf

> between choosing to obey the rules of a game which it does not matter whether you play or not, and choosing to obey the rules of life which you have to live whether you like it or not and where the rules are necessary for they do not cease to exist if you disobey them but operate within you to your destruction, this gulf is so infinite that all talk about . . . games being a preparation for . . . life is misleading twaddle.[25]

And it is, of course, the Kierkegaard of *Either/Or* and *Stages on Life's Way* who is being echoed in Auden's pronouncements on the frivolity of art, for the Idea of Poetry that he advances is, essentially, but a restatement of Kierkegaard's doctrine about the "aesthetic" point of view as that of the uncommitted spectator who lives merely on the surfaces of things, wholly absorbed by the ever-changing panorama of the world but viewing it from a position of neutrality which discourages his making any decisive choices or embracing any radical imperatives. "All poets," says Auden, "adore explosions, thunderstorms, tornadoes, conflagrations, ruins, scenes of spectacular carnage,"[26] for theirs is a world of play and game. So: "Art is not life and cannot be / A midwife to society"[27] or an agent in the upbuilding of the Just City.

Although *poiesis* is "a verbal rite"[28] and thus a kind of game, it is a game that aims to be "a game of knowledge."[29] Art is not life, but, as Auden says, "it *has* life"[30]—by which he means that, in its integral and absolute formality, in its strict patterning of what Susanne Langer called "virtual" worlds,[31] it presents us with evocative simulacra of what our lives would be like were *they* to be set in order. And in the degree to which the poet's mastery of his language enables him to reveal the plasticity of the world, to show its amenability to the shaping power of the human word, he does to that degree present us with a model of freedom, and one that, in declaring "that order is *possible,* . . . faces us with the command to make it *actual.*"[32] A work of art simply by way of its own formal order, makes a kind of analogy of that which is referred to in the second petition of the *Our Father* ("Thy Kingdom come. . . ."), and thus its effect—as "All we are not stares back at what we are"[33]—is, inevitably, in some measure indictive and admonitory: as Caliban says (in *The Sea and the Mirror*), "What else exactly *is* the artistic gift . . . if not to make you unforgettably conscious of the ungarnished offended gap between what you so questionably are and what you are commanded without any question to become . . . ?"[34]

So the poem, as Auden frequently liked to say, resembles a parable. The poet confronts two shapeless, chaotic "crowds," the vast crowd of words making up the vocabulary of his inherited language and that jumbled crowd of recollected occasions of feeling; and what he seeks to do is to fashion a verbal *society* (that is, a system whose members are optimally united into a whole whose mode of behavior is different from that of its component members), which will itself be capable of transforming the crowd of past occasions of feeling into a *community* (that is, an order whose component members, being free and equal, exist as a unity-in-tension). And the resulting poem thus presents "an analogy"—not an imitation but an analogy—"to that paradisal state in which Freedom and Law, System and Order are united in harmony."[35] "You cannot tell people what to do, you can only tell them parables."[36]

To be sure, Auden wanted to maintain (as he did in his inaugural lecture as Oxford's Professor of Poetry) that poetic statement originates in the poet's encounter with "the sacred"[37]—by which, however, he meant not to underwrite any sort of Longinian afflatus but only to remark, if in a somewhat eccentric fashion, the necessity of the poet's having somewhere located a dimension of radical significance in relation to which a proper weight may then be given to the various and sundry issues of proportion and order. But the poet qua poet does not undertake to be what Catholic Christianity speaks of as a "spiritual director": he offers only, as Auden was at most prepared to say (following Wilfred Owen), a word of "warning," and this of a highly indirect and oblique sort, through the formal concords of his poem—that (as he said in that famous line which he finally excised from his poem "September 1, 1939") "We must love one another or die."

Yet, however much Auden was inclined in theory to disavow didactic modes of poetic statement, the parables proposed by his poetry—from the period of his earliest publication into the middle years of his career—did entail a rather more direct commentary on the human scene of his time than anything that might have been merely an affair of his art, in its own formal order, adumbrating the Just City. Indeed, the prodigiously clever and intelligent young poet of *Poems* (1930), of *Look, Stranger!* (1936), and of *Another Time* (1940) makes us feel that his primary intentions were diagnostic and pedagogical and that, facing what seemed on all sides to be general disintegration, he wanted to see it "as the hawk sees it or the helmeted airman." The England in which he had come into maturity— and which he conceived to be but a microcosm of the modern West— struck him at the beginning of the 1930s as bearing, throughout the entire fabric of its life, the marks of seediness and decay. The economic system had been reduced to a shambles of stoppages and breakdown: men were without employment and were hungry and without hope: everywhere there was confusion and dismay. It was, as he observed in his book of 1930 (in poem XXII), a time of

> Smokeless chimneys, damaged bridges, rotting wharves
> and choked canals,
> Tramlines buckled, smashed trucks lying on their side
> across the rails.
> Power-stations locked, deserted. . . .

And, as he looked out upon the "civil anarchy" ruling the "dark dis-ordered city" of the age, this exigent young critic found it difficult not to be one—like the Voltaire he was later to describe in the poem "Voltaire at Ferney" (*Another Time*)—"Cajoling, scolding, scheming." For, as he said in the XVIth poem in the book of 1930, "It is time for the destruction of error," and the Auden of that period appears to have intended his pen to be a vigorous scalpel in its probing of blunder and perfidy.

This sense of travail in a "low dishonest decade" in which, as Auden said in *The Orators* (1932), "nobody is well," did not generally eventuate, however, in a poetry informed by the kinds of close social-political obser-vations which characterize the work of a writer of the English 30s such as George Orwell. Cecil Day Lewis trenchantly remarked at the time Au-den's tendency "to replace . . . the idea of the wickedness of society by the idea of the sickness of society."[38] Indeed, his habit of locating the source of collective distress in the failures of personal life did have the effect of giving a certain homiletical flavor to much of his early work, as social critique enforced some quasi-psychiatric lesson and this in turn a kind of Pascalian interrogation of the individual in the bleak, dreary win-ter of his isolateness ("So, insecure, he loves and love / Is insecure, gives less than he expects").[39] It is true that throughout these years he kept a steady interest in the new scene presented by the ever-darkening world over which the shadow of Hitler loomed—a world (as he said in the ded-icatory lines to Erika Mann in *Look, Stranger!*) of "external disorders, and extravagant lies, / . . . baroque frontiers, . . . surrealist police." And he knew that the "savaging disaster" had to be met by such a force of resistance as could be mustered only by the most carefully concerted political action. But, even as he faced the worsening public realities of a time in which the demonic atavism of the Nazis encountered in liberal democracy nothing more than a timorous aimlessness, his deepest concerns centered not so much on the problems arising out of the mechanisms of our social living as on what he took to be the ultimate and habitual source of these problems, in the crookedness and illiberality of the human heart.

By the mid-1930s Auden was, to be sure, prepared to acknowledge (as he did in *Look, Stranger!*) the fatuousness of his earlier belief that "one fearless kiss would cure / The million fevers," and the poem that carries this disavowal, being addressed to his friend Christopher Isherwood, bids Isherwood in his own writing to "Make action urgent and its nature clear." Yet the "Epilogue" of *Look, Stranger!* reiterates the contention that had already become a hallmark of Auden's testimony, that the menacing floods of history will be stayed only as we heed the example of those who "had unlearnt / Our hatred, and towards the really better / World had turned their face." It is still love that is being advocated, though now the insistence is on the necessity of a "disciplined love," one that by concerted action takes arms against a sea of troubles and, through a collective effort, seeks to bring them to an end. And, in the "Last Will and Testament" with which he and Louis MacNeice brought their *Letters from Iceland* (1937) to a close, the hope is expressed that "the good who know how wide the gulf . . . / Between Ideal and Real" may be granted

> . . . The power to take upon themselves the guilt
> Of human action, though still as ready to confess
> The imperfection of what can and must be built.[40]

Everywhere, in short, in the work Auden produced during the first decade of his career—in the poems, in the charade *Paid on Both Sides*, in the plays (*The Dance of Death, The Dog beneath the Skin, The Ascent of F6, On the Frontier*), and in the travel books with MacNeice (*Letters from Iceland*) and Isherwood (*Journey to a War*)—though he wanted to portray the human position as a point of juncture between the public world of society and the inner world of the spirit, his major stress fell not upon the events being recorded in daily newspapers "but on events and crises in the world of the moral imagination."[41] He wanted (as the closing poem in his book of 1930 says) to

> Cover in time with beams those in retreat
> That, spotted, they turn though the reverse were great;

> Publish each healer that in city lives
> Or country houses at the end of drives;
> Harrow the house of the dead; look shining at
> New styles of architecture, a change of heart.

But though his focus was on "the muddled heart," the poetry, in its strongest moments, moved within "a mode of public eloquence"[42] and has its background in the treacheries and evasions of the age.

In *New Year Letter*, the great poem of 1941 which presents a massive summary of the central themes and issues with which he had been occupied over the previous decade, Auden says (in part 3):

> There are two atlases: the one
> The Public space where acts are done,
> In theory common to us all . . .
> The other is the inner space
> Of private ownership, the place
> That each of us is forced to own,
> Like his own life from which it's grown,
> The landscape of his will and need
> Where he is sovereign indeed,
> The state created by his acts
> Where he patrols the forest tracts. . . .

Like his most significant poetry of the previous decade, what the *Letter* wants to do is to define the lines of relationship between these "two atlases," because Auden was convinced that there can be no true authenticity of life apart from a right understanding of the complex mutuality by which "the public space" and "the inner space" are interdependently held together. His reflections throughout the 30s had steadily deepened his belief that you do not have disorder in the City when there is order in the private lives of individuals, that the ultimate source of collective distress is to be found in "the error bred in the bone / Of each woman and each man." And, correlatively, he had furthermore been steadily moving toward a recognition of the ineradicable historicity of human life, of the fact that the individual is in large part the result not only of what he himself has done but also, perhaps even more crucially, of what others before him have been and done and thought. So, because each man's "parish of immediacy" is deeply wrought by the bequests of history, as he—midway the journey of this life[43]—undertook an appraisal of the condition and prospect of the human enterprise in the dark time of 1940, when the clouds of war were gathered over the entire world, there seemed no chance of finding "a sesame to light" except by way of canvasing anew the annals of the modern period and reassessing the whole repertoire of beliefs and philosophies, of programs and ideologies, that had prepared the impasse then in view.

New Year Letter, then, addresses itself to "the situation of our time," to the "political upheaveal" with which "our lives have been coeval." In its controlling perspective, its closest allegiances are with Dante and Pascal and Kierkegaard and, among Auden's contemporaries, with thinkers such as Karl Barth and Paul Tillich and Reinhold Niebuhr. But the poem is alert to the entire European tradition (the Greeks, the Church Fathers, the medieval Scholastics, the Reformers, Spinoza, Blake, Voltaire, Baudelaire, Rimbaud, Nietzsche, Wagner, Freud), and, at the close of one "scrambling decade" and the advent of still another that seemed to promise even more perilous emergencies, its alternately grave and witty couplets intend to stretch the secular mind of the age to the very limits of its memory, the limits beyond which there might remain nothing for it to know but that

> A day is drawing to a close . . .
> That all the special tasks begun
> By the Renaissance have been done.

True, Western liberalism did over a long period suppose that there was some simple path to felicity, either by way of science or education or universal suffrage. But these agencies of redemption were never able finally to break the stubborn recalcitrancies of the human polity. Thus, after the sudden mutation of "Old Russia . . . / Into a proletarian state," the earlier scriptures of Adam Smith and Comte and Spencer were replaced by the revelations of Marx—and, with the rise of the Soviet experiment, "Some dreamed, as Students always can, / It realized the potential Man":

> We hoped: we waited for the day
> The State would wither clean away,
> Expecting the Millennium
> That theory promised us would come,
> It didn't. Specialists must try
> To detail all the reasons why. . . .

Indeed, in that late moment when he wrote the *Letter*, Auden was struck by how much

> . . . even the best
> *Les hommes de bonne volonté*, feel
> Their politics perhaps unreal

> And all they have believed untrue,
> Are tempted to surrender to
> The grand apocalyptic dream. . . .

As he cautioned, however, "to surrender to / The grand apocalyptic dream" is to elect that history shall come to an end—which is precisely what the Devil desires, for abdication is confession of defeat. Nor must we, like poor Wordsworth, repent "of our last infraction" by seeking "atonement in reaction." For, in a time of shattered dreams and broken hopes, to surrender either to apocalypticism or to reactionism is to withdraw altogether from the rough, dark weathers of the historical arena. Daunted we may be by the relentlessness with which the modern age has mounted failure on failure, but at least "failures have one good result: / They prove the Good is difficult," and they provide the occasion for the necessary discovery that

> Aloneness is man's real condition,
> That each must travel forth alone
> In search of the Essential Stone. . . .

At the dawning in January 1940 of a new decade—as "Day breaks upon the world we know / Of war and wastefulness and woe"—Auden said that, though "The New Year brings an earth afraid," one great thing may at last be coming once again to be understood, that "true democracy begins / With free confession of our sins." And thus the poem concludes with the great prayer—

> O Unicorn among the cedars,
> To whom no magic charm can lead us . . .
> O Source of equity and rest . . .
> Disturb our negligence and chill . . .
> Send strength sufficient for our day,
> And point our knowledge on its way,
> O da quod jubes, Domine.

Point our knowledge on its way, the poet of the *Letter* prays; and the three long poems that followed the masterly epistle of 1941—*For the Time Being* (written in 1941–42),[44] *The Sea and the Mirror* (composed between 1942 and 1944),[45] and *The Age of Anxiety* (1947)—seem, indeed, as we look back upon them today, to have been dedicated to nothing other than a pursuit of the Way, of the Way and the Truth and the Life. By now, of course, he had entered deeply into the Christian commitments toward which he had been moving at the end of the 1930s. But, given the inveterate worldliness of his mind, his assent to the *skandalon* of Christianity needed to be of a piece with his facing and evaluating every major alternative to the Christian faith. As it is said in *For the Time Being,*

> . . . the garden is the only place there is, but you
> will not find it
> Until you have looked for it everywhere and found
> nowhere that is not a desert.

All the wrong roads had to be reconnoitered again, in order that they might be clearly seen to be only blind detours. So, as he confronted the Secular City of his time and what he took to be its incompetence at probing the "unrectored chaos" of the age, though knowing full well that "Art is not life and cannot be / A midwife to society," Auden wanted nevertheless to admonish and to warn and to trouble the common peace, even if this were to risk "the preacher's loose immodest tone." And it is precisely such an effort of catechizing and cross-examination which is being brilliantly undertaken in his work of the 1940s.

In his Christmas oratorio, *For the Time Being,* Auden found his "text" in the Gospel narratives and proceeded allegorically to render the anguished bafflement of people everywhere on the eve of the Second World War by analogizing it to the disquietude and confusion of the ancient world on the eve of the Nativity. Through a complex structure of choruses and solos and recitatives the oratorio takes us back into that remote time where, then as now, the type of the average man—whose mantelpiece clock had "nothing to recommend"—wanted nothing to happen. But a strange, new reality, an absolute miracle, was destined by way of a manger to come into Caesar's disconsolate world, and the drama of *For the Time Being* is an affair of the account it gives of the ambivalence and evasion that this miracle on all sides prompted—in Joseph, who was fearful of having been cuckolded; in the Wise Men, who followed the star unto Bethlehem only because their previous journeys had proved merely detours into failure; in Herod, the liberal bureaucrat, who angrily resented the intrusion of radical absurdity (the notion of the Word made flesh, of the God-Man) into his rational world; in the choralists who wanted to rest in the security of a world arranged and managed for them by the great all-powerful Caesar. And, of course, in the manner of Baudelaire's famous apostrophe, the poem wants to say "You!" "Hypocrite lecteur!—mon semblable,—mon frère!" Then, after the whole pageant has concluded with the flight into Egypt, the narrator brings us back into our own present, into the world of "the moderate Aristotelian city / Of darning and the Eight-Fifteen," the world of "the time being"—which, as we are told, we shall redeem from insignificance only by following "Him through the Land of Unlikeness," only by seeking "Him in the Kingdom of Anxiety," only by loving "Him in the World of the Flesh."

In *The Sea and the Mirror*, still another essay in histrionic exposition and one of the great triumphs of Auden's art, he found his "text" in Shakespeare's *The Tempest*. And, here—as he dazzlingly displays his command of Sapphics and elegiacs, of terza rima and the ballade, of the sestina and the villanelle—this poet, among the most consummately gifted artists in poetry of the modern period, wants (in the spirit of his own master Søren Kierkegaard) to warn us against trusting to the sorceries and enchantments of art for any ultimate redemption of our human estate. In the Shakespearean pastoral, Prospero, the Duke of Milan, has been banished from his realm through collusion between his traitorous brother, Antonio, and Alonso, the King of Naples; and we find him dwelling in retirement with his daughter, Miranda, somewhere in the Mediterranean between Tunis and Naples, on a lovely island the only other inhabitant of which is a strange, half-human creature Caliban, whom Prospero holds in servitude. Since he is a master of conjuration and wizardry, when he learns through his divining arts that a ship bearing his enemies is in the neighborhood of his coast, he prepares a storm as a means of causing the ship to founder on the island's shore.

With the help of Ariel, the angelic sprite who performs his bidding, Prospero then proceeds to arrange a drama of judgment, of forgiveness, and of reconciliation whereby, in the end, he is restored to his dukedom and all the estrangements that had ruptured his circle are healed, the lone final recidivist being the depraved Caliban on whose nature nurture cannot stick. So Auden takes Prospero to be a "personified type of the creative," to be indeed (most especially in his alliance with Ariel, who is but a metaphor of Imagination) the very type and example of the artist, of him who transmutes the discordancies of human existence into patterns of harmony and order. And through the elaborate conceit of his masque—which involves in effect Shakespeare's curtain being lifted for the sake of allowing his characters a final speech and of inviting speculation as to how in truth they will henceforth fare—Auden attempts to take some measure of how rough Prospero's "rough magic" really is. For, after "inveigling Caliban into Ariel's kingdom" and revealing its incapacity to deal with this "intrusion of the real," it then lets "loose Ariel in Caliban's" realm—but Caliban stands not for "a dream amenable to magic but [for] the all too solid flesh" of the human actuality in its elemental waywardness and intractability. Hence it is given to Caliban himself to remind us—through the long, rolling periods of his Jamesian rhetoric—of how inadequately "the mirror of art" reckons with "the sea" of reality, that sea out onto which Shakespeare's cast had finally to launch in their journey back from the magic isle to "the Grandly Average Place" in Milan and Naples where they had once again to enter into the human condition. "Art is not life and cannot be / A midwife to society."

It is in his "baroque eclogue" of 1947, *The Age of Anxiety*, that, after *New Year Letter*, we get the fullest account in his poetry of the 1940s of what was Auden's conception of the fundamental drift of contemporary society. The poem is a sequence of monologues and conversations and songs loosely organized (by a half-dozen "scenes") into a drama of quest and pilgrimage. But this eclogue presents no idyll of shepherds in a bucolic setting, and the poem may indeed be said to be an eclogue only perhaps in the sense carried by the Greek root, *eklegein* (to choose), from which the term derives—in the sense, that is, of its being a poem that explores a certain problem of choice, or the pathos consequent upon a certain paralysis of the capacity for making significant choices. We are taken into a New York bar on an All Souls' Night during the period of the Second World War, and there we meet four persons—the tired and aging widower, Quant, now hopelessly entrapped in the failed life of a shipping-office clerk; Malin, a middle-aged medical intelligence officer in the Canadian Air Force on a few days of leave in Manhattan; Emble, a young midwesterner in the Navy, who suffers "that anxiety about . . . his future which haunts, like a bad smell, the minds of most young men"; and Rosetta, an English émigrée now prospering as a buyer for a large department store. They sit on their bar stools, each listening to the radio's orchestration of news bulletins and inane commercials and each in inward musings trying to parse the grammar of a particular loneliness and of the inchoate yearnings it gives rise to. Once they fall into a casual camaraderie, they move into a booth with their drinks; and, there, the conversation—through its hollow periphrases and its broken, heavily alliterative lines—traverses the "seven ages" of man, from the baffled helplessness of childhood to the baffled hopelessness of old age and death. And, as they reflect on how elusive is "the route / Into hope and health," they launch into a second journey, now not across the "seven ages" but across the "seven stages" leading unto the Good Place. This voyage brings the pilgrims at last to "the hermetic gardens," there where "The ruined rebel is recreated / And chooses a chosen self." The charm and stillness of these gardens, however, is like an accusation: so they move on, and, because they have neither the faith nor the courage required to cross that dry region marking the seventh stage, "the world from which their journey had been one long flight [again] rises up before them."

As they travel across the city by taxi to Rosetta's apartment for a snack and a nightcap, the poem sounds a dirge that speaks about how the creaking and cracking of our "world-engine" betrays the need for another miracle of healing and grace. This little group, now half-seas over, amidst the coziness of Rosetta's flat, tipsily imagines that "love" may be the answer, as it is noticed that she and Emble are becoming attracted to each other: so Quant and Malin discreetly withdraw. But, after accompanying them to the elevator, Rosetta, on reentering the apartment, finds that Emble has passed out in her bedroom. "Blind on the bride-bed, the bridegroom snores, / Too aloof to love." And, as Quant sullenly makes his way homeward through the empty streets, Malin in his subway train sadly reflects on the futility of this evening of "vaguely disquieting adventures" and on the heartache that must be suffered by those who are

> . . . unwilling to say Yes
> To the Self-So which is the same at all times,
> That Always-Opposite which is the whole subject
> Of our not-knowing, yet from no necessity
> Condescended to exist and to suffer death
> And, scorned on a scaffold, ensconced in His life
> The human household.

These four, in short, exemplify the world of the Slump: they dwell in a wilderness of their own contriving and make manifest the diminution of spirit suffered in a time whose sign is that of the *désacralisé*.

At the beginning of the 60s the late Philip Larkin began an essay on Auden by suggesting that, in a discussion between one who knew only his work prior to 1940 and another who knew only the work produced after that date, it would be inevitable that "a mystifying gap" should open between them.[46] And the burden of Larkin's argument—that the post-1940 phase expressed a great falling off in animation and cogency—entailed an attempt at defining what the nature of this gap would be. The essay is not untouched by animus and wrong-headedness, but its experiment in trying to imagine such a conversation as it proposed is more than a little suggestive, for, when one takes a broad view of the *oeuvre* representing Auden's total achievement, it does most assuredly seem to fall into two major phases, though the watershed separating the one from the other is to be located not, as Larkin alleged, at the beginning of the 1940s but rather at the end of the decade. In a conversation between one who knew Auden's poetry only up through *The Age of Anxiety* and another who knew only his work from *Nones* (1951) on—in such a conversation the mystifying gap that would open would be very large indeed.

The penultimate poem in *Poems* of 1930 begins, "Consider this . . ."— and then, after remarking a "cigarette-end smouldering on a border / At the first garden party of the year," it goes on, like a roving camera eye, to notice the international set in winter at a sports hotel ("easy, in furs, in uniform / And constellated at reserved tables"), impoverished farmers sitting in their "kitchens in the stormy fens," the decadent insipidity of the academic cloisters ("Amid rustle of frocks and stamping feet / They gave the prizes to the ruined boys"), highborn gentlemen in their limousines "humming down arterial roads"—all this and more seen panoramically, "As the hawk sees it or the helmeted airman": it is (the English scene at the time of the Crash) a world of "strangled orchards" and "diseased youngsters," of "classic fatigue" and spreading decay. "Consider this and in our time / . . . ."And it is a similar injunction being sounded by the Auden of *The Orators* and *Look, Stranger!*, of *Another Time* and *New Year Letter*, of *For the Time Being* and *The Sea and the Mirror* and *The Age of Anxiety*—"Consider this. . . ."

Through the first twenty years of his career in poetry Auden's policy was that of launching—sometimes playfully, sometimes mordantly—a direct assault on a civilization and a cultural polity that, in his sense of the matter, represented failure. Stephen Spender has recorded his suspicion that, in the early years of his career, Auden's "secret fantasy of the poet" resembled "Cocteau's image in *Orphée* of Death as the surgeon with white coat and rubber gloves."[47] He was, of course, always "a marvellous talker, with all the gifts of an orator at his finger-tips,"[48] and, over a long period, the spirited and brilliant talk carried on by his poetry was that of one bent on diagnosing and arraigning and instructing a delinquent age. In an essay of 1940 in which he was setting forth the respects in which he felt Thomas Hardy to be his "poetical father," he said that what he "valued most in Hardy . . . was his hawk's vision, his way of looking at life from a very great height."[49] And it was a similar vantage point that he himself had wanted to win, for it was "time for the destruction of error," and, if the crucial faults and infirmities were to be ferreted out with clinical precision, one needed to attain and to keep something like the aerial view—of "the helmeted airman."

As Auden looked down from a great height on the unstable world of his time, his focus did, of course, periodically shift from one to another phase of the general "crisis and dismay." In the early poems he was frequently preoccupied with the "underground proliferation of mould" that lay beneath a society of frozen credit and tottered combines, of "rotting

wharves and choked canals," where what was required was "death . . . /
Death of the old gang." Sometimes, as it seemed, "the error" was to be
located not in the malfunction of social-political structures but in the evasions of the individual, and thus he would interrogate those "nervous
people who will never marry," choosing instead to live on dividends in
lonely cottages, "With an animal for friend or a volume of memoirs."
Then, again, the poetry would move within the world of "the flat ephem-
eral pamphlet and the boring meeting" and stare at "Imperialism's face /
And the international wrong." And, recurrently, it would sound its sum-
mons to "build the Just City." But, whatever may have been his particular
interest at a given moment, the young poet of *Poems* (1930) and *Look,
Stranger!* and *Another Time* was a specialist in cultural diagnostics for
whom the great idea, as Spender says, was "Symptom and Cure."[50] Or,
when he was not (in Geoffrey Grigson's phrase) a "benign wizard casting
out devils,"[51] he was playing the part of Schoolmaster unto his age, saying with raised forefinger, "Consider this. . . ."

Auden's poetry of the 40s, records a very profound shift in basic perspective. For, as he moved from *New Year Letter* into the period of his
Christmas oratorio and *The Sea and the Mirror* and *The Age of Anxiety*, it
became apparent that no longer was he under the tutelage of his earlier
mentors, of Freud and (more remotely) Marx, of Georg Groddeck and
Homer Lane and D. H. Lawrence. His progress had at last brought him
onto the terrain of the Christian faith into which, indeed, he was to enter
ever more deeply throughout the remaining thirty years of his career; and
the guides presiding over this *metanoia* were figures such as Augustine
and Pascal and Kierkegaard, Reinhold Niebuhr and Paul Tillich and
Charles Williams. Yet, now as a Catholic obedient to Anglican tradition,
the distinguishing style of his speech and thought did in no way undergo
any significant alteration, for he kept his old belief that the "duty of a
poem . . . is to bear witness to the truth": as he faced the secular forums
of his day from the standpoint of his newly embraced orthodoxy, the
central stress of his poetry continued to be aggressive, polemical, admonitory—and the note of triumphalism is often to be heard in the under-
tones of his work of the 1940s, as when he is bidding us to make "free
confessions of our sins" and (as his "Star of the Nativity" says in *For the
Time Being*) to

> Descend into the fosse of Tribulation,
> Take the cold hand of Terror for a guide.

In *Nones*, his book of 1951, and *The Shield of Achilles*, which followed it
in 1955, a new poetic personality, however, began to make itself felt, and
this even more decidedly so through the 60s and early 70s in Auden's last

books—in *Homage to Clio* (1960), *About the House* (1965), *City without Walls* (1969), *Epistle to a Godson* (1972), and the posthumous volume of 1974, *Thank You, Fog.* In these wonderfully nuanced and deeply affecting volumes of his full maturity, his extraordinary adroitness in the management of meter and diction and syntax continues to be the prodigy it had always been, and, as he goes about his elaborately mannerist procedures, he remains one who (as he puts it in one of the finest poems in *The Shield of Achilles*—"'The Truest Poetry Is the Most Feigning'") wants to say to himself

> Be subtle, various, ornamental, clever,
> And do not listen to those critics ever
> Whose crude provincial gullets crave in books
> Plain cooking made still plainer by plain cooks,
> As though the Muse preferred her half-wit sons. . . .

But the old pugnacious, bullying, vigilant strictness is gone, or does at least now come to the fore only very rarely. He is still "a marvellous talker," but the talk being heard in the late poetry is the quiet, equable, urbanely courteous talk of one who has chosen for his *ars poetica* "the wry, the sotto-voce, / Ironic and monochrome." And, in his late books, the caustic, imperious, exigent wittiness of an earlier period has deepened into a profoundly comic compassionateness and equanimity. Here, it is no longer the "hawk's vision" that he covets, for he has come to realize (as he says in the beautifully composed "Memorial for the City" in *Nones*) that

> The steady eyes of the crow and the camera's candid eye
> See as honestly as they know how, but they lie.

"The eyes of the crow and the eye of the camera open / Onto Homer's world, not ours." And Homer's world, as he had earlier said in an essay on Greek culture,

> is unbearably sad because it never transcends the immediate moment; one is happy, one is unhappy, one wins, one loses, finally one dies. That is all. Joy and suffering are simply what one feels at the moment; they have no meaning beyond that; they pass away as they came; they point in no direction; they change nothing. It is a tragic world but a world without guilt for its tragic flaw is not a flaw in human nature, still less a flaw in an individual character, but a flaw in the nature of existence.[52]

Homer's world, therefore, is not the world in which we dwell: as the "Memorial" reminds us,

Our grief is not Greek: As we bury our dead
We know without knowing there is reason for what we bear,
That our hurt is not a desertion, that we are to pity
Neither ourselves nor our city;
Whoever the searchlights catch, whatever the loudspeakers blare,
We are not to despair.

Because we are hobbled neither by some essential defect in the nature of existence nor by some inherent defect in the nature of the human faculty, our tears need never be tears of self-pity but only tears of remorse and repentance. So the detached, objective, aerial view—of the crow and the camera, of the hawk and the helmeted airman—does not, in the end, afford a proper perspective on our human condition: it may, from its altitude, offer a fair prospect of the craggy, mountainous uplands of the world, but, in the late poems, Auden wants to say that the scene "Of green and civil life" (as the *New Year Letter* calls it) is the

. . . places where we have really been, dear spaces
Of our deeds and faces, scenes we remember
As unchanging because there we changed, where shops have names,
Dogs bark in the dark at a stranger's footfall
And crops grow ripe and cattle fatten under the kind
Protection of a godling or goddessling
Whose affection has been assigned them, to heed their needs and
Plead in heaven the special case of their place.[53]

We are, in short, imperfect, conditioned, earth-bound creatures; and, however far we may venture out beyond our wonted precincts or however high we may climb those treacherous mountains that Hopkins called "cliffs of fall" ("Frightful, sheer, no-man-fathomed"),[54] we are still of the earth and earthy. And, in its intention to find its own fulcrum in the mundane, unexceptional region of our everyday habitancy, the poetry of Auden's last years shows itself to be controlled by persistently comic sympathies, for it is, indeed, the special tendency of the comic vision to assert our deep, unsunderable involvement in the things of earth, and to do this in a spirit of praise and thanksgiving. Moreover, despite the infrequency with which the late poems avail themselves of Christian theological concepts as an arsenal for polemic or disputation, it may be just in their readiness to affirm the dignity of "the ordinary universe" that they prove how deeply formed by the perspectives of an Incarnational faith the mind of this poet in his late maturity had come to be.

It was the great poem in *Nones*, "In Praise of Limestone," that presented what was perhaps the first major expression of Auden's late style.

He had earlier in *New Year Letter* declared his affection for those limestone moors chained by the Pennine uplands in the countryside of northern England, identifying this as the locality that came to mind whenever he tried to imagine where it might be that "the human creature" could perhaps best be brought "to sense and decency." And here, in *Nones*, he explains what it is that prompts his fondness for the landscape:

> If it form the one landscape that we the inconstant ones
> Are consistently homesick for, this is chiefly
> Because it dissolves in water.

The impermanence of this limestone world is like the transiency of the human thing itself; and, furthermore, it is a "region / Of short distances and definite places," a region "Where everything can be touched or reached by walking"—"sometimes / Arm in arm, but never, thank God, in step." It is thus a place whose gently "rounded slopes / With their surface fragrance of thyme" invite us to remember how deeply rooted we are in the finite creaturality that belongs to the things of earth, to remember that we are men and women and not angels. This may be why, as the poem's speaker surmises, "The best and worst never stayed here long but sought / Immoderate soils": the would-be saint is drawn to "granite wastes" and "Intendant Caesars" to clayed and gravelly plains where "there is room for armies to drill" and where "rivers / Wait to be tamed." But this calm terrain, this backward and dilapidated province, this human place, makes an analogue of the scene and site of the common life, of the well-trodden, middling world in which the generality of humankind actually dwells. Yet, though it may be scorned by the tigers of wrath, it is not without its own peculiar power to disturb, for it "calls into question /All the Great Powers assume": by thrusting forward the rock-bottom earthiness of human life and by reminding us how incorrigibly finite all human things are, it exposes the fraudulence of all attempts (whether by art or by science or by religion) at leaping out of the human condition into Magnificence and Glory: "it dissolves in water" and thereby makes us remember that we must "look forward / To death as a fact." So when he tries to imagine the Good Place, says Auden, "what I hear is the murmur / Of underground streams, what I see is a limestone landscape."

The poem in *Nones* entitled "Memorial for the City," in its swift résumé of two thousand years of Christendom, reviews the great patterns of the *civitas terrena* in Western history. It recalls that New City resulting from the precarious balance of papal and imperial power—which was followed by the Sane City of the high Middle Ages, where "disciplined logicians" held at bay "the eccentricities of the private brain." This dispensation, however, in due course was denounced by Luther as the Sinful City; and, amidst the fragmentations brought by Reformation and Renaissance, reason and science claimed the primacy, so there came a time when "history marched to the drums of a clear idea" and all was aimed at the Rational City—whose shadow falls across the whole modern quest for the Conscious City, where we may be "Faithful without faith." But, as the poem wants eventually to say, the last state of things is worse than the first, for, in our own late time, the modern experiment in secularization issues only in "the abolished City," where the world seems "a chaos of graves" and where "the barbed-wire stretches ahead / Into our future till it is lost to sight."

So, then, says Auden, *"Let Our Weakness speak,"* and this is what the concluding section of the poem wants to give voice to—the duplicity and opportunism, the recreancy and sharp practice, the mulishness and illiberality that are the despair of social engineers and all those who would build "Metropolis, that too-great city." The poem wants finally to hold up our bloody beastliness as that which has no doubt ever and again subverted the enterprise of *communitas* but which, in its very intractability, bespeaks a certain stoutness in our flesh that offers a kind of hope for the human future. And though this gritty, gamy waywardness of the race may, to be sure, exasperate those who would reduce the world to the tidiness of a chessboard, the richly ironic poem in *Nones* called "The Managers" suggests that, so far as they are concerned—the quiet men who work too hard in rooms too big, eating with one hand little luncheons of sandwiches brought in a tray while handling with the other "papers a couple / Of secretaries are needed to file"—

> . . . no one is really sorry for their
> Heavy gait and careworn
> Look, nor would they thank you if you said you were.

This insistently comic perspective provides the basic point of view controlling not only "In Praise of Limestone" and "Memorial for the City" and "The Managers" but also many of the other poems in *Nones*—among them, "Their Lonely Betters" (with its strikingly devised echoes of Robert Frost), "Ischia," "Pleasure Island," "Under Which Lyre." It is a poetry carrying much complexity of theme and argument, but—in its colloquial idioms, its easy mingling of wit and gravity, its relaxed conversational tone, its preference for loosely stressed accentual lines—studiedly avoiding the large gesture. For, as he says in the dedicatory lines "To Reinhold and Ursula Niebuhr," the language of "the grand old manner," of the "resonant heart," is "soiled, profaned, debased" and has been too much used "to befuddle the crowd." So, in the elected manner of his oblique informality, Auden's great technical virtuosity begins in his poetry of the 1950s to be dedicated to an essentially comic work, of declaring amidst the ruins of the Rational City that, however intractable the Managers may find the human reality to be, there is, just in its very recalcitrancy and waywardness, a kind of sign, a sign of a certain obstinate sturdiness in things—in the scents of flowers and the songs of birds, as well as in the frowardness of men—that no rationalist technicism can bring to heel. And thus, in the spirit of that sense of deep encouragement which ensued, he was moved to make the great testimony voiced by the poem in *Nones* called "Precious Five":

> I could . . .
> Find reasons fast enough
> To face the sky and roar
> In anger and despair
> At what is going on,
> Demanding that it name
> Whoever is to blame:
> The sky would only wait
> Till all my breath was gone
> And then reiterate
> As if I wasn't there
> That singular command
> I do not understand,
> *Bless what there is for being.* . . .

Indeed, what is most remarkable in the books of Auden's last years—in *The Shield of Achilles,* in *Homage to Clio,* in *About the House,* in *City without Walls* and *Epistle to a Godson*—is this Blakean impulse by which they are all touched, the impulse to celebrate and doxologize the holiness of the world. And they are books in which the world is being looked at not through the narrow end of the telescope, where the view is of the enormous and dreadful abysm of existence: things instead are being looked at through the larger end of the instrument—which is, of course, the comic vantage point, where "everything has become not sea incarnadine but a disconcertingly small puddle."[55] Auden's telescope, in short, is turned around: so it brings into view the common, average, ordinary circumstances and realities of life, and it is in these that holiness is descried.

It should not, therefore, be considered odd that many of the late poems are focused on pastoral themes and situations, for, when a poet so deeply steeped in urban ethos as Auden always was begins to reflect on the sustaining continuities of the quotidian realm, it is no doubt to be expected that he (perhaps most especially he) will feel an impulse to recall the various supportive agencies in the natural order by which human life is upborne. And, indeed, the poems of Auden's last years are recurrently to be found performing rites of homage to that good lady, Dame Kind— "our Mum"—who, Coarse Old Party that she is, keeps all the vitalities of nature unimpaired. For She gives our bodies their solid structures of bone which "Are no discredit to our kind." She gives us hands that "reckon, beckon, demonstrate," so that, even when we wander in foreign lands, "We command a rhetoric / Which makes us glad we came." And we are indebted to Her not only for the marvelously pleasurable and efficient "corporal contraptions" we are but also for all the wonderfully variegated creatures and processes that form the environing theater of our life in the world, things so astonishing in their power to nourish and to heal that this poet, with his old propensity for parables, was moved again and again in the latter phase of his career to proffer one or another kind of parable recording a meditation initiated by some wonderment at the miraculous prodigality and beneficence of the order administered by Dame Kind. The *pietas,* expressed always wryly and sotto voce, is not at all Wordsworthian—five minutes of gazing at some vista in the Lake District would be "awfully long"—but, for all the ironic qualifications with which it may hedge itself about, it is something very deeply felt.

Auden's pastoral mode attains one of its finest expressions in the sequence of seven poems in *The Shield of Achilles* entitled "Bucolics." In "Winds," inscribed not surprisingly to Alexis Léger (St.-John Perse), he reminds us that the agitated airs of the world "make weather," and he prays that, in all seasons and all weathers, the Goddess of winds will grant that he, her clerk and minstrel, may so perform "every verbal rite" as to make it an act of "anamnesis / Of what is excellent" in all the things and creatures of earth. The iambic pentameters of "Woods" challenge the old convention that opposes the decorum of human society to the murder and rapine of sylvan thickets; and they suggest that the world's forest tracts (which are often to be found "massacred to the last ash") are at the mercy of humankind, that their condition reveals "a lot about a country's soul"—"A culture is no better than its woods." "Mountains" speaks a word of warning against "steep places" that may attract "unsmiling" men reaching after Heaven but that do not make a good terrain for most of us, "uncatlike" as we are. Similarly, "Lakes" also expresses a preference for the small, domiciliated scale of things:

> A lake allows an average father, walking slowly,
>> To circumvent it in an afternoon,
> And any healthy mother to halloo the children

Back to her bedtime from their games across:
(Anything bigger than that, like Michigan or Baikal,
    Though potable, is an "estranging sea").

"Islands," in its brisk and witty quatrains, catalogues the various types
who dwell on keys and island shelfs—saints on millstones, pirates in
their lairs, convicted criminals, exiled emperors—but the poem insists
that the broad majority of men must find "a mainland livelihood." In
"Plains," the poet confesses that he cannot see a stretch of flats—"where
all elsewheres are equal" and where all "roads run level"—"without a
shudder," though, as he recalls how he has often lost his way in valleys
and lowlands, he also admits that perhaps "I've reason to be frightened /
Not of plains . . . but of me." Then, in "Streams," the last and most beautiful of these eclogues, he speaks of that for which he has the greatest
affection, "clear water," convivial and cheering in all its streams, seeming
always "glad—though goodness knows why—to run with the human
race":

as you dash or loiter through life who does not love
    to sit beside you, to hear you and see you,
        pure being, perfect in music and movement?

Air is boastful at times, earth slovenly, fire rude,
    but you in your bearing are always immaculate,
        the most well-spoken of all the older
        servants in the household of Mrs. Nature.

It should be apparent, then, that in these essays in *paysage moralisé*, as
in his numerous other poems in a bucolic mode, Auden does not permit
himself any kind of Arcadian sentimentality. For the natural order that
he confronts, though finally inviting homage and reverence, presents itself at least initially in the form of moral ambiguity, besmudged as it is
with all the improprieties of men. Nor does his tutelage under the great
masters of Christian anthropology ever allow him to suppose that there
is some balm in nature that offers a quick and easy cure for the ailments
of the human heart. Indeed, the great sequence of poems with which *The
Shield of Achilles* concludes—"Horae Canonicae"—wants to insist on how
incontrovertibly and inexorably, throughout all the rhythms of each daily
round, we are as much implicated in the crucifixion of Christ as were
those who nailed him to his cross on that Friday afternoon of long ago.

This cycle of seven texts, as its title indicates, offers a series of meditations marking those seven canonical hours that are laid down by the old
breviaries of the Western Church as the times for saying the offices of
daily prayer. "Prime" (6:00 A.M.) speaks of that moment at the beginning

of the day when, "Recalled from the shades to be a seeing being," the self wakes to consciousness, still—in the moment of waking—"wholly in the right." But no sooner does the body stir into its first movements than "this ready flesh" becomes the accomplice and the creature of the will—whose inveterately self-regarding motivation immediately ordains that "I" shall *fall* into "my historical share of care / For a lying self-made city"; thus, as the poem suggests, to "draw breath . . . is . . . to die."

By 9:00 A.M. ("Terce") "I" will have shaken the paws of my dog, quietly closed the door of the bedroom of my wife, who is having one of her headaches, and started off on the day's affairs, with such a prayer as

> "Let me get through this coming day
> Without a dressing down from a superior,
> Being worsted in a repartee,
> Or behaving like an ass in front of the girls;
> Let something exciting happen,
> Let me find a lucky coin on a sidewalk.
> Let me hear a new funny story."

(But by sundown "I" "shall have had a good Friday," shall have managed, however obscurely or unimpressively situated my life may be, to have dealt another blow to the fearfully bruised face of Christ.)

By 12:00 P.M. ("Sext"), indeed, the great machine of the world's business is awhir, and you will find "a cook mixing a sauce, a surgeon / making a primary incision, / a clerk completing a bill of lading"—all wearing "the same rapt expression, / forgetting themselves in a function." And, apart from the various technical specialists and functionaries who perform the work of civilization, there is the *fourmillante cité*, which sees only what the crowd can see and "only believes in that / in which there is only one way of believing."

By 3:00 P.M. we are well into the heat of the day, and "Nones" is set therefore in the siesta hours, when "the faceless many" lie sprawled in slumber, none able now to "remember why / He shouted or what about / So loudly in the sunshine this morning." This, in the chronology of the New Testament narrative, is the time that followed the Crucifixion, when indeed "the faceless many" then, if challenged, would have replied:

> —"It was a monster with one red eye,
> A crowd that saw him die, not I."—

So now, as then, their "projects under construction, / Look only in one direction." "The shops will re-open at four": meanwhile, there is "time / To misrepresent, excuse, deny, / Mythify" that event which occurred at the place of a Skull and which is reenacted over and again each day in all the other places of man's habitation.

"Vespers" brings us to the time of early evening (6:00 P.M.), and, here, "in this hour of civil twilight," Auden's speech relaxes into a prose idiom, as "two paths cross"—that of "an Arcadian" (who is the speaker) and that of "a Utopian":

> Neither speaks. What experience could we possibly share?
> Glancing at a lampshade in a store window, I observe
> it is too hideous for anyone in their senses to buy:
> He observes it is too expensive for a peasant to buy.
> Passing a slum child with rickets, I look the other
> way: He looks the other way if he passes a chubby
> one. . . .
> You can see, then, between my Eden and his New
> Jerusalem, no treaty is negotiable.

Yet this encounter is "also a rendezvous between two accomplices," because their Victim is one "on whose immolation" both Arcadias and Utopias are founded: that is, when all the relativities of our tastes and perspectives are viewed in relation to the Primal Fact (of, in the Evangelist's phrase, the "ransom for the many" that sinlessness was required to pay), they prove to be relativities that do not entail any very great difference.

"Compline" marks the hour (9:00 P.M.) when the day is over and when one would like to be able, in an "instant of recollection," to shape its happenings into some pattern of significance—but all that can be recalled

> . . . are doors banging,
> Two housewives scolding, an old man gobbling,
> A child's wild look of envy,
> Actions, words, that could fit any tale. . . .

And, as the poem's speaker tellingly admits, "I cannot remember / A thing between noon and three" (the time of the Crucifixion). But, as he gradually lapses into sleep, a prayer (from the Ordinary of the Mass) is wrung from his lips—"*libera me*"—and, "in the name of a love / Whose name one's forgotten," he asks that the time may come when he "shall know exactly what happened . . . between noon and three."

So it is a very stringent measure indeed that Auden was prepared to take of that "village of the heart" wherein "ordinary decent folk," with all their transgressions and evasions, daily dwell. Yet it is in these inglorious precincts, amidst the commonplace mutualities of the human household, that we are summoned to be obedient to the requirements of *agape:* as Justin Replogle reminds us, Auden shared with Robert Frost the conviction that "The earth's the right place for love."[56] But there shall be no love on earth unless the things and creatures of earth themselves are loved: so "Lauds," the beautiful lyric that brings the "Horae" to an end, as it listens at dawn to the warbling of small birds and the crowing of the cock, sings out its imploration:

> God bless the Realm, God bless the People;
> God bless this green world temporal. . . .

Now it is the great canticle with which the "Horae" conclude—"God bless this green world temporal"—that, from our present vantage point, may be seen to have prefigured the line Auden would be taking in the work of his last years. For in the collection of his poems that he issued in 1960, *Homage to Clio*, and in the book that followed it five years later, *About the House*, it is, indeed, Clio who (as in the later volumes also) is his Muse. She is, of course, the goddess of time, the guardian spirit who presides over our steady passage through all the finite, limited moments of our journey amidst "this green world." And whenever we are seized by any "angelic" passion for some specious "eternity" and are thus prompted to conceive these finite, limited moments as something to break out of and to escape from, it is a part of Clio's office to arrange for us to be reminded that our residence is not in the heavens, that we are irrevocably committed to the ordinary, unexceptional world of our earth-bound career, and that we had, therefore, better learn to take our lives on the terms of their concrete actuality.

So it is appropriate that Clio, unlike Artemis and Aphrodite, should be one for whom the arts have no ready icon, that she (as Auden says) should "look like any / Girl one has not noticed"—for, as the goddess of time, her special realm is that of the quotidian; and this is precisely the region explored in the wonderfully rich books of Auden's final years. Here, under Clio's guidance, he is taking stock not of lords and saints but of "all poor s-o-b's who never / Do anything properly," of those who merely breed good horses and find decent answers to their questions, who pay their bills promptly, and who (as the Eliot of *The Cocktail Party* would say) keep the hearth. His Representative Man is he who, however audacious and far-ranging his nocturnal dreams, finds himself con-demned (or privileged) to be only human and who—Voice of "Our Weak-ness" that he is—scrapes up a supportable bulwark against the mortifi-cations of life by blessing *what there is for being*, by forswearing both Paradise Losts and New Jerusalems, by being grateful to Dame Kind that, though "She mayn't be all she might . . . She *is* our Mum," by facing into the fact of his commitment to time, and by being glad for the shelter over his head under which, as he says, "I needn't, ever, be at home *to* / those I am not at home *with*. . . ."

The genial, seasoned, gray eminence that Auden had become at the end—the man who had found "an angle of experience where the dark is distilled into light" and where our daily bumblings with work and friends may be seen to go "straight to the key which creation was composed in"[57]—this poet (in his desire to bless what there is for being) proved, as at times he still does, to be for many only a disappointing backslider who had strangely lost the prophetic rectitude of an earlier time. The technical virtuosity of the later poems, the astounding range of the vocabulary he commands, the clarity he manages to keep in syntactical constructions of frequently great complexity, his well-nigh unexampled genius as a metrist, the extraordinary contrapuntalism with which he orchestrates voices and tones (coarse heartiness, mock solemnity, circus horseplay, high eloquence), the enormous breadth of learning and scholarship that supports his reflections, the outrageous ease with which he turns out odes and clerihews and villanelles and ballades and *haiku*—all this remains as impressive as ever before. But this poet who now finds his "catholic area" to be his living room, where friends gather after dinner for music or gossip; who forswears "the preacher's loose immodest tone," believing that in our rackety and clamorous age a truly human speech must now be quiet and intimate; who obstinately focuses his later poetry, therefore, not on the public spaces of the age but on the domestic scene, where men and women may meet "without papers" to enjoy a good dinner; and who wants, amidst the civil amenities and formalities of the domestic life, to sound a *Benedicite*—this, in the judgment of numerous arbiters, is a poet who had given up his earlier intention to promote "new styles of architecture" and to be a "conscript to our age." Indeed, as it is sometimes charged, the Auden of *About the House* and *City without Walls* and *Epistle to a Godson*—"overdined and overwined"[58]—is one who had suffered a sad "change of life"; and the sclerosis of the last years, it is said, when viewed in relation to the insouciantly *engagé* figure of the 30s and 40s, can only be taken to represent an unfortunate decline into reactionist "apoliticalism."[59] So Philip Larkin's question of 1960—"What's become of Wystan?"—is recurrently raised, the tense now of course, unhappily, needing to be preterit.

Yet, surely, any careful reconsideration of Auden's line of progress, if not controlled by hostile bias, ought to indicate that the case is by no means so simple as it is made out to be by those who think of him as having been in his last years a Lost Leader. And what needs particularly to be heeded in that line of progress is the steadiness with which, from the 1940s on, he ever more firmly resolved not to give his own suffrage to the ominously darkening world of the new *Masse-Mensch*. For life in our own century, as he came more and more deeply to feel over the last twenty-five years of his career, is perilously drifting toward a polity comprised of such entities as arise when men and women are simply added together into the kinds of collectives that may be efficiently controlled and manipulated by the managerial élite brought to a position of world-rulership in this present postheroic stage of bourgeois capitalism, at the end of the modern era.

One suspects, indeed, that Auden was very greatly influenced not only by the Kierkegaard of *Either/Or* and *Stages on Life's Way* but also by the Kierkegaard of that brilliant little book of 1846 called *The Present Age*, which announced that all the basic structures of modern society are calculated to keep a person from saying "I." It is the crowd, said Kierkegaard, that is fast becoming the fundamental form of human existence. Anticipating that line of testimony that was later to come from thinkers such as Jaspers and Ortega and Marcel and Berdyaev, he contended that the people of the modern period are no longer prepared to risk any attempt at straightforwardly reckoning with their individual selfhood: instead, they form a committee—and "in the end the whole age becomes a committee."[60] In Kierkegaard's estimate, the result is the invasion of the world by that new phantom he called "the public"—"a kind of gigantic something, an abstract and deserted void which is everything and nothing,"[61] and which begins to come into existence when we give up our individuality for the sake of buying the cheap sort of safety to be had when one is engulfed, as an anonymous component, into a social collective. Then, "all inwardness is lost,"[62] and the world enters into an "age of levelling."[63] And, of course—as we have been reminded again and again by that tradition of modern sociology running, say, from Georg Simmel and Max Weber to Jacques Ellul—this great indolent human mass constituting "the public" breeds that strange dispensation in which the bureaucratic ethos takes the ascendancy, where those for whom life must be something like a vast committee elect that their fate shall be conjured with by the inscrutable men comprising the cadre of Technicians, of Experts, of Managers, whose overriding concern is "to wipe out the blots . . . [that] personal determination introduces into the perfect design of the organization."[64]

Now it is this Myth—which, regrettably, has proved to have a remarkable power to illumine the drift of the age—that began, as it would seem, at some time in the 40s to organize one phase of Auden's thought. He was not, to be sure, any sort of systematic theorist of the relations between *Gemeinschaft* and *Gesellschaft*, but the decline from the one to the other may be seen at various points to have been something he was deeply pondering over a long period. As early as 1941, in his essay "Criticism in a Mass Society," Auden was already remarking the failure of the modern populace in the liberal democracies "to acquire the habits [of thought] that an open society demands,"[65] was remarking how much "the great majority prefer opinion to knowledge, and passively allow the former to be imposed upon them by a centralized few."[66] Or, again, in an essay of 1948 on Yeats, he said: "No private citizen to-day thinks seriously, 'Here is superior me and there are all those other people'; but 'Here are we, all in the same boat, and there is It, the Government.' "[67] Two years later, he was observing that revolutions may often be graphically represented by a symbolic figure—the American, say, by a pioneer, the French by an intellectual—and that perhaps the appropriate symbol of the revolution we are in the midst of today is "a naked anonymous baby," since

it is for the baby's right to health, not for the freedom of any person or class to act or think—for a baby is not yet a person and cannot choose or think—that the revolution is being fought everywhere in one way or another. A baby has to be controlled, it has to be indoctrinated, it cannot be told more of the truth than it can profitably understand, so the present revolution is authoritarian and believes in censorship and propaganda. Since its values are really derived from medicine, from a concept of health, it is hostile to any nonconformity, any deviation from the norm. . . .

What will happen is anybody's guess. Perhaps history is forcing the intellectual, whether scientist or artist, into a new conception of himself as neither the respectable bard nor the anarchic aesthete, but as a member of the Loyal Opposition, defending, not for his own sake only but for all, the inalienable rights of the individual person against encroachment by an overzealous government, with which, nevertheless, even though the latter deny it, he has a bond, their common love for the Just City.[68]

Nor does one have any difficulty at all in adjusting to this kind of argument a poetic statement such as "The Managers" (in *Nones*) makes, about those for whom "there will be places on the last / Plane out of disaster"— the New Men who have "The last word on how we may live or die." And a large number of similar citations may be gathered from Auden's writings of the 1950s and 60s, from both his poems and his essays.

In the whole course of his reflections in this vein, it was no doubt his reading of Hannah Arendt's *The Human Condition*[69] that constituted a major event, and it is surprising that, among those who have attempted to reckon with Auden's late phase, it is Richard Johnson alone who has sensed the depth of Arendt's impact.[70] The very careful review of the book that Auden published in the English magazine *Encounter* was obviously the result of enormous pains having been taken to master the great complexities of her dialectic; and it is not unlikely that *The Human Condition* requires to be associated with that select group of books—Kierkegaard's *Stages on Life's Way,* Charles Williams's *He Came Down from Heaven,* Charles Norris Cochrane's *Christianity and Classical Culture,* Reinhold Niebuhr's *The Nature and Destiny of Man,* Denis de Rougemont's *L'Amour et l'Occident*—which, beyond all others, must be taken account of in any comprehensive plotting of his mature thought. Indeed, as he said in his review, "Every now and then, I come across a book which gives me the impression of having been especially written for me. In the case of a work of art, the author seems to have created a world for which I have been waiting all my life; in the case of a 'think' book, it seems to answer precisely those questions which I have been putting to myself. . . . Miss Hannah Arendt's *The Human Condition* belongs to this small and select class."[71]

In Arendt's book of 1958, her subject remained what it had been in the book by which, seven years earlier, she had first won a large reputation, *The Origins of Totalitarianism*—though, now, she was concerned not with the kind of outrageous despotism fostered by Stalin and Hitler but, rather, with the equally virulent tyrannizing of the human spirit which is effectuated in the modern period by the totalitarianism of mass society. In the terms of Arendt's own lexicon, however, the familiar locution "mass society" would need to be denominated a redundancy, for what she takes to be the great distinguishing fact of the modern scene is "the emergence of the social realm,"[72] the rise to ascendancy of a type of consociation amongst people whereby they are related to one another only by reason of their belonging to the human species and of their concern for its perpetuation, but united not at all on the basis of their sharing a common spiritual world. Indeed, when the human community has become a kind of vast household in which the major activities are housekeeping activities calculated to guarantee the maintenance of life for the individual and the species; when (as in a family) there is no longer any distance between people, so that, instead of acting as individuals, they "play roles" and behave like robots; and when the conduct of this household's affairs is taken over by anonymous bureaucrats, so that the predominant form of government becomes that of "rule by nobody" (which may be "one of . . . [the] cruelest and most tyrannical versions"[73] of government)—when this is the reigning state of affairs (as Arendt takes it to have been, with ever-increasing inordinacy, over the past two hundred years), then, as she would say, the human world has fallen under the sway of "society," which is in its very essence a *mass* reality.

The bench mark in relation to which Arendt takes her measure of the human City in our time is that which is for her represented by the Greek *polis* of the great Athenian age of the fifth century, the age of Pericles and Thucydides, of Plato and Isocrates. And, when she moves back from the drifting, muddled world of the present to that exemplary moment made by the Greek city-state, what she finds to be of greatest interest in that ancient mode of life is its containment of "society" within the realm of the private household. For, as she maintains, the Greeks conceived the home and the family to be the center of all the various forms of merely social companionship that may be necessary for the satisfaction of our natural wants and needs. Here, in the realm of the household, the presiding figure was the *paterfamilias* who, in the style of an unchallengeable autocrat, so governed the family circle and its enslaved retainers as to provide for all the necessities of the domestic order and to sustain the ongoing processes of life: here it was, under the guardianship of the penates, that the man labored to provide nourishment for the individual and the woman labored (in giving birth) to provide for the survival of the species. And it was from out of the dim, sheltered interior of this nonpolitical (or prepolitical) realm of the household that a freeman stepped forth into the life of the City, into the world of "action," into that public space of the *politikos* where, by well chosen words and courageous deeds, he joined his equals in the pursuit not of life but of "the good life."

In the context of the Greek city-state, as Arendt insists, the household was the domain of necessity—where the slaves labored that their master might be liberated from all gross employments, where the woman labored to bring forth new life; and it was only in the public forums of the commonwealth that freedom dwelt, where men, having left the dark alcoves of the private region, moved among their equals to initiate common enterprises and to conduct the business of the *polis*. Here it was, indeed, in the world of the *politikos*, that, having been liberated from those necessities of nature served by the household, men could truly become individuals, as they embarked on important civic undertakings and (by their words and deeds) strove with one another for glory. Indeed, the whole raison d'être of politics was that of providing an unpolluted, invigorating public space in which, as they attended to the affairs of the City, men might so test one another as to discover whom it was who deserved to be admitted into the fellowship of the brave and the true. This meant, of course, that the reality of the *polis* was something incommensurable with that range of meanings presided over by our modern concept of "ideology," for politics—namely, that enterprise which concerned the *polis*—

was in no wise conceived to be any kind of superstructure of social and economic interests, for these touched not the life of the *polis* but belonged wholly to the private sphere of the household. Nor was politics an affair of rulership and legislation. True, a stable structure of law was required, for, apart from established ordinances, "a public realm could no more exist than a piece of property without a fence to hedge it in; the one harbored and inclosed political life as the other sheltered and protected the biological life process of the family."[74] But the making of laws was not the *content* of political action. And rulership had no place in the political sphere, because the *polis* knew only *homoioi* (equals), who neither commanded nor submitted to commands. Instead, what was of the essence of things in the public realm was not the administering of institutions or the enactment of laws or the policing of the rabble, but rather the affiliation in great enterprise of men who, only by acting together, found their freedom and thus came into their full human stature. "The public realm, in other words, was reserved for individuality; it was the only place where men could show who they really and inexchangeably were. It was for the sake of this chance, and out of love for a body politic that made it possible to them all, that each was more or less willing to share in the burden of jurisdiction, defense, and administration of public affairs."[75]

In the contemporary world, however, as Arendt argues, the basic terms of the Greek situation are quite radically reversed. For, in our own time, "society" has invaded the public realm, so much so that this latter is now but the ancient household writ large. The despotic rule of the Greek *paterfamilias* has been replaced by the various impersonal machineries of our modern bureaucratic ethos, to be sure, but "rule by nobody" represents rulership, nevertheless, often of the most severely tyrannous kind. And what Arendt considers most decisively characteristic of the modern world is its way of gathering us together in the manner in which the members of a Greek household were constituted twenty-five hundred years ago. Just as, anciently, the private household was the realm where men were united toward the end of sustaining the life process, of providing for individual survival and the continuity of the species, so now the public realm is, most essentially, a vast community of laborers and jobholders organized around activities necessary for the sustenance of life. And, just as the polity of the ancient household allowed no real room for individuality (which, for the freeman, was to find its expression *outside* the household, in the public realm of the *polis*), so, again, our own world, under the dominion now of "society," tends to accord the person a purely abstract and functional identity: he becomes merely a commodity in the marketplace, to be "packaged" in the manners and styles of behavior appropriate to his "role."

In short, what Marx called the "socialization of man" has so completely transformed the public spaces of the modern age that, far from affording today the kind of environment for self-realization offered by the public realm of the Greek *polis*, they now represent precisely that from which men want to flee in their quest of the chance for a human life. "The emergence of society—the rise of housekeeping, its activities, problems, and organizational devices—from the shadowy interior of the household into the light of the public sphere, has not only blurred the old borderline between private and political, it has also changed almost beyond recognition the meaning of the two terms and their significance for the life of the individual and the citizen."[76] For whereas, anciently, the "privacy" of the household did indeed represent a privative principle, when viewed over against the realm of the *polis* which was the sphere of freedom, today the opposite of privacy is not the world of the *politikos* but the realm of "society" which is something like a slave-economy, in which persons are identified merely by the functions they perform, in which they are governed by the iron laws of conformity and "shuffled together like grains of sand."[77] So, as a consequence, says Arendt, the private realm, far from being (as it was in Greek antiquity) the realm of the not-yet-human, has become for us—opposed as it now is to the dominion of "society"—the sphere of intimacy. Thus it is a world no longer barren and unpropitious, but rather one felt to be rich and manifold, offering the one remaining shelter against the mediocrity and confusion of mass life, offering indeed the one region in which a person may hope to be free.

So great is her sense of the fearful losses entailed by this whole development that Arendt is noticeably reluctant to invite the conclusion that the private realm deserves now to be regarded as an important base for "political" action, for action intended to rehabilitate and to fortify the *polis*. True, she is not quite prepared to account "the modern discovery of intimacy" as merely a flight from the discouragements of the public scene into the less daunting world of individual subjectivity. But "the consequences for human existence when both the public and private spheres of life are gone, the public because it has become a function of the private and the private because it has become the only common concern left"[78]—the consequences of this whole chain of circumstance appear to her to be so expensive that she is not eager to push forward any consoling principle of compensation.

Yet, after looking at essentially the same developments and issues that engaged Arendt, many of those over the past generation or so whom we think of as among the more thoughtful analysts of our condition—and people representing such diversity in fundamental viewpoint, say, as

E. M. Forster and Martin Buber, George Orwell and Gabriel Marcel, Simone Weil and Ignazio Silone—have not hesitated to embrace the possibility that, now, at the end of the modern age, a politics looking toward the redemption of the City may need to be carried on, at least in part, within the regions of the personal life. In this connection it should not go unnoticed how careful Auden himself was, in his review of Arendt's book, approvingly to remark her lesson that "What a modern man thinks of as the realm where he is free to be himself and to disclose himself to others, is what he calls his private or personal life, that is to say, the nearest modern equivalent to the public realm of the Greeks is the intimate realm."[79] And, indeed, it is just in this range of ideas, so masterfully charted by Hannah Arendt's *The Human Condition,* that we may locate the main ballast of the poetry of Auden's last years.

Throughout, of course, the whole stretch of his career Auden conceived the name and nature of the human world to be that of the City: that is, in both its early and its late stages, he took it for granted that the primary fact of human existence is that we are members one of another. True, the particular cities of the world—those "Built by the conscience-stricken, the weapon-making, / By us"—are often to be found "unlucky," "assaulted" and "starved." But, over a long period, their failure to be places "where / The will of love is done" only prompted Auden's poetry to bid us, again and again, to seek the Just City, to (as he said in *Look, Stranger!*) "rebuild our cities, not dream of islands." Yet, as his Page-Barbour Lectures at the University of Virginia (*The Enchafèd Flood*) indicate, he was already at the end of the 1940s beginning to be deeply troubled by the strange inexorability with which urban democracy in our time turns the individual "into a cypher of the crowd, or a mechanical cogwheel in an impersonal machine."[80] And a decade later, no doubt largely helped by Arendt's influence, he had become convinced of the disappearance altogether of the Public Realm as a sphere of authentically human life: as he said in one of the leading essays ("The Poet & The City") in *The Dyer's Hand,*

> To the Greeks the Private Realm was the sphere of life ruled by the necessity of sustaining life, and the Public Realm the sphere of freedom where a man could disclose himself to others. Today, the significance of the terms private and public has been reversed; public life is the necessary impersonal life, the place where a man fulfills his social function, and it is in his private life that he is free to be his personal self.[81]

Again, as it is said in the fine poem "The Shield of Achilles" (after which his book of 1955 was entitled), now we dwell not in the "Marble well-governed cities" of the Greeks but on an unfeatured plain where there is "no sign of neighborhood," where "An unintelligible multitude"—"A million eyes, a million boots in line"—waits "for a sign," as ragged urchins loiter, as "girls are raped" and "two boys knife a third." "The mass and majesty of this world" have fallen into the hands of "bored officials" who give statistical proof that some cause is just to those who've "never heard / Of any world where promises were kept, / Or one could weep because another wept." And in such a time, as Auden concluded, the heroic image is to be sought "neither [in] the 'Great Man' nor [in] the romantic rebel . . . but [in] the man or woman in any walk of life who, despite all the impersonal pressures of modern society, manages to acquire and preserve a face of his own."[82]

"When little was left standing / But the suburb of dissent," it seemed necessary, then, to turn from "Metropolis, that too-great city," toward this remaining purlieu, in order there to explore the new "conditions [to which] we must bow / In building the Just City now." Auden's vision of this bordering region wherein one may learn anew "To serve mankind's *imperium*," though it was to be fully developed only in the series of books begun in 1965 with *About the House*, had already been beautifully prefigured in *New Year Letter*, in which, early on in part 3, amidst the festivities signalizing the arrival of New Year 1940, he began all of a sudden directly to address Elizabeth Mayer, to whom the poem was dedicated:

> Warm in your house, Elizabeth,
> A week ago at the same hour
> I felt the unexpected power
> That drove our ragged egos in
> From the dead-ends of greed and sin
> To sit down at the wedding feast,
> Put shining garments on the least,
> Arranged us so that each and all,
> The erotic and the logical,
> Each felt the *placement* to be such
> That he was honoured overmuch,
> And Schubert sang and Mozart played
> And Gluck and food and friendship made
> Our privileged community
> That real republic which must be
> The State all politicians claim,
> Even the worst, to be their aim.

And it is, indeed, in such an excellent fellowship as this, in the generous civility that prevails in "the *polis* of our friends," that, as Auden came to feel, we may now find our best image of the true City and a kind of outpost from which to begin the work of renewing the ruined walls of "that too-great city," that "dread Leviathan," called Metropolis.

It is in the poems that he brought together in his book of the mid-60s, *About the House*—and most especially in the long, beautiful sequence entitled "Thanksgiving for a Habitat"—that we get what is perhaps the decisive statement of the deeply chastened, yet wonderfully sunny, sobriety marking Auden's late maturity. In the late 1950s he had bought a house in the little village of Kirchstetten in southern Austria, less than thirty miles out of Vienna and only ninety kilometers removed from "where minefield and watchtower say *No Exit*": what he had never dared hope for was, as he said (in *About the House*), at last, "in my fifties, mine, a toft-and-croft / where I needn't, ever, be at home *to* / those I am not at home with. . . ." And it is this rustic seat that the book of 1965 makes an image of the House, of those places of intimacy "haphazardly scattered over the earth" where we may meet "without papers"—to cultivate "authentic comity."

The great opening cycle of poems, in speaking its thanks for this Habitat, performs a little eucharist for each of its rooms. "The Cave of Making," which is an elegy for Louis MacNeice, speaks of the room—"more private than a bedroom even"—which was Auden's study, where (amongst Olivetti portable and heaps of paper and the very best dictionaries money could buy) he served that

> unpopular art which cannot be turned into
> background noise for study
> or hung as a status trophy by rising executives,
> cannot be "done" like Venice
> or abridged like Tolstoy, but stubbornly still insists upon
> being read or ignored. . . .

"Down There" is devoted to the "cellar underneath the house" which is very much unlike the other rooms, for, "When trunks are being packed, and when, without warning, / We drive up in the dark, unlock and switch lights on, / They seem put out" and wear an injured look— but the cellar, keeping in all seasons its wine and conserves and other good things ripened by the sun, "never takes umbrage": though visited only when its stores are needed, "It takes us as we are, explorers, homebodies. . . ."

"Up There" celebrates the attic that "no clock recalls . . . / Once an hour to the household it's a part of" and where all sorts of things—old letters and bulging boxes and galoshes—"Wait unworshipped."

"The Geography of the House" is devoted to the "white-tiled cabin" in which one sits at stool after breakfast, and the poem's parenthesis says:

(Orthodoxy ought to
Bless our modern plumbing:
Swift and St. Augustine
Lived in centuries,
When a stench of sewage
Ever in the nostrils
Made a strong debating
Point for Manichees.)

"Encomium Balnei" extols the one room in the house which "has only an inside lock," the room in which, lying snugly in hot water, one may "present a Lieder Abend / to a captive audience of . . . [one's] toes." "Grub First, Then Ethics" is devoted to the fine modern kitchen Auden had installed in the little Kirchstetten house, "For Friends Only" to the bedroom for guests, and "The Cave of Nakedness" to his own bedroom.

Of all the poems taking us on this tour, it is perhaps "The Common Life," which is devoted to the living room, and, even more especially, "Tonight at Seven-Thirty" (whose setting is the dining room) which offer the fullest hints of what these parables are proposing. The six stanzas of the latter poem speak of a dinner party at which six congenial guests are assembled, and six because in these days one's likely to find it necessary to be one's own "chef, servitor and scullion." The gathering is "small and unpublic," and, though a sparklingly festive occasion, a certain requisite formality is carefully kept, for this "is a worldly rite that nicknames or endearments / or family / diminutives would profane": to be the means of grace that it ought to be, a dinner party must be informed by the virtues of deference and courtesy. And thus "two doters who wish / to tiddle and curmurr between the soup and fish / belong in restaurants." For those who come together around the board are there—if, as may be hoped, they have "stalwart digestions"—to enjoy the food, but also to enjoy one another and to talk to one another as wittily and courteously and attentively as they can:

. . . a brawler may not
be put to death on the spot,
but he is asked to quit the sacral dining area
instanter, and a foul-mouth gets the cold
shoulder.

Nor does one want saints at table, and surely not a god, for

> he would be too odd
> to talk to and, despite his imposing presence, a bore,
>   for the funniest
> mortals and the kindest are those who are most aware
> of the baffle of being, don't kid themselves our care
> is inconsolable, but believe a laugh is less
>   heartless than tears, that a hostess
> prefers it.

What one hopes for, at seven-thirty of an evening, is six lenient, politic, graceful people amongst whom there is much "well-liking" and who are adept at keeping "the eye grateful / for what Nature's bounty and grace of Spirit can create"—

> . . . men
> and women who enjoy the cloop of corks, appreciate
>   depatical fare, yet can see in swallowing
>   a sign act of reverence,
> in speech a work of re-presenting
>   the true olamic silence.

What the poem conjures up, in short, is a microcosm of that more spacious co-inherence which the *civitas terrena* was meant to be, an image of that hither side of "the demanded *caritas*"[83] which is not "glory" but thoughtful generosity and "civility": the little banquet that the poem arranges intends to be but a small simulacrum of the civic world to which we are summoned in all the larger relations of life.

It is a similar image that "The Common Life" wants to invoke. The poem is dedicated to Chester Kallman, with whom Auden shared his life over many years, and it cannot resist marveling at how each has managed to forgive in the other "impossible behavior, / to endure by some miracle / conversational tics and larval habits / without wincing," and at how they have thus created "a common world / between them":

> It's a wonder that neither
> has been butchered by accident,
>
> or, as lots have, silently vanished into
>   History's criminal noise
> unmourned for, but that, after twenty-four years,
>   we should sit here in Austria
>
> as cater-cousins, under the glassy look
>   of a Naples Bambino,

> the portrayed regards of Strauss and Stravinsky,
>   doing British crossword puzzles,

> is very odd indeed.

Yet the poem is not all marveling, for, as it contemplates that "catholic area" of the living room which each is free to "enter / without knocking, leave without a bow," and where "There's no *We* at an instant, / only *Thou* and *I*," it suggests that, in not having carelessly flung themselves upon each other and in having prudently chosen not to trespass upon each other's solitude, the real secret of this "common life" which they have built together lies in its having been so ordered as to allow for "two regions / of protestant being which nowhere overlap." And thus we are given another parable of what the modern City would be like, if it were what "The Cave of Nakedness" calls a "Country of Consideration."

So the statement being made in "Thanksgiving for a Habitat" (as in many of the other poems in *About the House*), far from representing any sort of "apoliticalism," expresses a profoundly *political* concern. The careless, or the shortsighted, reader may quickly conclude that this celebrant of a merely domestic *polis* was one who, unfortunately, had been driven by the adversities of the age into the special kind of amnesia suffered by the thoroughly privatized man. And one or another version of this judgment has been rendered with tiresome regularity over the past thirty years. But what is too much disregarded in the quasi-official view of the presumed *trahison* represented by Auden's late phase is precisely his own conviction that the Private Realm has in our time become what the Public Realm anciently was—namely, the place in which a truly human language is spoken and in which by our words and deeds we may disclose ourselves to one another with forthrightness and candor. In the Great World of our period, in what political economists call "the public sector," as Auden felt—and he was surely not mistaken—we have in effect come to what Daniel Bell at the end of the 50s was declaring to be "the end of ideology."[84] Though Auden himself never made use of Bell's phrase, it does very exactly render his general sense of the modern landscape. For, with a splendidly commonsensical kind of clarity, he saw that *out there,* in the Great World, no real debate any longer goes on, because capitalism and socialism and communism are all seeking essentially the same goal: which is to say, as he defined the matter, that they are all seeking "to guarantee to every member of society, as a psychophysical organism, the right to physical and mental health." But such a goal, he believed—as a thinker like Hannah Arendt also contended—is hardly a *political* goal, because, as he said, "it is not concerned with human beings as persons and citizens but with human bodies, with the precultural, prepolitical human creature."[85] Politics, in other words—or that field of activity having to do with our distinctively human relations with one another—concerns, most principally, not the basic necessities of life, not the issues that fell under the superintendence of the ancient household, but that level of the human enterprise related to the dimension of freedom. So when the Public Realm has become the sphere of housekeeping and the Private Realm the sphere of what Arendt calls "action," it is, as Auden expected us to realize, to be supremely *political*—and supremely committed to the renovation of "the public sector"—to focus in on that area of the world where we can still be truly human: to wit, the department of life which for the ancients was opposed to the *polis* but which is *for us* the very center of the *polis*, namely, the sphere of intimacy, where a climate still prevails in which "regions of protestant being" may freely meet.

In his last years, then, though long since having forsworn any kind of *Agit-Prop*, he remained a poet under conscription to the City, but wanting—in his "suburb of dissent"—very greatly to deepen our contemporary conception of what it means to be a politically engaged person, wanting indeed (as Lionel Trilling already in the mid-1940s was urging us to do) "to force [back] into our definition of politics every human activity and every subtlety of every human activity." "There are," said Trilling, "manifest dangers in doing this, but greater dangers in not doing it. Unless we insist that politics is imagination and mind, we will learn"— as Auden might have said, from the Managers—"that imagination and mind are politics, and of a kind that we will not like."[86] And, in all the wonderfully complex and graceful pirouettes that this poet of the Loyal Opposition was making his language perform in the work of the closing years of his career, he was attempting, over and above the "argument" he advanced, to execute a political gesture, to present what he hoped might be an invigorating model of the punctiliousness and *esprit* with which a man ought to undertake to talk to other men. He wanted, in short, not only to rehabilitate politics (in its classical sense), and this for the sake of the City, but also to make us remember again that a truly human politics *is* imagination and mind, in their fullest and most consequential intensity. The concluding passage of "Thanksgiving for a Habitat," after speaking of the Kirchstetten house as a place where one need not be at home *to* those one is not at home *with*, says that it is "not a cradle, / . . . and not a windowless grave, but a place / I may go both in and out of." And so it is with this miniature *civitas* of Auden's Private Realm which is located in a suburban precinct: it is a place one goes out of again and again into the Great World, there to treat with Caesar's minions and to serve, as best one can, "mankind's *imperium*."

The final books—*City without Walls, Epistle to a Godson,* and *Thank You, Fog*—though they contain many impressive declarations of this great old Horatian, do not add any new dimension to the funded testimony of the period initiated by *Nones.* It is a quiet, gentle, conversational speech we hear, of one who does not now intend (as François Duchene puts it) "to be entangled in youth's false airs and graces"[87]—though, as he says in the dedicatory lines in *Epistle to a Godson,* "at Twenty I tried to / vex my elders, past Sixty it's the young whom I hope to bother."

Auden liked to think of Ariel as the genius of poetic *divertissement* and of Prospero as the tutelary of poetry in its sapient mode, and both, together, seem to preside over the last poems. A quite typical instance of the characteristic manner and tone (when any large subject is being approached) is presented by the opening poem in *City without Walls.* Here, three voices are heard, and it is the first, with its savage account of the contemporary scene, which speaks at greatest length:

> "Those fantastic forms, fang-sharp,
> bone-bare, that in Byzantine painting
> were a short-hand for the Unbounded
> beyond the Pale, unpolicied spaces
> where dragons dwelt and demons roamed,
>
> "colonized only by ex-worldlings,
> penitent sophists and sodomites,
> are visual facts in the foreground now,
> real structures of steel and glass:
> hermits, perforce, are all today. . . ."

And this first voice goes on to speak of how, in this "Gadgeted Age" of "Hobbesian Man . . . mass-produced," "all has gone phut"—of how we dwell now in the lawless marches of Asphalt Lands, "where gangs clash and cops turn / robber barons"; of how

> "Every workday Eve fares
> forth to the stores her foods to pluck,
> while Adam hunts an easy dollar:
> unperspiring at eventide
> both eat their bread in boredom of spirit.
>
> "The weekend comes that once was holy,
> free still, but a feast no longer,
> just time out, idiorhythmic,
> when no one cares what his neighbor does:
> now newsprint and network are needed most. . . ."

Indeed, in stanza after stanza, this first voice is to be heard dryly mar-
shaling the various signs and evidences of the stuntedness and vacancy
that prevail in the False or the Unreal City of this late, bad time—till
finally the voice is broken off by Auden's saying, "Thus I was thinking at
three a.m. / in mid-Manhattan. . . ." Then, as he says, these musings
were suddenly "cut short" by another voice, "a sharp voice":

> "What fun and games you find it to play
> Jeremiah-cum-Juvenal:
> Shame on you for your *Schadenfreude.*"

And, at the end, the irony is *re*doubled, as the poet's debate with the
second voice is interrupted by a third voice:

> "My!" I blustered, "how moral we're getting.'
> A pococurante? Suppose I were,
> so what, if my words are true."

> Thereupon, bored, a third voice:
> "Go to sleep now for God's sake!
> You both will feel better by breakfast time."

Now it is just such a steady, affable equanimity as this that gives to the
final poems their special kind of charm. The man who is speaking to us
is one by no means forgetful that "never as yet / has Earth been without /
her bad patch, some unplace with / jobs for torturers"—and he does not
fail to remark "how glib all the faces I see about me / seem . . . to have
become." "Housman was perfectly right. / Our world rapidly worsens: /
nothing now is so horrid / or silly it can't occur." But, as he says to himself, "Why . . . should I badger?" "No rheum has altered my gait, as ever
my cardiac muscles / are undismayed, my cells / perfectly competent."
So, despite his frequently hinted confidence that death was not far off,
he wanted to live *gratefully,* to view all that had been granted by Dame
Kind eucharistically, to make his days (in the great old phrase of the Anglican Prayerbook's anaphora) a "sacrifice of praise and thanksgiving."
And thus he beautifully toasts old friends—Nevill Coghill, Marianne
Moore, William Empson, physicians who have treated him, the remarkable old peasant who was his housekeeper in Kirchstetten for ten years;
he prepares an "Epistle" to Philip Spender, his godson (bidding him on
the Quest Perilous to keep his toes turned out as he walks and to remember that he is a Spender), as well as an "Epithalamium" for Peter Mudford
and Rita Auden; in syllabic meters and alliterative structures of extraordinary refinement he, in numerous occasional poems, explores the ordinary fears and embarrassments that beset most of us, those who are not

amongst "the top intelligent few"; he produces wonderfully turned out little *haiku*, which write various kinds of marginalia on the great central themes of his work; he now and again, after talking to Goethe and to dogs and mice and *contra* Blake, talks quite directly to himself—

> Time, we both know, will decay You, and already
> I'm scared of our divorce: I've seen some horrid ones.
> Remember: when Le Bon Dieu says to You *Leave him!*,
> please, please, for His sake and mine, pay no attention
> to my piteous *Don'ts*, but bugger off quickly.

And always the background against which these last poems are written is that garrisoned *civitas* of the Private Realm, whose goodly fellowship of faithful friends and true neighbors, as Auden says in *Epistle to a Godson* ("The Garrison"), is intended by his poetic designs "to serve as a paradigm / now of what a plausible Future might be"—of that future in which "the story / Of our human city" would

>   . . . move
> Like music, when
> Begotten notes
> New notes beget,
> Making the flowing
> Of time a growing,
> Till what it could be
> At last it is,
> Where even sadness
> Is a form of gladness,
> Where Fate is Freedom,
> Grace and Surprise.

It must be apparent, then, even to his most cursory readers, that those modern theorists who claim that the poet does in no way supervise any kind of propositional discourse would be ill-advised to seek evidentiary support of their position in the poetry of Auden. For, from beginning to end, it is a poetry untouched by any scepticism about its own capacity to handle systematic ideas, and it is deeply committed to its chosen task of bearing "witness to the truth." If something like this were being said in a university classroom, the force of the conventions prevailing there would doubtless prompt one's students to make an act of obeisance to the pieties of the graduate school by demanding that careful notice be taken of the ways in which Auden's various "forms" *establish* his meanings. And, faced with such a demand, one would not in desperation be driven back against the blackboard, since, given his profound integrity of "vision" and given a virtuosity of craftsmanship rivalled in the English-speaking world of the modern period perhaps only by Yeats and Frost, Auden's work presents one of the great examples in the poetry of our time of "'unified' utterance."[88] But, after the requisite responses had been made in a university seminar to the demand for certification of unity of "form" and "content," Auden's poetry would still be found to be wanting, in very nearly a forensic sense, to be *heard,* wanting its drift and purport to be tried and appraised. And thus—particularly with the late poems whose emphasis so collided with many of our most deeply settled presumptions—we cannot finally evade that question which dons generally consider it gauche for critical discourse to undertake to confront in a simple and direct way: namely, may the deliverances of this poet be conceived to be in any sense true?

We, of course—or, let us say, most of the people who make themselves heard in the public forums of our period—take it for granted that the Just City is chiefly served by those who circulate petitions and join picket lines, who attend boring meetings and who distribute equally boring pamphlets, who treat with the agents of sectarian conclaves and who engage in the choreography of "confrontation"-politics. And such a testimony as comes out of Auden's last years—about the spheres of life in which we may find our clearest paradigms of the "plausible Future"—will doubtless seem to many to entail nothing other than an advocacy, while Rome burns, of a virtual abdication from the historical arena. It will perhaps be acknowledged that he was not, to be sure, a patron of those young Gnostics who in his last years espoused everyone's doing his own "thing," but, as some may impatiently insist, there is no large final difference between the individualistic antinomianism promoted by the new Bohemia of the 60s and this retreat (however precautious) from the jungles of Metropolis into "the *polis* of our friends" —differences in cultural tone, yes, as between the puerile crudity of the one and the assured urbanity of the other, but no final difference as regards the essential substance of what is held forth as a program for life.

Yet it may be just here, in the supposition that the Auden of *Nones* and *About the House* and *City without Walls* is primarily committed to the espousal of a kind of program that says, Back to the catacombs, or the barracks, or the cottages—it may be just here, in this supposition, that a primary mistake is made. Auden did, of course, believe that people dwelling amidst disorder in their private lives are not likely, in the larger relations of their social business, to fashion anything good and humane, and he also felt that to have kept peace in one's own household is, there-fore, to have contributed to the well-being of one's community, to have offered to one's compatriots a sign and pledge of what James Joyce called "the fair courts of life." But he was not a sentimental fool, and he was never for a moment by way of supposing that the affairs of the Great World will somehow take care of themselves, if the *honnête homme* simply keeps his hearth. Yet he did want steadily to keep his eye on what is often well-nigh forgotten by the fashionable forms of contemporary serious-ness—namely, that the real goal of all the petitions and boring meetings and picket lines is not merely more petitions and more picket lines but what Shakespeare's Ferdinand speaks of in *The Tempest* as "quiet days, fair issue, and long life." He knew, as we have noticed he was also careful to say, that the House—or the realm where one abides with family and friends and neighbors—is a place one both goes in and *out* of; but all that we do *out there*, in our efforts to promote *shalom* in the City, is done in order that there might be peace and blessedness in those precincts where boys and girls fall in love and children are born and the old and the young peer at family albums by lamplight. Which is to say that in the plausible future, in the world of the Just City, men and women will not be straining after some new stratagem in the politics of "confrontation" but will, as we ought surely to hope, be at ease—taking their Sunday baths, tooting at neighbors across the backyard fence, reading Colette, marveling at the progeny of Balanchine, and at martini time drawing the curtains and choosing a composer they would like to hear before sitting down with friends at table before some good savory mess.[89] And it is of these "fair courts" that Auden's late poems want to bring news: they are, in other words, poems stirred by "the old vision of the noble life,"[90] and they are deeply informed by the conviction that "the norm [for the hu-man City] . . . is one of order, peace, honour, and beauty"[91]—which is a vision of the world that, finally, will be declared *un*true perhaps only by "the possessed," by those who take the ideal human condition to be one in which things are being wrenched apart and broken up and brought to an end.

Auden was one, however, who most stringently disavowed all the var-ious forms of Gnostic contempt for Creation, because he had been taught by the Christian faith and by his own experience to conceive the world as everywhere filled with rumors of angels and touched with Glory. As he said in the final lines of "Whitsunday in Kirchstetten" (*About the House*),

> . . . about
> catastrophe or how to behave in one

I know nothing, except what everyone knows—
if there when Grace dances, I should dance.

The *Benedicite* of the Church's Morning Office bids the sun and the moon, the showers and the dews, the frost and the cold, the fowls of the air and all green things on earth, the mountains and hills, and all the children of men to "bless the Lord," to "praise Him, and magnify Him for ever." And it was in this spirit, of Catholic obedience, that he made that great declaration in *Nones*—

> I could (which you cannot)
> Find reasons fast enough
> To face the sky and roar
> In anger and despair
> At what is going on,
> Demanding that it name
> Whoever is to blame:
> The sky would only wait
> Till all my breath was gone
> And then reiterate
> As if I wasn't there
> That singular command
> I do not understand,
> *Bless what there is for being,*
> Which has to be obeyed, for
> What else am I made for,
> Agreeing or disagreeing.

It is, indeed, with an iteration of this doxology—"Bless what there is for being"—that an account of Auden's service as a poet to the City ought to close, since what was so much of the essence of his faith and thought was the certainty that, when the relations of life that give substance and graciousness to the City are dismantled, we shall be rescued from the *Blick ins Chaos* only by a supernatural love. And so eloquently did he bear witness to this belief that, as he went about his work of disclosing "some of the room still left on a sadly crowded planet in which human freedom might grow,"[92] we—even in a secular age—felt him to be, after Eliot's death, beyond doubt the great poet of the age.

CHAPTER FOUR

Theodore Roethke's Doxology

*I*n his brilliant book of 1954 on the nature of symbolic language, *The Burning Fountain*, Philip Wheelwright proposes that there are four basic ways whereby the imagination may be considered, in one or another of its phases, to reckon with the world's multifarious reality. He suggests that it may choose simply to contemplate, in an attitude of the strictest attention, the various particulars that experience brings its way, seeking with great intensity to grasp these particulars in their radical individuality. As he says, this is the way taken by the "Confrontative Imagination," and it leads toward such a pure concentration upon what is unique in the given reality that the self finds that reality "confronting it as a *thou* and becomes in turn a *thou* before the presence of its object."[1] But quite a different approach may be taken: instead of igniting the object with the kind of mesmerizing power by which it is endowed when responded to in the dimension of the simplicity of its sheer presence, the imagination may choose to act "upon its object by stylizing and distancing it."[2] This is the way of the "Stylistic Imagination," whose principal effort involves "a kind of distancing . . . which consists of 'putting the phenomenon, so to speak, out of gear with our practical, actual self' and thereby looking at it with a fresh objectivity."[3]

When, however, the concrete reality or event (*Phänomen*) is perceived as an "Eminent Instance" of some primordial or generic reality (*Urphänomen*), the way being taken, says Wheelwright, is that of "the Archetypal Imagination, which sees the particular object as embodying and adumbrating suggestions of universality."[4] Here the self is given over to an impression of what is paradigmatic in the specific things and happenings of life, and they are appropriated in terms of "the perduring archetypes which they express and symbolize."[5] But, of course, the fusion that the mind performs may not be so much between the concrete and the general as between two or more concrete units of experience. This, in Wheel-wright's scheme, represents the fourth great mode of imaginative percep-tion, the way of the "Metaphoric Imagination," which involves the mind's unification of a given multiplicity into an organic whole, but with a kind of tact that preserves in some significant degree the heteroge-neousness of the various elements being unified.

Now, of these four types of imagining, it is perhaps the confrontative and the archetypal that most nearly define that way of receiving the world which deserves to be called sacramental. For, wherever the sacra-mental imagination is at work on the material of human experience, the dictates of what Heidegger calls "calculative" reason[6] have been so hushed as to permit an attitude of simple enchantment before the irrev-ocability whereby the things and creatures of this world are what they are, in their utter specificity. All the particular realities making up our earthly environment are approached in a spirit of radical amazement (at their sheer givenness), of acquiescence, of "letting be"; each is so heark-ened to that it becomes, as it were, a *thou*, the human subject itself in turn becoming a *thou* in the presence of its object. But then, inevitably, as the concrete particular is confronted with such intensity, it takes on the luster of a "something more" and is felt to be an outward and visible expression of something *else* which is wonderful and has value. In short, it is conceived in some sort to be a sign or token of a "numinous" reality, of the tremendous mystery of the Holy. Thus it is that the confrontative and archetypal modes of imagining are joined in a sacramental apprehen-sion of the things and events of human life.

It is of this type of imagination that the late Theodore Roethke presents in his poetry a great example, for his entire career was a search for ways of turning "the wild disordered language of the natural heart" into a song whose "broken music" might be an adequate sacrifice of praise and thanksgiving for all the marvelous things of earth. And in American po-etry over the past generation he offers a crucial instance of a truly sacra-mental vision of our human inheritance.

Indeed, there is rarely to be found in the literature of our period a body of poetry so predominantly psalmic and doxological as Roethke's: almost everywhere, it seems, the poet's voice is lifted up in jubilant alleluias announcing "the soul's immediate joy" and praising the glory and great-ness of the world. In the remarkable sequence of poems "Four for Sir John Davies," which appeared in his book of 1953, *The Waking*, he speaks of his "need [for] a place to sing," of how his very blood leaps "with a wordless song." In the poem "The Renewal," which is included in *Words for the Wind* (1958), he says: "I teach my sighs to lengthen into songs." And his verse, even after having descended into the darkest things imaginable, wants to sound a hymnic note and to be a sort of lay canticle, for this poet (as he notes in "The Dying Man," *Words for the Wind*) is one whose

> heart sways with the world.
> I am that final thing,
> A man learning to sing.

As he says in one of the last poems ("Sequence, Sometimes Metaphysical," included in the posthumous volume of 1964, *The Far Field*), "I'll make a broken music, or I'll die."

But the resonance of song which is so constantly to be heard in Roethke's poetry is by no means the consequence of something merely willed by a resolutely gladsome spirit. For his jubilation is not only often a narrowly won achievement on the further side of despair: it is also always, finally, a response to a music that is *heard*—in the spheres and in those places of the world that we regularly inhabit. Indeed, he finds "the earth itself a tune," whose rocks and birds and trees and living souls are all minstrels "singing into the beyond." And thus the habit Roethke's poetry has of recurrently breaking into song represents, as Heidegger would say, his way of "hailing" a world whose *presence* is itself conveyed as a kind of music. This is what lies behind his venturing, in the beautiful poem "O Lull Me, Lull Me" (*Praise to the End!* [1951]), so risky a declaration as

> I could say hello to things;
> . . . .
> I see what sings!
> What sings!

Or again, as he says with a moving brevity and terseness in the great cycle of poems "Meditations of an Old Woman" (*Words for the Wind*):

> In my grandmother's inner eye,
> . . . .
> A bird always kept singing.
> She was a serious woman.

In a love poem written toward the end of his life, "Light Listened" (*The Far Field*), Roethke concludes his song about one than whose "ways with a man" nothing "could be more nice" by saying, "Light listened when she sang." This puts us in mind of the great line in the opening poem of "North American Sequence" (*The Far Field*), in which the poet declares: "The light cries out, and I am there to hear." One might say that, for Roethke, the earth is a singing earth whose things and creatures answer and listen to one another in their singing, so all their songs make up a vast universal dialogue and one great antiphonal hymn wherein the infinitely varied minstrelsy of Creation sings "into the beyond" its perpetual exultets and magnificats.

A vulgar literalism will, of course, immediately nominate such a sense of reality animistic or panpsychist, and Roethke's vision will be conceived to represent a curiously self-indulgent primitivism. Yet this is by no means the inevitable response. What this man understood (through processes of poetic intuition)—and what certain systematic philosophers occasionally perceive—is that the myth of the world as nothing but a huge and silent *res extensa* is no less improbable than the crudest animism. For things that are merely things-in-themselves simply do not exist. Any truly cognitive encounter with the world inevitably involves its being drawn into a kind of family relationship with human consciousness, for things do not even begin to exhibit any sort of significant meaning or value until we identify ourselves with them. As Conrad Bonifazi has reminded us, the act of knowing "is born and nourished in some kind of *enthusiastic* association."[7] Or, as Edmund Husserl never tired of saying, "What things are . . . they are as things of experience"[8]—by which he meant that, though they exist in their own right, they can be known only as they are experienced, and to be experienced they must be drawn into dynamic interrelationship with human consciousness.

As Husserl was also at pains to tell modern philosophy, human experience does not move wholly within the dimensions of the fact-world, which is spread out before us in space and time. We take this world for granted, of course, and it is one of the great limiting boundaries of the human enterprise. But sensory perception—which, in its most highly disciplined forms, is our way of grasping the fact-world—is not at all our only means of access to reality, and the world of human consciousness embraces far more than simply the contents of sensory perception. Indeed, the insight with which Husserl inaugurated the whole program of modern phenomenology consisted very largely in his discerning that there is no such thing as "experience" until something more than a merely perceptual act occurs.

Husserl's basic contention was that a thing does not really enter into our selfhood, into our sense of the world and of our own existence, until we have done something more than merely glance at it. For the world that is "out there" must be "immanentized," must be not simply glanced at but attended to; and only then do we receive its meaning (through an act of radical intuition) and appropriate it as a matter of "experience," of "intentionality." Things are not enabled fully to declare themselves as what they truly are until we have turned toward them "intentionally," permitting them thus to step forth out of their amorphous facticity and to disclose their essential qualities.[9]

It was not, of course, a part of Husserl's purpose to offer any defense of distinctively poetic modes of vision and statement. But his distinction between the world as merely perceived and as fully experienced suggests a line of thought whereby a kind of vindication of *poiesis* may be possible. Recent phenomenology, following his lead, maintains not that the fact-world is itself somehow a function of human consciousness but, rather, that it finds its depth of meaning in the intentionality that the human percipient brings to it. It seems, therefore, that room is by way of being made for poetic "myth," however eccentric or radical it may be, if it does permit the various entities with which we dwell on this earth to stand forth in the clear, bright actuality of their being.

At a certain point in *I and Thou*, for example, Martin Buber remarks two quite different ways in which we may face a tree. He suggests that it may be regarded simply as a stiff column reared against a background of blue sky and, in the nature of its leafage and structure, as an example of a certain species. Or we may even "subdue its actual presence and form so sternly" that it is recognized "only as an expression . . . of the laws . . . in accordance with which . . . [certain] component substances mingle and separate." We may regard the tree simply as a phenomenon of the fact-world. But, as Buber says, we *may* consent to become so "bound up in relation" to this tree before which we stand that it ceases to be merely an *it*, merely an item of the fact-world, and—being valued for its own sake, being permitted to "speak," and the mysterious communication that it bodies forth being "listened to"—becomes a kind of *thou*.[10] Yet there is no question here of any sort of animism, of the tree being possessed by an occult power that makes it in some way itself a center of consciousness. Instead, the mutuality of our relationship with the tree is wholly grounded in the affectionateness and sympathy with which it is approached, in a delicacy and tact that permit it to stand forth in the radiant particularity of its concrete presence. It would be very much like Michelangelo's "listening" (as Rilke imagined) to the uncut stones, as his hands caressingly explored their unhewn surfaces in the moment before the chisel made its first indentation.[11]

So the world "sings" for Theodore Roethke, plants and animals, fire and water, the sun and the moon—indeed, all living creatures. They sing to one another: they send out their songs "into the beyond." And only the stupidest sort of prosaicism would register any objection to this way of envisaging what is most primitively marvelous in Creation. Roethke's hailing the world with song and his listening to the melodies that are everywhere to be heard being sung by the things of earth do not present us with another instance of Ruskin's "pathetic fallacy." For this imagination of reality as a vast antiphony rests not upon the world's being invested with human qualities but, rather, upon a lively intuition that both the human and the nonhuman modes of existence are animated and empowered by some primal reality that may be denominated simply as Being itself.

This is the *otherness* in which the creatures of earth participate, the absolute presence of Being. And the genitive relationship in which all things stand with respect to the Mystery of Being makes possible the world's great choral fugue. So, at the dying of the day, when "two wood thrush sing as one," it is, as Roethke suggests, simply because "Being delights in being . . ." Or, as he says in the same poem ("A Walk in Late Summer," *Words for the Wind*), the "late rose [that] ravages the casual eye" is nothing other than "a blaze of being. . . ." And it is the dynamic presence in things of this primal Leaven that accounts for what happened on the day when, as the poet says (in "Words for the Wind"),

> I cried, and the birds came down
> And made my song their own.

Now it is this profound and abiding sense in Roethke of all creaturely existence as instinct with Being which gives to his poetic persona its predominantly contemplative cast. As he says in "The Abyss" (*The Far Field*), "Being, not doing, is my first joy." And it is a morality of contemplation which prompts him to find something not only maladroit and indelicate but nearly blasphemous in that rationalist spirit which is so dominated by the intention to bring the world under the reign of the Idea that, as a consequence, nothing is seen or experienced in the dimension of holiness, or with any reverential amazement at the way in which—whether it be a garden slug or a flowing stream or a shock of ragged corn beside a country road—it is simply steadied and supported by the sheer presence within it of Being itself. The irritation with which meddling intellect is dismissed in "I Cry, Love! Love!" (*Praise to the End!*) marks a characteristic note:

> Reason? That dreary shed, that hutch for grubby schoolboys!
> The hedgewren's song says something else.

"Stupor of knowledge lacking inwardness" ("The Pure Fury," *Words for the Wind*) is conceived to be a kind of sickness; and the poetry expresses, again and again, its desire to "break through the barrier of rational experience."[12] "O to be delivered from the rational into the realm of pure song," he cries in "What Can I Tell My Bones?" (*Words for the Wind*).

In one of the late poems, "Infirmity" *(The Far Field)*, Roethke says:

> A mind too active is no mind at all;
> The deep eye sees the shimmer on the stone . . .

And the second line does, in a way, summarize a good part of his testimony. For throughout his life he was committed to an ocular perspective on reality, feeling that the eye, though it has sometimes been held to be the "instrument of lechery," is yet, of all the senses, least drastic in its way of taking hold of the world. As he said in an early poem, "Prayer" *(Open House* [1941]):

> Its rape is gentle, never more
> Violent than a metaphor.

So, because "the Eye's the abettor of / The holiest platonic love," he prays that "Light" may "attend" him "to the grave," for the "deep eye"— which "sees the shimmer on the stone"—is that faculty which is most adept in helping us to approach the world in what Heidegger would call the spirit of "letting-be."[13] Indeed, Roethke considers this the most generous and the most truly human position vis-à-vis our world environment: it is the attitude of paying heed to "the sigh of what is," of being willing simply to "hum in pure vibration, like a saw," and to marvel at the miraculous way in which things "flame into being." To refuse (again as Heidegger would phrase it) this "releasement toward things" is to condemn oneself to the sterile emptiness of Hell. Thus, in the fourth of the "Meditations of an Old Woman":

> I think of the self-involved:
> The ritualists of the mirror, the lonely drinkers,
> The minions of benzedrine and paraldehyde,
> And those who submerge themselves deliberately in trivia. . . .
>
> How I wish them awake!
> May the high flower of the hay climb into their hearts;
> May they lean into light and live;
> May they sleep in robes of green, among the ancient ferns;
> May their eyes gleam with the first dawn;
> May the sun gild them a worm;
> May they be taken by the true burning;
> May they flame into being!

What one finds, then, as a central quality of Roethke's poetry and a distinctive mark of his basic vision of the world is a profound sense of all earthly reality as invested with a power and presence and as touched by a kind of glory that make it our principal obligation to offer, in turn, a humble *pietas* as our primary response to the mysteriousness with which all created things reflect the splendid fecundity and holiness of Being. He is a poet who wants very much to exchange (as a phrase of Albert Camus puts it) a "smile of complicity" with all the enchantments of the earth, even those belonging to mute, insensate things. He conceives the world to be a place enwrapt in glory, and the reverence that he proposes as a basic norm for human life does, undoubtedly, represent the judgment of an essentially sacramental imagination.

Yet, though the earth itself is such "a tune" as makes him feel the need (in "Four for Sir John Davies") for "a place to sing, and dancing-room," and

> Though dancing needs a master, I had none
> To teach my toes to listen to my tongue.

His confession of being without a dancing-master is Roethke's way of remarking his sense of having nothing but his own unaided imagination to depend upon for reckoning with the ultimate mysteries and astonishments of life. Nor does he misstate his situation here, for he was, most assuredly, one who felt himself to be without any revelation, who felt himself to be *alone* with the universe and therefore under the necessity himself of building up out of his own experience such coordinating principles as might give coherence and meaning to that experience. Indeed, it seems that it was precisely his sense of being without a "dancing-master" which convinced him that his only chance of finding any order at all lay in listening to his own inner history with the utmost patience and in attempting thereby to repossess his earliest encounters with the circumambient world. And it is these researches into the basic material of his own selfhood which are chronicled in his first book, *Open House*, and more crucially in the books of 1948, *The Lost Son and Other Poems*, and 1951, *Praise to the End!*

The record suggests, of course, that the decisive experience in Roethke's early years was his enchantment by the world of his family's greenhouse. He was born (in 1908) and reared in eastern Michigan, in the placid town of Saginaw, where his father, Otto, and his paternal uncle, Charles Roethke, presided as co-owners over what was then the largest enterprise of its sort in the region; the establishment embraced twenty-five acres within the town, with approximately a quarter-million feet under glass. The family residences of the two brothers, Otto and Charles, were immediately adjacent to the vast, multistructure, *L*-shaped nursery, and thus it was the greenhouse property that made the scene and setting of much of Roethke's childhood play and exploration. Here it was that he early learned the yearly seasons of this huge conservatory, "which flowers were planted from seeds, which from slips, which from bulbs; the various manures and fertilizers in extravagant detail; the flowers' diseases and their cures, . . . the different periods of growth into maturity, and how fine the timing and the temperature had to be."[14]

It was amidst this glassed-in universe of luxuriantly teeming plant life, as well as in the woods and fields beyond the greenhouse, that Roethke's "vegetal radicalism" (as Kenneth Burke calls it)[15] doubtless first began to develop. It would appear to have been in this environment, as he studied the minute motions of life in his "narrow vegetable realm" ("'Long Live the Weeds,'" *Open House*), that he first began to feel a "steady storm of correspondences" ("In a Dark Time," *The Far Field*) between the human and the nonhuman modes of being, between the life of persons and the "minimal" domain of weeds and flowers, of newts and beetles and all "simple creatures." Thus it was quite early in his life that he decided that his heart should keep "open house," with "doors . . . widely swung" before the strangely wondrous "epic of the eyes" presented by the "small things" of the world, even "things unholy, marred by curse, / The ugly of the universe."

The poems in *Open House* carry occasional intimations of this deep sense of relationship and correspondence between the inner life of the soul and the life of the natural order—as when, for example, in "The Light Comes Brighter," the coming of spring puts the poet in mind of how

> Soon field and wood will wear an April look,
> The frost be gone . . .
>
> And soon a branch, part of a hidden scene,
> The leafy mind, that long was tightly furled,
> Will turn its private substance into green,
> And young shoots spread upon our inner world.

But it is in the "greenhouse poems" in *The Lost Son* that we get the first sustained development of Roethke's vision of the world as something akin to Baudelaire's "forest of symbols," as an order whose things and creatures are not only "in vigorous communication with one another"[16] but in equally vigorous communication—or at least in a relationship of reciprocity—with the human spirit itself. Here it is, as he looks back on "those fields of glass," that he records how "the whole scheme of life" was disclosed in his experience of "the natural order of things." His father was, of course, constantly receiving orders for bouquets and floral arrangements; and he remembers, for example, something of the pathos that he felt in the cut flowers, in

> This urge, wrestle, resurrection of dry sticks,
> Cut stems struggling to put down feet,
> What saint strained so much,
> Rose on such lopped limbs to a new life?
> ("Cuttings [*later*]")

Or he remembers how

> Bulbs broke out of boxes hunting for chinks in the dark,
> Shoots dangled and drooped,
> . . . .
> And what a congress of stinks!—
> Roots ripe as old bait,
> Pulpy stems, rank, silo-rich,
> Leaf-mould, manure, lime, piled against slippery planks.
> Nothing would give up life:
> Even the dirt kept breathing a small breath.
> ("Root Cellar")

The poems imply that a formative influence on the boy's deepening awareness of the world was his intuition that this lust for life in dirt and roots and flowers is the same great lust by which the human reality itself is also moved—that, "underground," that same "sucking and sobbing" wherewith plants and flowers struggle to be born are to be heard

> In my veins, in my bones . . .
> The small waters seeping upward,
> The tight grains parting at last.
> When sprouts break out,
> Slippery as fish,
> I quail, lean to beginnings, sheath-wet.
> ("Cuttings [*later*]")

But, as the boy assisted his father in the daily labors of the greenhouse, digging away at aggressive weeds,

> Under the concrete benches,
> Hacking at black hairy roots,—
> . . . .
> Digging into the soft rubble underneath,
> Webs and weeds,

. . . .
With everything blooming above me,
Lilies, pale-pink cyclamen, roses,
Whole fields lovely and inviolate,—
("Weed Puller")

what he was most moved by, it seems, was just the stoutness and simplicity with which the little things of the world manage to be what they
are. The boy did somehow come to be touched by that most elementary,
that most primitive shock—at the fact that there is *something* rather than
nothing. And the poems in *The Lost Son* record this utter enchantment by
things so rudimentary as the bulging of little cells and the search of bulbs
for light, the breathing of limply delicate orchids through their "ghostly
mouths," "the twittering of swallows above water," or

. . . the lives on a leaf: the little
Sleepers, numb nudgers in cold dimensions,
Beetles in caves, newts, stone-deaf fishes,
Lice tethered to long limp subterranean weeds,
Squirmers in bogs,
And bacterial creepers
Wriggling through wounds
Like elvers in ponds
Their wan mouths kissing the warm sutures,
Cleaning and caressing,
Creeping and healing.
("The Minimal")

Nor do Roethke's "minute particulars run out into great universals" (as it
was once said by someone to be the case with Robert Frost's): he has no
interest at all in devouring his snails and frogs and slugs and fungi in
some system of moralizing analogy. What is truly marvelous is not any
message that is conveyed by the "littles" of the world but, rather, simply
their showing forth of Being and of the infinite generosity with which it
lets things be.

The poems of *The Lost Son*, however, not only speak of the amazing
songs that are sung by small things, but also honor those who were long
ago a part of that greenhouse world and whose gracefulness in relation
to its "lovely diminutives" expressed the kind of sanctity which does itself help to keep "creation at ease." The poet remembers, for example,
the hands of men who worked for his father—men who were, many of
them, cantankerous and full of odd crotchets,[17] but whose hands were a
marvel to watch

> . . . transplanting,
> Turning and tamping,
> Lifting the young plants with two fingers,
> Sifting in a palm-full of fresh loam,—
> One swift movement,—
> Then plumping in the bunched roots,
> A single twist of the thumbs, a tamping and turning,
> All in one . . .
>
> ("Transplanting")

Or, again, he remembers

> That hump of a man bunching chrysanthemums
> Or pinching-back asters, or planting azaleas,
> Tamping and stamping dirt into pots,—
> How he could flick and pick
> Rotten leaves or yellowy petals,
> Or scoop out a weed close to flourishing roots,
> Or make the dust buzz with a light spray,
> Or drown a bug in one spit of tobacco juice,
> Or fan life into wilted sweet-peas with his hat,
> Or stand all night watering roses, his feet blue in rubber boots.

In one of his most beautiful and moving poems—and one of the great poems of his career—"Frau Bauman, Frau Schmidt, and Frau Schwartze," in *The Waking*, he remembers those

> . . . three ancient ladies
> Who creaked on the greenhouse ladders,
> Reaching up white strings
> To wind, to wind
> The sweet-pea tendrils, the smilax,
> Nasturtiums, the climbing
> Roses, to straighten
> Carnations, red
> Chrysanthemums; the stiff
> Stems, jointed like corn,
> They tied and tucked,—
> These nurses of nobody else.
> Quicker than birds, they dipped
> Up and sifted the dirt;
> They sprinkled and shook
> They stood astride pipes,
> Their skirts billowing out wide into tents,

Their hands twinkling with wet;
Like witches they flew along rows
Keeping creation at ease;
With a tendril for needle
They sewed up the air with a stem;
They teased out the seed that the cold kept asleep,—
All the coils, loops, and whorls.
They trellised the sun; they plotted for more than themselves.

This is Roethke's definition of sanctity—plotting for more than oneself, for the care of the good earth, in order that things might simply be what their entelechies intend that they shall be.

The act that is performed, then, by Roethke's early work is an act of anamnesis whereby a poet who conceives himself to be without a "dancing-master" undertakes to lay hold of the most basic certitudes afforded him by his earliest contact with the world. Like the Wordsworth of *The Prelude*, he found those "spots of time, / That with distinct pre-eminence retain / A renovating virtue" to be "moments / . . . Taking their date / From our first childhood" (book 12). For it was then and there—in that lost and faraway vegetal world of his Saginaw childhood—that, as he came to understand, he first learned "to woo the fearful small," to "sing / The soul's immediate joy," and "not to fear infinity, / The far field, the windy cliffs of forever," because things are gathered together in a great Coinherence in which "everything comes to One, / As we dance on, dance on, dance on"—

Where ask is have, where seek is find,
Where knock is open wide.[18]

So, as a result of the investigations recorded in *Open House* and *The Lost Son*, this poet was enabled to discern that, even if "angels are [not] around any more," he might still "say hello to things; / . . . Talk to a snail; / . . . see what sings!" Although, to be sure, there was no "dancing-master," he could yet say (in "First Meditation," one of the great poems in *Words for the Wind*):

In such times, lacking a god,
I am still happy.

A few weeks after Roethke's death (1 August 1963), John Ciardi, in a memorial piece in the *Saturday Review*, spoke of his verse as "poetry as a medicine man's dance is poetry"[19]—by which he meant to remark a certain incantatory element in Roethke's style. Although Ciardi's phraseology should be felt to be wildly inapposite to the early and the late poems, it may not betray many of the poems in the remarkable book of 1951, *Praise to the End!* For, having found in the lost greenhouse-world of his Saginaw Eden the source of those basic certainties that permitted him to be happy while "lacking a god," in the period immediately following the appearance of *The Lost Son* (1948) Roethke was attempting, indeed, to achieve a kind of total recovery of the childhood experience. And the myriad, evanescent intuitions of childhood are conjured up by means of an incantatory rhetoric so drenched in the "anguish of concreteness" and so radically primitivistic as to make the language of *Praise to the End!* one of the most elusive vocabularies in modern poetry.

The psychologist Jean Piaget suggests that the child's way of taking hold of his or her world involves a tendency at once to "juxtapose" and to "syncretize" the various items of experience. That is, children are so enchanted with the diversity and multiformity of the world, and their appetite for novelty is so great, that they are not intent on finding principles wherewith to codify and categorize the things and events that come their way. They are content to be nothing more than connoisseurs of the sheer profusion and variousness of reality: instead of attempting to classify things and locate them in some system of order, they simply collect them and hold them in juxtaposition, without much regard for questions of logical propriety. They handle the contents of their experience by way of juxtaposition because they feel that "the world is a wedding" in which everything splays off onto everything else. So their habit of mind is one not only of juxtaposition but also of "syncretism," which Piaget defines as the "tendency on the part of children to take things in by means of a comprehensive act of perception instead of by the detection of details, to find immediately and without analysis analogies between words or objects that have nothing to do with each other, to find a reason for every chance event; in a word, it is the tendency to connect everything with everything else."[20]

What is most fundamentally expressed, of course, by the syncretism and juxtaposition of the child's reasoning is a sense of reality in which the subject-object distinction has not yet come to play any decisive part. For, in the earliest period of life, the child does not say, "I am I, and thou art thou." The world is not yet experienced as a vast not-self, outside and over against one's own being. Instead, everything is experienced from the inside: nothing is enclosed within frameworks of identity and causality, and nothing requires mediation, for no distance is felt between ego and world. Usually, it is not until they enter the second or third year of life that children begin to deal with reality not merely in the terms of play but also in the terms of inquiry and analysis. Initially, in the earliest stages of development, they receive the world simply as a marvelous discothèque with whose music they sway, in jubilation and delight and amazement.

Now, because it was in this "first" world that Roethke found what it was that had perduringly sustained his life, even in the absence of "a god" or a "dancing-master," the recollective effort, which in his early work had been largely focused on the greenhouse world of his Saginaw childhood, came gradually to broaden out into an attempt at recovering the whole adventure of childhood and the whole evolutionary process whereby the individual wins the identity of selfhood. And the result of this effort was the astonishing poetry of *Praise to the End!*, whose brilliantly orchestrated chaos (though sometimes defeating for even the most careful reader) represents Roethke's way of miming the primary chaos of psychic life itself.

The title of this book is drawn from a passage in book 1 of *The Prelude* (in the version of 1805–6) in which Wordsworth says:

> Praise to the end!
> Thanks likewise for the means! But I believe
> That Nature, oftentimes, when she would frame
> A favor'd Being, from his earliest dawn
> Of infancy doth open out the clouds,
> As at the touch of lightning, seeking him
> With gentlest visitation; not the less,
> Though haply aiming at the self-same end,
> Does it delight her sometimes to employ
> Severer interventions, ministry
> More palpable, and so she dealt with me.

Wordsworth's avowal of the creative role played in the ripening of the self by the adversities and tribulations suffered in one's early years represents precisely the perspective guiding Roethke's own meditation. But his method is hardly Wordsworthian, for the poems of *Praise to the End!* are "all interior drama; no comment; no interpretation,"[21] and it is very clearly "the spring and rush of the child"[22] that he wants to render in these lines from "Where Knock Is Open Wide":

> I'm somebody else now.
> Don't tell my hands.
> Have I come to always? Not yet.
> One father is enough.
>
> Maybe God has a house.
> But not here.

—or in the concluding lines of "O Lull Me, Lull Me":

> Soothe me, great groans of underneath,
> I'm still waiting for a foot.
> The poke of the wind's close,
> But I can't go leaping alone.
> For you, my pond,
> Rocking with small fish,
> I'm an otter with only one nose:
> I'm all ready to whistle;
> I'm more than when I was born;
> I could say hello to things;
> I could talk to a snail;
> I see what sings!
> What sings!

The early poems in *Praise to the End!*—such as "Where Knock Is Open Wide," "I Need, I Need," and "Bring the Day!"—are written from the standpoint of the child protagonist. The lines are short, and the language is a "dream language" that so mingles the material of nursery rhyme and childish fancy as to convey a direct impression of the inwardness of the child's *Lebenswelt*. Roethke felt that

> in this kind of poem, the poet, in order to be true to what is most universal in himself, should not rely on allusion; should not comment or employ many judgment words; should not meditate (or maunder). He must scorn being "mysterious" or loosely oracular, but be willing to face up to genuine mystery. His language must be compelling and immediate: he must create an actuality. He must be able to telescope image and symbol, if necessary, without relying on the obvious connectives: to speak in a kind of psychic shorthand when his protagonist is under great stress. He must be able to shift his rhythms rapidly. . . . He works intuitively.[23]

It is this aesthetic that is controlling the first of the two parts of the book, in which the poetry is rendering that jumbled and irregular landscape of the fledgling whose identity is still in process of formation. And the drama reflected in these poems is that which Jung took to be the essence of the child's adventure—"the conquest of the dark,"[24] the journey from the night of unconsciousness into the day of awareness and comprehension. As it is said in the beautiful exclamation with which "Bring the Day!" closes:

O small bird wakening,
Light as a hand among blossoms,
Hardly any old angels are around any more.
The air's quiet under the small leaves.
The dust, the long dust, stays.
The spiders sail into summer.
It's time to begin!
To begin!

Part 2 of *Praise to the End!* consists of the series of poems that had concluded *The Lost Son* ("The Lost Son," "The Long Alley," "A Field of Light,"
"The Shape of the Fire") and three others—"Praise to the End!" "Unfold!
Unfold!" and "I Cry, Love!" Here the journey begun in part 1—in search
of identity and selfhood—is continued, but, the protagonist being now
older, the prevailing emphasis falls more heavily on those "severer interventions" (as Wordsworth calls them) which are employed by the executive powers to "frame / A favor'd Being." "The Lost Son," which makes
one of the crucial statements in this whole group of poems, places its
opening scene in a cemetery:

At Woodlawn I heard the dead cry:
I was lulled by the slamming of iron,
A slow drip over stones,
Toads brooding in wells.
All the leaves stuck out their tongues;
I shook the softening chalk of my bones. . . .

And the pilgrim's journey, as it is traced out in part 2 of the book, seems
often to be along the dark underside of things—the disquiet aroused by
the dead father's ghost, the unease consequent upon sexual sins and
alienations, the dismay provoked by an industrial society's desecration of
air and water and earth, the haunting awareness of death as the ultimate
and unavoidable emergency of life. So it comes to be that, for the lost
son, there is no dodging the question:

Which is the way I take;
Out of what door do I go,
Where and to whom?

Always, however, the basic order of perception is that which has been
found to be the determining framework of Roethke's vision—namely, the
sense of the human situation as, most fundamentally, one of our simply
standing (as Heidegger would say) in-the-neighborhood-of-Being, in the

outright *presence* of that-which-is. The gesture that his poetry performs is one of *Gelassenheit*, of abandonment, of surrender to the sheer presence of Being in the things and creatures of earth. For this poet, as he recalls in "Unfold! Unfold!," was

> privy to oily fungus and the algae of standing waters;
> Honored . . . by the ancient fellowship of rotten stems.

So he says (in "A Field of Light"):

> Listen, love,
> The fat lark sang in the field;
> I touched the ground, the ground warmed by the killdeer,
> The salt laughed and the stones;
> The ferns had their ways, and the pulsing lizards,
> And the new plants, still awkward in their soil,
> The lovely diminutives.
> I could watch! I could watch!
> I saw the separateness of all things!
> My heart lifted up with the great grasses;
> The weeds believed me, and the nesting birds.
> There were clouds making a rout of shapes crossing a
>   windbreak of cedars,
> And a bee shaking drops from a rain-soaked honeysuckle.
> The worms were delighted as wrens.
> And I walked, I walked through the light air;
> I moved with the morning.

In February 1963, just a few months before his death—in a statement prepared for a public forum at Northwestern University which is often astonishing in the naked simplicity of his self-revelation—Roethke asserted his belief that "everything that lives is holy" and declared the governing intention of his art to be that of invoking "these holy forms of life." "One could even put this," he said, "theologically: St. Thomas says, 'God is above all things by the excellence of His nature; nevertheless, He is in all things as causing the being of all things.' "[25] Therefore, he concluded, such a poetry as his own, in calling upon snails and weeds and nesting birds and all the various "lovely diminutives" of the world, is indeed calling upon God. And it is this persuasion, it is this faith, that constitutes the vital center of Roethke's vision.

His poetry, however, speaks only rarely of God, and never in the accents of any sort of mystical religion. He was a man who had no desire to transcend the finites and definites that make up the common occasions of life; his poetry is uninfluenced by any great lust for infinities and eternities. Nor was he a poet of Supreme Fictions, and he seems never to have had any impulse to make such a claim as Stevens':

Out of my mind the golden ointment rained,
And my ears made the flowing hymns they heard.
I was myself the compass of that sea:

I was the world in which I walked, and what I saw
Or heard or felt came not but from myself;
And there I found myself more truly and more strange.[26]

On the contrary, it was in the world of the actual—established, as he felt it to be, independently of the human intelligence—that Roethke found his house of prayer. But it was a house of prayer, and he was no mere "facer of facts," of facts that say only "that nothing much can come out of our reality."[27] For he found an engrossing but unfathomable density in the Is-ness of everything that exists, in the mysterious munificence with which even dirt and weeds and garden slugs are indwelt by Being. So his characteristic mode of predication is not the subjunctive or the imperative but the indicative, and it is his deep piety toward all the concrete, tangible things of earth that fills his poetry with exclamations. He makes us feel that he was a man who was always prepared to cry out with Landor, "Good God, the violets!"

Roethke never did have any taste for eschatological abstentions from the world. And, though he believed that God is in a worm, his poetry does not touch manure and cockroaches and geraniums only just enough to yield the *visio dei*. They are not taken "as a bag of tricks, or as a set of notes to be played lightly and delicately, in order to send the soul shooting up, one knows not how, into some kind of infinite or absolute." The mud of earth is not used as "a sort of resilient, rubbery surface off which to rebound as quickly as possible into various parts of the sky"—which is to say that Roethke is not intent on getting "as much as possible of heaven out of as little as possible of earth."[28] He is, instead, a true "literalist of the imagination" for whom (in Teilhard de Chardin's previously quoted phrase) the "within" of all things is "coextensive with their without."

Although Roethke is prepared to affirm that God is in a worm, his intention is not, of course, to assert a relationship of *identity* between the creature and the creative Ground of existence. One might imagine him saying to the worm (in the language of *The Cloud of Unknowing*), "He is thy being, but thou art not his." And thus any heavy-handed leveling of the charge of pantheism would constitute only a stupidly vulgar response to this vision of Being as permeating all things with the clarity and luster of its luminous presence. Roethke was not a pantheist, for his "minute particulars" are never swallowed up in some vast encircling unity in which all diversity and distinction are ultimately annulled.[29] His grains of sand, his mud and roots and moles, his plants and flowers, his frogs and snails are not creatures behind whose illusoriness is descried the reality of the Transcendent. Rather, the mystery of Being is bodied forth in the very creatureliness of the things of earth, in their very contingency and finitude, through which it glows, charging everything with a grandeur that (as Hopkins says) flames "out, like shining from shook foil." This is doubtless what prompted Roethke, as he contemplated the world's marvelous "epic of the eyes," to say, "I recover my tenderness by long looking" ("What Can I Tell My Bones?" *Words for the Wind*). And his poetry wants *us* finally to say, "The poetry does not matter." "What I love is near at hand, / Always, in earth and air," he says. These are the things that matter, the things that are "near at hand," for therein it is that he comes upon what he speaks of in one of the finest of his last poems, "The Marrow" *(The Far Field)*—with its echo of Paul Tillich, whose thought he was then discovering—as the "Godhead above my God."

The Irishman Denis Donoghue strikes a somewhat surprising note in an essay on Roethke when he remarks what he considers the tenuousness of his involvement in things "American," his lack of relationship to the established American tradition in literature, whether of New England or of the South (itself, of course—that is, the dualistic conception of American tradition—being very much such a mistake as a native American would be most unlikely to make). Indeed, says Donoghue, "it is quite possible to think of Roethke as one of the best modern poets without troubling about the fact that he was, after all, an American poet."[30] But surely this is an impermissible conclusion. For Roethke's characteristic mode of vision is one that leads him to respond to the world in terms of a profoundly reverential astonishment and wonder—at the marvelous fecundity and amplitude of Being wherewith the things of earth are steadied and exalted, and by which they manage to last. And, as Tony Tanner reminds us in his book *The Reign of Wonder*, it is precisely in this order of perception that American literature has very often found its central commitment. For whether one turns to Emerson or to Mark Twain, to Thoreau or to Gertrude Stein, to Whitman or to William Carlos Williams, to Henry James or to Hemingway, what one finds being constantly stressed is "the radical importance of a true way of seeing; the generous, open, even naive, undulled and reverent eye—as opposed to the self-interested squinting and peering of the greedy utilitarian social eye, and the cold myopia of the scientific, analytic eye. Their ideal is an eye of passive wonder."[31] Judgment, says the narrator of Saul Bellow's *Dangling*

Man, is "second to wonder"—which neatly summarizes what has tended to be a major premise of the American imagination, that the first and most proper response to be offered the world is one of simple marveling at the variousness and multiplicity of its enchantments.

Roethke deserves to be considered deeply American not only in his commitment to wonder as a primary mode of vision, but also in his conformity to Carlyle's portrayal of Emerson as "*a Soliloquizer* on the eternal mountaintops only, in vast solitudes where men and their affairs all lie hushed in a very dim remoteness; and only *the man* and the stars and the earth are visible."[32] The tendency of our literature to be suspicious of social reality and to find its ballast in what Emerson called "the simple genuine self against the whole world" has been often noted, and there is no gainsaying that it marks a deeply settled habit of thought among our classic writers of both the nineteenth and the twentieth centuries. "Of the great formative works of the American imagination one is set on a river *(Huckleberry Finn)*, one on an open road *(Song of Myself)*, one on the sea *(Moby Dick)*, . . . one by a pond *(Walden)*."[33] And many of the most exemplary personages—Ahab, Hester Prynne, Huck Finn, Nick Adams, Isaac McCaslin, Jack Burden, and Eugene Henderson—are fugitives from society. Fitzgerald tells us that "out of the corner of his eye Gatsby saw that the blocks of the sidewalk really formed a ladder and mounted to a secret place above the trees—he could climb to it, if he climbed alone, and once there he could . . . gulp down the incomparable milk of wonder." And it is toward such a point, above the flurry of the human City— "where men and their affairs all lie hushed in a very dim remoteness"— that our literature often seems to have been aiming.

Roethke's poetic personality is very much that of an *isolé*, and in this also, surely, he may be felt to be a thoroughly American poet. He does, of course, admit into his poetry a number of very remarkable personages—some of whom are identified and others of whom are without name—such as his mother and father, his sister, his Aunt Tilly, his Uncle Charles, "the three ancient ladies / Who creaked on the greenhouse ladders," various "chums" of childhood, and the old woman listening "to the weeds' vesperal whine" as her life draws to a close. But, though his poetry by no means expresses a vision that is merely egocentric, Roethke seems never to have found any high significance in the realm of what Martin Buber calls "the interhuman" or to have believed that "it is from one man to another that the heavenly bread of self-being is passed."[34] The ontological mystery was not for him a preeminently human mystery, and the dialogical drama of our human togetherness did not constitute for him the essential medium or agency through which the self encounters Being.

The famous line in Auden's poem "September 1, 1939"—"We must love one another or die"—makes a kind of announcement which is in no way of a piece with the basic stress of Roethke's poetry. For though he loved, as he said, what "is near at hand, / Always, in earth and air," it seems that the tensions and fulfillments that make up our human sociality were never felt to be quite so near at hand as sprouting bulbs and wriggling worms, as sighing weeds and the "midnight eyes" of all the little creatures of the earth. He could join the Yeats who listened to the "sweet everlasting Voices" that "call in birds, in wind on the hill, / In shaken boughs, in tide on the shore."[35] But there was another Yeats, whose mind and art moved in a dimension altogether beyond Roethke—the Yeats, for example, who prefaced the following lines with an epigraph from Thomas Mann which says that "In our time the destiny of man presents its meaning in political terms":

> How can I, that girl standing there,
> My attention fix
> On Roman or on Russian
> Or on Spanish politics?
> Yet here's a travelled man that knows
> What he talks about,
> And there's a politician
> That has read and thought,
> And maybe what they say is true
> Of war and war's alarms. . . . [36]

"Ye littles, lie more close!" says Roethke in the poem "In Evening Air" (The Far Field); and this "minimalism," which is recurrently echoed throughout his work, does unfortunately shut out large tracts of experience—nearly all those regions in which "the destiny of man presents its meaning in political terms," in the terms of our life together in the human polis. He was a man "more responsive to intimations of being when they offer themselves in plants than in people,"[37] so that finally, in his vast solitudes, men and their affairs do lie all too hushed, in a very dim remoteness indeed. And the result is an impoverishment, a failure to carry the sacramental principle to its full and decisive limit.

But, however sparsely populated Roethke's universe may be, at least lovers are not excluded; and many of the love poems in Words for the Wind and The Far Field belong among the great modern triumphs in this genre, with the finest lyrics of Yeats and Graves and Auden. Here again, as at so many other points in his poetry, we see how thoroughly unplatonic was the essential cast of Roethke's mind, for what he values in heterosexual love is not some ethereal felicity to which it gives access, not some pallid empyrean into which it leads: on the contrary, it is the riot and romp and frolic of sexual joy that he celebrates, and the poetry sounds a pure hosanna in behalf of the fleshly delights of the partnership between man and woman. The poem "Words for the Wind" closes, for example, with the following lines:

> I kiss her moving mouth,
> Her swart hilarious skin;
> She breaks my breath in half;
> She frolicks like a beast;
> And I dance round and round,
> A fond and foolish man,
> And see and suffer myself
> In another being, at last.

Or, again, the second stanza of "I Knew a Woman" says:

> How well her wishes went! She stroked my chin,
> She taught me Turn, and Counter-turn, and Stand;
> She taught me Touch, that undulant white skin;
> I nibbled meekly from her proffered hand;
> She was the sickle; I, poor I, the rake,
> Coming behind her for her pretty sake
> (But what prodigious mowing we did make).

And it is a similar reveling in the joyous privilege of sensuality which the love poems express again and again. "We did not fly the flesh. Who does, when young?" Roethke's candor about the itch of desire is unsullied by any smirking embarrassment or uneasiness of conscience, and his exuberance gives to the rhetoric of his love poetry a fervency and an eloquence that make it something very remarkable indeed.

It would be, however, a miscalculation to conceive the love poems as dedicated to nothing more than the careless raptures of sensual joy. For, despite all their rollicking carnality, they carry a larger freight of meaning. One clue to this additional dimension is given in the beautifully executed cycle of poems "Four for Sir John Davies," which appeared in *The Waking* and was reissued in *Words for the Wind*. "The Dance," the first poem in the sequence, is perhaps most heavily dependent on Roethke's reading of Sir John Davies, for this minor poet of the English sixteenth century, in the long poem *Orchestra* (1594), was proposing that the harmonious interrelationships among the various realms of Being are conceivable as all constituting a sort of cosmic dance in which the whole of reality participates. This notion activates the meditation recorded in the opening poem of Roethke's cycle, in which he wonders if this metaphor retains any relevance for the modern imagination:

> Is that dance slowing in the mind of man
> That made him think the universe could hum?

But, as for himself, he seems to be saying, the "great wheel" continues to turn, and he likens the clumsiness of his own dancing to the ungainly romping of a bear. "Though dancing needs a master, I had none / To teach my toes to listen to my tongue." Yet, even so, "I was dancing-mad, and how / That came to be the bears and Yeats would know."

To dance, however, one needs a partner. So, in the second poem of the sequence ("The Partner"), the poet is joined by a woman (who "would set sodden straw on fire"). The form of his dance now becomes that of sexual union:

> We played a measure with commingled feet:
> The lively dead had taught us to be fond.
> . . . .
> Light altered light along the living ground.
> She kissed me close, and then did something else.
> My marrow beat as wildly as my pulse.

In the last line of the poem, these two are playing "in that dark world where gods have lost their way." Here, immediately, we feel a new seriousness, for this "dark world" is presumably the world in which Sir John Davies' cosmic dance begins now to be "slowing in the mind of man" because no dancing-master is to be found. Roethke seems to suggest that what the protagonist and his companion have together is that which will alone make this darkness tolerable.

Indeed, what is only hinted at in the closing lines of "The Partner" is made quite explicit in the opening lines of "The Wraith":

> Incomprehensible gaiety and dread
> Attended what we did. Behind, before,
> Lay all the lonely pastures of the dead;
> The spirit and the flesh cried out for more.
> We two, together, on a darkening day
> Took arms against our own obscurity.

This makes as plain a declaration as is to be found anywhere in Roethke's love poems of what he considers the true office of love. It is, he intends to say, our best, perhaps our only, way of taking arms against our frailty, our "obscurity," our defenselessness before the infinite hazards to which we are exposed. It is our way of ringing ourselves round with a campfire that staves off the environing dark of the nighttime wilderness looming beyond. But the lines that immediately follow this stanza may remind us how inappropriate it would be to take what Roethke is saying here as his conception of the "spiritual" meaning of love. For, even as the cycle deepens down into the "dark world where gods have lost their way," the actual physicality of human love remains the primary datum of the poem:

> Did each become the other in that play?
> She laughed me out, and then she laughed me in;
> In the deep middle of ourselves we lay;
> When glory failed, we danced upon a pin.

Sexuality is not, in other words, merely a metaphor whereby one speaks of the really important thing, which is something "spiritual." For (unlike Shelley) Roethke never conceives felicity to be any sort of "unbodied joy," and his love poetry is always fully committed to the claims of the flesh. But, there, the stress of body against body casts a spell wherewith, as he says in the concluding poem of the cycle ("The Vigil"), "We undid chaos" and "mocked before the black / And shapeless night that made no answer back."

It is this whole undercurrent of meaning in the love poems which leads on into what increasingly became one of Roethke's major concerns in the final years of his life—namely, the last great emergency that we face, which is none other than the certain eventuality of death. For even those lovers who are most intensely involved in each other's lives are only pawing the dark,[38] as Roethke very clearly wants to say in one of his most memorable poems, "The Sensualists" (*Words for the Wind*), which deserves to be quoted in full:

> "There is no place to turn," she said,
> "You have me pinned so close;
> My hair's all tangled on your head,
> My back is just one bruise;
> I feel we're breathing with the dead;
> O angel, let me loose"
>
> And she was right, for there beside
> The gin and cigarettes,
> A woman stood, pure as a bride,
> Affrighted from her wits,
> And breathing hard, as that man rode
> Between those lovely tits.

"My shoulder's bitten from your teeth;
    What's that peculiar smell?
No matter which one is beneath,
    Each is an animal,"—
The ghostly figure sucked its breath,
    And shuddered toward the wall;
Wrapped in the tattered robe of death,
    It tiptoed down the hall.

"The bed itself begins to quake,
    I hate this sensual pen;
My neck if not my heart, will break
    If we do this again,"—
Then each fell back, limp as a sack,
    Into the world of men.

Here Roethke offers, through the drama of his poem, a kind of evidence of how impossible it is, finally, for love effectively to confer anything like the sort of ultimate solace which Matthew Arnold's "Dover Beach" envisages. For, after its ecstasy, the lovers must fall "back . . . / Into the world of men"—the "dark world," in which one cannot avoid the disquieting chill of "the shifting midnight air." "All sensual love's but dancing on a grave" ("The Dying Man," *Words for the Wind*).

In the great sequence of poems concluding *Words for the Wind*, "Meditations of an Old Woman," the protagonist is one who has felt the frosty touch of "the shifting midnight air." So, in the "late afternoon" of her life, after long years of yearning "for absolutes that never come," she is unprepared to give any quick assent to Eliot's assurance in "Little Gidding" that

All shall be well, and
All manner of thing shall be well.

For, as she says,

It is difficult to say all things are well,
When the worst is about to arrive. . . .

She is a woman who has journeyed far—"into the waste lonely places / Behind the eye; the lost acres at the edge of smoky cities." But a lifetime's effort is without any crown, and

On love's worst ugly day,
The weeds hiss at the edge of the field,
The small winds make their chilly indictments.

As she draws "near the graves of the great dead," she wonders what she can tell her bones. The five poems making up the cycle create a profoundly poignant drama of self-interrogation and search. But these "Meditations" do not move toward the embrace of a resurrection-faith. Instead, the old woman says (in "Her Becoming"), "I have learned to sit quietly"—which is to say that she has learned (as Roethke says in one of the poems in *The Far Field*, "The Abyss") to "wait, unafraid, beyond the fearful instant."

This is, indeed, the essential *action* in the poems in which she figures, an action of meditation and of waiting. As Roethke says in one of his late poems, "The Right Thing" (*The Far Field*), "Let others probe the mystery if they can." But the ancient lady of the "Meditations" is no longer a "time-harried prisoner of *Shall* and *Will*": she has learned to prefer "the still joy," to listen to a "snail's music"—and simply to wait. To be sure, as she says, "In the days of my slowness . . . / I've become a strange piece of flesh," infirm and "whiskery." But, as she declares in the great final lines of the "First Meditation," even "lacking a god, / I am still happy." For there is to be heard the call of

> The cerulean, high in the elm,
> Thin and insistent as a cicada,
> And the far phoebe, singing,
> The long plaintive notes floating down,
> Drifting through leaves, oak and maple,
> Or the whippoorwill, along the smoky ridges . . .

Thus, even as one faces the last great extremity of life, a certain nonchalance or poise is possible. "Birds are around," mice are still capering in the straw, stones can still be caressed; and the old woman has come to believe that there is "wisdom in objects," for the speech that passes between birds and trees, between salmon and shallow streams, between sun and earth is a speech that testifies of the presence of Being beneath and above and within all the things and creatures of this world. So, she says, "I become the wind" and "recover my tenderness by long looking."

Indeed, it is very much in this way that the disquiet aroused by the prospect of death is in some measure allayed in many of the remarkable poems making up Roethke's posthumous volume *The Far Field*—in the poems forming the cycle "North American Sequence," in "The Abyss," and in several of the magnificent poems of "Sequence, Sometimes Metaphysical" ("In Evening Air," "Infirmity," "The Right Thing," "Once More, the Round"). They all tend to reach a similar conclusion—that, baffling and fearful as the thought of death may be, once the spirit gathers itself together to "embrace the world," it will find itself no longer fearing "infinity, / The far field, the windy cliffs of forever," since when one breathes

> . . . with the birds,
> The spirit of wrath becomes the spirit of blessing,
> And the dead begin from their dark to sing. . . .

Thus it is that the poet comes upon "the true ease of myself" and unlearns "the lingo of exasperation"—by not insisting upon too much reality (which "can be a dazzle, a surfeit") and by simply faring forth into the things of earth which do themselves, for all their finitude (as "The Far Field" says), "reveal infinitude."

On days of mottled clouds, of thinly misted mornings or evenings, we may still "rock between dark and dark," waiting for God. But there is one deeply felt intuition on which Roethke's entire poetry is built—that, miraculously, the universe in which we dwell is so ordered that Being never deserts the things and creatures of earth, that it bestows itself upon them with a most handsome munificence, and that, even when we must wait "in a dark time" for the gods, one need not "outleap the sea— / The edge of all the land" in order to discover that in ourselves by which we are steadied and "in which all creatures share. . . ." In short, even in the darkest time, one can still say (as in "The Abyss"):

> I receive! I have been received!
> I hear the flowers drinking in their light,
> I have taken counsel of the crab and the sea-urchin,
> I recall the falling of small waters,
> The stream slipping beneath the mossy logs,
> Winding down to the stretch of irregular sand,
> The great logs piled like matchsticks.

> I am most immoderately married:
> The Lord God has taken my heaviness away;
> I have merged, like the bird, with the bright air,
> And my thought flies to the place by the bo-tree.

> Being, not doing, is my first joy.

So this poet was one who could say, with enormous gusto and conviction, "I count myself among the happy poets."[39] He adored his life "with the Bird, the abiding Leaf, / With the Fish, the questing Snail," and he wanted to "dance with William Blake / For love, for Love's sake. . . ." One of the lines in his poem "I Cry, Love! Love!" declares: "I proclaim once more a condition of joy." And to proclaim a condition of joy was an abiding intention of his verse. For, despite his recurrent bouts with a most baffling and often humiliating mental illness,[40] he was indeed a happy poet. So the cadence that his poetry sounds, with a deeply moving kind of repetitiveness and with an eloquence unique in the literature of modern poetry, is that of reverence for life—and of thanksgiving:

> I could watch! I could watch!
> I saw the separateness of all things!
> My heart lifted up with the great grasses;
> . . . .
> And I walked, I walked through the light air;
> I moved with the morning.

And there is perhaps no other passage in the whole of Roethke's poetry that more beautifully expresses his distinctive *pietas* than the great exclamation with which "The Shape of Fire" (*Praise to the End!*) closes:

> To have the whole air!
> The light, the full sun
> Coming down on the flowerheads,
> The tendrils turning slowly,
> A slow snail-lifting, liquescent;
> To be by the rose
> Rising slowly out of its bed,
> Still as a child in its first loneliness;
> To see cyclamen veins become clearer in early sunlight,
> And mist lifting out of the brown cattails;
> To stare into the after-light, the glitter left on the lake's surface,
> When the sun has fallen behind a wooden island;
> To follow the drops sliding from a lifted oar,
> Held up, while the rower breathes, and the small boat drifts quietly
>   shoreward;
> To know that light falls and fills, often without our knowing,
> As an opaque vase fills to the brim from a quick pouring,
> Fills and trembles at the edge yet does not flow over,
> Still holding and feeding the stem of the contained flower.

CHAPTER FIVE

Elizabeth Bishop—Poet without Myth

N early sixty years ago Basil Willey, in his still indispensable book *The Seventeenth Century Background*, proposed that we take Words-worth as the largest exemplar of one of the two courses remaining open to poetry once "the Locke tradition" had had its full impact. In Willey's view of it, this was a tradition extending from Bacon though Hobbes to Locke—and on, of course, to Hartley and Hume and Bentham. And the kind of hardheaded empiricism represented by this line of thought said in effect that, though "the air of Parnassus may be pleasant, . . . its soil is barren."[1] Empiricist philosophy in the morning-time of the modern period was striving above all else to inculcate the belief that the fact-world is the true locus of reality, and it accorded, therefore, a privileged status to that faculty of the mind which Locke's *Essay Concerning Human Understanding* nominates as "Judgment," for Judgment weighs all things in relation to "the severe Rules of Truth, and good Reason." Moreover, in the Lockean calculus, Judgment "is a way of proceeding quite contrary to Metaphor and Allusion, wherein for the most part, lies that entertain-ment and pleasantry of Wit, which strikes so lively on the Fancy, and therefore so acceptable to all People; because its Beauty appears at first sight, and there is required no labour of thought, to examine what Truth or Reason there is in it." Which was, of course, to say that he who deals with experience in terms of metaphor—that is, in terms of the language of the literary imagination—is simply a trifler whose "pleasant Pictures, and agreeable Visions" may, to be sure, conduce to diversion and amuse-ment but will not, however, be found "perfectly conformable" to truth and reason.[2]

So it was that all the enabling myths in which the poetic enterprise had traditionally found its vital principle were suddenly enervated by what Keats's "Lamia" calls "the touch of cold philosophy." For, as it seemed at the point of this new extremity, none of the existing mythologies "could express the 'real,' as the 'real' was now felt to be. . . . The new poet must therefore either make poetry out of the direct dealings of his mind and heart with the visible universe, or he must fabricate a genuine new mythology of his own (not necessarily rejecting all old material in so doing). Keats and Shelley," says Willey, "often follow the second of these methods; Wordsworth typically follows the first."[3] For the poet of the *Lyrical Ballads* and *The Prelude* forswears all "abstractions, . . . symbols, . . . myths . . . [which might] stand between the mind and its true object . . . To animise the 'real' world, the 'universe of death' that the 'mechanical' system of philosophy had produced, but to do so without either using an exploded mythology or fabricating a new one, this was the special task and mission of Wordsworth."[4] Which meant that, "alone" as he was with the universe, his poetic mission could validate itself only by "a record of successes; of successful imaginative dealings with the world of eye and ear."[5]

Now these notations of Willey's on Wordsworth will surely remind us of how searching is the floodlight that can be thrown on Anglo-American poetry of our own period by the whole venture of the English Romantics. For what Willey says about Wordsworth's situation suggests such an estimate of where a poet like Elizabeth Bishop stands than which none could be more exact. The English critic John Bayley is quite wrong when he says of Conrad: "He has no myth with a view to insight: he has scenes and he has people."[6] But no more apt a formula could be devised for Bishop: she is, indeed, a poet without myth, without metaphysics, without commitment to any systematic vision of the world, perhaps the most thoroughly secular poet of her generation[7]—and it makes an impressive attestation to her extraordinary record of successes in her dealings simply with the world of eye and ear that, even so, she was well-nigh universally regarded at the time of her death (October 1979) as one who had *added* something to our literature in the ways that only genius can.

Since by some quirk of misfortune she won no "myth with a view to insight" such as a Yeats or a Stevens or an Auden was granted, it was no doubt inevitable that her poetry should always be (as one of her critics has remarked)[8] a kind of *expedition*, just as her own life was that of the constant voyager to Brittany and Paris, to North Africa and Spain, to Mexico and Scandinavia and Brazil. When she was awarded the Neustadt International Prize for Literature at the University of Oklahoma in the spring of 1976, she spoke in her words of acceptance about how all her life she had "lived and behaved very much like . . . [a] sandpiper—just running along the edges of different countries and continents, 'looking for something.' "[9] Which is not unlike what her poetry is doing, what indeed it *has* to be doing, since there is no controlling myth to chart and guide its motions: it is forever turning to this and that and something else and saying (as does the final line in the great poem "The Monument"), "Watch it closely." "I require of you only to *look*," says St. Teresa—which might be thought to be the imperative in which the morality of Bishop's art is grounded. For, being unregulated by any metaphysic wherewith the things and creatures of earth are proportionated and ordered into a system of total meaning, hers is a poetry that must be continually searching for significances, looking here and looking there till (in the final phrase of "Over 2,000 Illustrations and a Complete Concordance") it has "looked and looked our infant sight away." We dwell in a world whose variousness and multiformity are beyond all calculation, a world of continents and cities and mountains, of oceans and mangrove swamps, of buzzards and alligators and fireflies, of dews and frosts, of light and darkness, of stars and clouds, of birth and death, and of all the millions of other things that make up the daily round of experience. And, amidst "the bewilderingly proliferating data of the universe," Bishop must take it for granted that "not until the senses have all but eroded themselves to nothing in the process of doing the work assigned to them can anything approaching a moment of understanding take place."[10] The attention bestowed upon whatever comes one's way must be so pure, so absolute, so intransitive, as to allow us, as it were, to hear "the elements speaking: earth, air, fire, water."[11] And, in this way, even without myth or metaphysic, we may win through to knowledge, fundamental knowledge—

> dark, salt, clear, moving, utterly free,
> drawn from the cold hard mouth
> of the world. . . . [12]

What one ought to want in art, said the poet in a letter to Anne Stevenson, "is the same thing that is necessary for its creation, a self-forgetful, perfectly useless concentration"[13]—on all the various particulars that surround us and that are freighted with meanings so abundant that we may find the consolations of systematic philosophy to be quite inessential.

Indeed, the posthumously issued *Complete Poems* might well have been given the title that Bishop chose for her book of 1965, *Questions of Travel*, for, in its search for significant particulars, the poetry is constantly moving from Wellfleet, Massachusetts, to Paris, from Florida to Nova Scotia, from New York to Brazil, and on to still other scenes and regions. "There are in her poems," says David Kalstone, "no final visions—only the saving, continuing, precise pursuits of the travelling eye."[14] This may well

be why, as one moves through her work from her first book, *North &
South* (1946), to *A Cold Spring* (1955), and from *Questions of Travel* (1965) to
Geography III (1976) and on to the last poems, one has no sense of any
progress or growth, as one does in contemplating the whole career of
Eliot or Auden or Lowell: poem after poem is recording utterly discrete
perceptions, and though, taken poem by poem, her work is powerfully
unified and cogent, the poems altogether seem an affair of "Everything
only connected by 'and' and 'and' " ("Over 2,000 Illustrations," in *A Cold
Spring*).

So, for the reader approaching Bishop's poetry for the first time, it
makes little difference where one begins, because, in whatever one turns
to, one finds oneself in the hands of a poet who is saying, "But surely it
would have been a pity / not to have seen" this or "not to have pondered" that—as she does in the beautiful poem "Questions of Travel,"
which invites us to contemplate a luxuriant Brazilian landscape that is all
an *affaire de trop*: "too many waterfalls," "streams [that] hurry too rapidly
down to the sea," and "so many clouds on the mountaintops." "But,"
says the poem,

> surely it would have been a pity
> not to have seen the trees along this road,
> really exaggerated in their beauty,
> not to have seen them gesturing
> like noble pantomimists robed in pink.
> —Not to have had to stop for gas and heard
> the sad, two-noted, wooden tune
> of disparate wooden clogs
> carelessly clacking over
> a grease-stained filling-station floor.
> (In another country the clogs would all be tested.
> Each pair there would have identical pitch.)
> —A pity not to have heard
> the other, less primitive music of the fat brown bird
> who sings above the broken gasoline pump
> in a bamboo church of Jesuit baroque. . . .
> —Yes, a pity not to have pondered,
> blurr'dly and inconclusively,
> on what connection can exist for centuries
> between the crudest wooden footwear
> and, careful and finicky,
> the whittled fantasies of wooden cages. . . .
> —And never to have had to listen to rain

so much like politicians' speeches:
two hours of unrelenting oratory
and then a sudden golden silence
in which the traveller takes a notebook, writes:

"Is it lack of imagination that makes us come
to imagined places, not just stay at home?
Or could Pascal have been not entirely right
about just sitting quietly in one's room?

Continent, city, country, society:
the choice is never wide and never free.
And here, or there . . . No. Should we have stayed at home,
wherever that may be?"
                    (*CP*, 93–94)

And the tone in which the closing question of the poem is asked clearly indicates that this poet wants it to be answered in the negative. For she takes a sceptical view of Pascal's injunction that we forswear the temptations of *divertissement* and remain quietly in our own chambers. So she rarely situates her poetic *topos* "at home, / wherever that may be": she wants to be in *other* places, for, as Stevens says,

From this the poem springs: that we live in a place
That is not our own and, much more, not ourselves
And hard it is in spite of blazoned days.[15]

The world that Bishop looks out upon, for all its blazoned days, often appears hard indeed. Hers was, of course, a sensibility too chaste for her ever to have moaned about falling on the thorns of life or about how cruel and terrifying the world is, and she had nothing but impatience with "the tendency . . . to overdo the morbidity" in much recent "confessional" poetry: "You just wish," she said, "they'd keep some of these things to themselves."[16] Yet she reserved a certain mistrust for the "vulgar beauty of irridescence" (*CP*, 37). In "Florida," for example, she remarks the irony that "the state with the prettiest name"

        . . . floats in brackish water,
    held together by mangrove roots
    that bear while living oysters in clusters,
    and when dead strew white swamps with skeletons,
    dotted as if bombarded, with green hummocks
    like ancient cannon-balls sprouting grass.
                    (*CP*, 32)

Or, in the strange poem "The Unbeliever," we are told that he—whoever he is—"sleeps on the top of his mast / with his eyes closed tight" and that, when a "gull inquired into his dream," it turned out to be

"I must not fall.
The spangled sea below wants me to fall.
It is hard as diamonds; it wants to destroy us all."
(CP, 22)

Or, again, in "Question of Travel," she speaks of how, as one peers up at the Brazilian highlands, "the mountains look like the hulls of capsized ships, / slime-hung and barnacled." And in the great poem "Crusoe in England" in *Geography III*, she has the solitary back at home on his native isle remembering his former place of exile, which—unlike the rough, craggily grand landscape that Defoe's protagonist subdued—was "a sort of cloud-dump" over which "all the hemisphere's left-over clouds" appeared to hang. The volcanoes were "miserable, small . . . —volcanoes dead as ash heaps." Everywhere there was aridness and desiccation: the waterspouts would "come and go, advancing and retreating," and they offered "not much company." Even the little volcano that he christened *"Mont d'Espoir* or *Mount Despair"* seemed never to confirm either designation. And the goats and the gulls as they went *"Baa, baa, baa* and *shriek, shriek, shriek,"* offered only "equivocal replies" to his tacit questions. It was a mute world that held forth not the merest promise of any kind of reciprocity, an "island [that] had one kind of everything" ("one tree snail," "one variety of tree," "one kind of berry"), but with nothing seeming inclined to become for this *isolé* (as Martin Buber would say) a *thou* (CP, 162–66).

Bishop views the world with an unblinking clarity, and she has no recourse to any kind of sentimental pastoralism. Indeed, her way of rendering the natural order would have made it wholly appropriate for her to say, with Alain Robbe-Grillet, "Man looks at the world, and the world does not look back at him."[17] Yet, hard as it is, for all its blazoned days, she bestows upon it and all its creatures an attention so passionate that very often the distinction between the self and the not-self seems nearly altogether to have been dissolved, so much so that the confession of Byron's Childe Harold could be hers:

I live not in myself, but I become
Portion of that around me . . .
. . . . I can see

> Nothing to loathe in nature, save to be
> A link reluctant in a fleshly chain. . . .
>
> Are not the mountains, waves, and skies a part
> Of me and of my soul, as I of them?
> (*Childe Harold's Pilgrimage,*
> Canto III—LXXII, LXXV)

Indeed, Bishop's meditation, for all its secularity, cannot but paradoxically put one in mind of the meditative methods underlying the religious poetry of the English seventeenth century which Louis L. Martz has scanned so profoundly in his book *The Poetry of Meditation.* Martz has shown quite conclusively how the immense body of Continental treatises on meditation which were an issue of the Counter Reformation drifted into England toward the end of the sixteenth century and during the early decades of the seventeenth century from Spain and Italy and France (in English versions printed at Antwerp, Louvain, Rouen, Paris, Douay, and Rheims). He has also shown how the Catholic spirituality transmitted in this way onto the English scene helped widely to disseminate the influence of Ignatius of Loyola and of his *Spiritual Exercises,* which was perhaps the decisive landmark in this entire body of literature. But the main burden of Martz's book concerns the large extent to which the sensibilities and the poetic procedures of those writers whom we usually speak of as "metaphysical," such as Donne and Herbert, were formed by this European "art of meditation." This art of applying the understanding to things for the sake of exciting holy affections began with what Ignatius called the "composition of place, seeing the spot": that is, the scene or object (or, more preferably, as Ignatius specifies, "Christ our Lord") prompting the meditation needed to be *seen* by "the eyes of the imagination"[18] with the greatest possible intensity. Then the meditant needed most strenuously to reflect on the import of what was beheld for the ultimate profit of the "whole soul." And, finally, for the empowerment of the affections, there needed to be a "colloquy," preferably with God, though permissibly also with oneself, or even, as St. Francis de Sales allowed, with "insensible creatures."[19] And the great fascination of Martz's book grows out of its various disclosures of how deeply English meditative poems of the seventeenth century were affected by this discipline, even when they departed in one particular or another from the prescriptions laid down by devotional manuals of the period.

Now Elizabeth Bishop did, to be sure, keep a great admiration for George Herbert,[20] but her own idioms suggest that she was perhaps far more immediately influenced by Hopkins and Stevens and Marianne Moore than by the Metaphysicals in general. And certainly she was most insistent on her neutrality in regard to any form of religion.[21] Yet, again and again, her own style of thought moves from a "composition of place" or object to reflection on its anagogical import and on to a "colloquy" either with herself or with her reader. The central masterpiece in *A Cold Spring*, "At the Fishhouses," presents a case in point. The setting of the poem is a town in Nova Scotia, in the district of the local fishhouses. And the "composition" of the scene, for all its apparent casualness, is wrought with the utmost care:

> Although it is a cold evening,
> down by one of the fishhouses
> an old man sits netting,
> his net, in the gloaming almost invisible,
> a dark purple-brown,
> and his shuttle worn and polished.
> The air smells so strong of codfish
> it makes one's nose run and one's eyes water.
> The five fishhouses have steeply peaked roofs
> and narrow, cleated gangplanks slant up
> to storerooms in the gables
> for the wheelbarrows to be pushed up and down on.
> All is silver: the heavy surface of the sea,
> swelling slowly as if considering spilling over,
> is opaque, but the silver of the benches,
> the lobster pots, and masts, scattered
> among the wild jagged rocks,
> is of an apparent translucence
> like the small old buildings with an emerald moss
> growing on their shoreward walls.
> The big fish tubs are completely lined
> with layers of beautiful herring scales
> and the wheelbarrows are similarly plastered
> with creamy iridescent coats of mail,
> with small iridescent flies crawling on them.
>
> (*CP*, 64)

With a most deliberate and meticulous kind of literality, the scene is "composed" with such an exactness as locks us up within the closet of that which is to be meditated. Later in the poem the speaker declares herself "a believer in total immersion," and this is what she wants for us: total immersion in the tableau presented by this old fisherman weaving his net on a bleak, cold evening down at the waterfront, where everything seems either iridized by the waters lapping against the strand or caked and plastered and rusted over by the erosive power of the sea. Indeed, it is not until we have been fully drawn into this scene that the poem allows it to quiver into life: the speaker offers the old man a cigarette, and they begin to "talk of the decline in the population / and of codfish and herring," as "he waits for a herring boat to come in."

So, then, we are

> Down at the water's edge, at the place
> where they haul up the boats, up the long ramp
> descending into the water. . . .
>
> (CP, 65)

And, as the speaker contemplates the "cold dark deep and absolutely clear" waters of the sea, waters "bearable . . . to fish and to seals" but "to no mortal," she remembers a particular seal she has often seen here:

> He was curious about me. He was interested in music;
> like me a believer in total immersion,
> so I used to sing him Baptist hymns.
> I also sang "A Mighty Fortress Is Our God."
> He stood up in the water and regarded me
> steadily, moving his head a little.
> Then he would disappear, then suddenly emerge
> almost in the same spot, with a sort of shrug
> as if it were against his better judgment.
> Cold dark deep and absolutely clear,
> the clear gray icy water. . . .
>
> (CP, 65)

And now, the scene having been fully composed, the meditation begins, developing finally into a colloquy with the reader who is directly addressed as "you":

> The water seems suspended
> above the rounded gray and blue-gray stones.
> I have seen it over and over, the same sea, the same,
> slightly, indifferently swinging above the stones,
> icily free above the stones,
> above the stones and then the world.
> If you should dip your hand in,
> your wrist would ache immediately,
> your bones would begin to ache and your hand would burn
> as if the water were a transmutation of fire
> that feeds on stones and burns with a dark gray flame.

If you tasted it, it would first taste bitter,
then briny, then surely burn your tongue.
It is like what we imagine knowledge to be:
dark, salt, clear, moving, utterly free,
drawn from the cold hard mouth
of the world, derived from the rocky breasts
forever, flowing and drawn, and since
our knowledge is historical, flowing, and flown.

(*CP*, 65–66)

By this point the lone fisherman and his shuttle and net have quite faded into the background, and the speaker has realized that what most urgently asks to be pondered is the sea itself, "dark, salt, clear." And the rippling sibilance with which it is described—"slightly, indifferently swinging above the stones, / icily free above the stones"—does, as it echoes the rising and falling of the waters, make for a very intense realization of the briny, inscrutable abysm beyond the land's edge. But the *result* of this meditation is the grave recognition that the sea is much like something in the affairs of human life with which we must reckon, and thus the poem is ready at last to eventuate in the final colloquy, which the speaker addresses at once to herself and to her reader. "If you should dip your hand in, / your wrist would ache immediately, / your bones would begin to ache. . . ." "If you tasted it, it would first taste bitter, / then briny, then surely burn your tongue." And then, with what is for her an uncharacteristic explicitness, Bishop specifies the referent of which the sea is a symbol:

It is like what we imagine knowledge to be:
dark, salt, clear, moving, utterly free,
drawn from the cold hard mouth
of the world, derived from the rocky breasts
forever, flowing and drawn, and since
our knowledge is historical, flowing, and flown.

(*CP*, 66)

Here it is that the poem at its end formulates the idea to which it would have the "whole soul" give heed, that a truly unillusioned awareness of our place and prospect is won only by facing into the cold, hard, bedrock realities of our mortal condition and that, however circumspect and sober it may be, even at its best it remains something "historical," something needing to be revised over and over again, flowing and flown—like the sea. So to render Bishop's final lines is, of course, to betray them, but it is to something like such a conclusion as this that she is brought on that cold evening in a Nova Scotia town, down by one of the fishhouses where an old man sits netting, as he waits for a herring boat to come in. It is undoubtedly her deep formation by the kind of meditative discipline underlying this poem which accounts for the extraordinary sympathy with which Bishop approached a world that, however intently it is scanned, seems not to look back at us. In this connection one thinks of poems such as "The Weed" and "Quai d'Orléans" and "Roosters" in *North & South,* "The Riverman" and "Sandpiper" in *Questions of Travel,* and "The Moose" in *Geography III.* And certainly one will think of the beautiful prose poems "Giant Toad" and "Strayed Crab" and "Giant Snail," which make up the sequence "Rainy Season; Sub-Tropics." The Giant Snail, for example, gives this account of his situation:

> The rain has stopped. The waterfall will roar like that all night. I have come out to take a walk and feed. My body—foot, that is—is wet and cold and covered with sharp gravel . . . I have set myself a goal, a certain rock, but it may well be dawn before I get there. Although I move ghostlike and my floating edges barely graze the ground, I am heavy, heavy, heavy. My white muscles are already tired. I give the impression of mysterious ease, but it is only with the greatest effort of my will that I can rise above the smallest stones and sticks. And I must not let myself be distracted by those rough spears of grass. Don't touch them. Draw back. Withdrawal is always best . . . .
>
> Rest a minute; relax. Flattened to the ground, my body is like a pallid, decomposing leaf. What's that tapping on my shell? Nothing. Let's go on.
>
> My sides move in rhythmic waves, just off the ground, from front to back. . . . I am cold, cold, cold as ice. . . . Ah, but I know my shell is beautiful, and high, and glazed, and shining. I know it well, although I have not seen it . . .
>
> But O! I am too big. I feel it. Pity me.
>
> (*CP,* 141)

Here, like Wordsworth, she is looking steadily at her subject, but—again, like Wordsworth—not from a merely analytical, matter-of-fact perspective: on the contrary, she is facing a wordless creature with so much affectionate responsiveness that not only (in Coleridge's phrase) does "nature [become] thought and thought nature"[22] but there occurs even an interchange of roles, the snail becoming a speaking *I* as the poet becomes a listening *thou.* And the result is a well-nigh preternatural commingling of love and awe before the sheer otherness of the things of earth.

Perhaps the most notable instance in Bishop's poetry of this genius for empathy is "The Fish," the great poem in *North & South* that has been so frequently anthologized. The poet has caught "a tremendous fish" and is looking at him, as she holds him half out of water beside her boat:

> He didn't fight.
> He hadn't fought at all.
> He hung a grunting weight,
> battered and venerable
> and homely. Here and there
> his brown skin hung in strips
> like ancient wallpaper,
> and its pattern of darker brown
> was like wallpaper:
> shapes like full-blown roses
> stained and lost through age.
> He was speckled with barnacles,
> fine rosettes of lime,
> and infested
> with tiny white sea-lice,
> and underneath two or three
> rags of green weed hung down.
>   (*CP*, 42)

She watches his gills "breathing in the terrible oxygen," and she notices his eyes,

> which were far larger than mine
> but shallower, and yellowed,
> the irises backed and packed
> with tarnished tinfoil
> seen through the lenses
> of old scratched isinglass.
> They shifted a little, but not
> to return my stare.
>   (*CP*, 43)

Then, as she admires "his sullen face" and "the mechanism of his jaw," she sees

> that from his lower lip
> —if you could call it a lip—
> grim, wet, and weaponlike,

hung five old pieces of fish-line,
or four and a wire leader
with the swivel still attached,
with all their five big hooks
grown firmly in his mouth.
A green line, frayed at the end
where he broke it, two heavier lines,
and a fine black thread
still crimped from the strain and snap
when it broke and he got away.
                              (*CP*, 43)

Like Hemingway's old Santiago—who, after he hooks his great marlin, yet pities him in his wounded, massive dignity and pain—this poet is deeply moved by the pathos that belongs to this scarred survivor of our predatoriness:

I stared and stared
and victory filled up
the little rented boat,
from the pool of bilge
where oil had spread a rainbow
around the rusted engine
to the bailer rusted orange,
the sun-cracked thwarts,
the oarlocks on their strings,
the gunnels—until everything
was rainbow, rainbow, rainbow!
And I let the fish go.
                              (*CP*, 43–44)

And the victory that fills up the little rented boat? To whom does it belong? It is a question by no means simple. It belongs in part, of course, to the fish, which in the end manages to escape "the terrible oxygen" and to return to his watery home. But the greater victory surely belongs to the poet herself, who, despite her first satisfaction in winning her prey, yet succeeds in quelling the sportswoman's aggressiveness to the point of being able to respond to "that which is within the thing, that which is active through form and figure . . . —the *Natur-geist*." And thus, the fish being allowed "its moment of self-exposition,"[23] everything becomes "rainbow, rainbow, rainbow!"

Bishop's remarkable powers of sympathy are not, however, reserved merely for fish and snails, for birds and weeds, for rocks and mountains, for the insensible or subhuman things of earth: they also extend far into the realm of "the interhuman," and she presents many poignantly drawn and memorable personages. Her readers will tend perhaps most especially to recall the Brazilian portraits in *Question of Travel* which focus not on people of importance but on the humble and the lowly, on those who perch ever so lightly on some narrow and incommodious ledge of the world. One thinks, for example, of "Squatter's Children," with its picture of "a specklike girl and boy" playing "on the unbreathing sides of hills / . . . near a specklike house" and of how, as clouds pile up and a great storm gathers, "their laughter spreads / effulgence in the thunderheads." And there is "Manuelzinho," with its account of a young man—"half squatter, half tenant (no rent)"—who is supposed to supply a friend of the poet with vegetables, but who, as the friend says, is "the world's worst gardener since Cain":

> The strangest things happen, to you.
> Your cow eats a "poison grass"
> and drops dead on the spot.
> Nobody else's does.
> And then your father dies. . . .
> I give you money for the funeral
> and you go and hire a *bus*
> for the delighted mourners,
> so I have to hand over some more
> and then have to hear you tell me
> you pray for me every night!
> (CP, 97)

Manuelzinho is shiftless and improvident and unreliable, but, with his "wistful face," this "helpless, foolish man" is irresistible: so Bishop's friend says:

> I love you all I can,
> I think.

Affectionate sarcasm and lenity give way to a tone of unqualified solicitude and pity in the moving ballad "The Burglar of Babylon." The setting of its narrative is "the fair green hills of Rio," which are fearfully stained by the hordes of the displaced and the impoverished who build their little shacks there "out of nothing at all" and who on these uplands that rise above the city cling and spread "like lichen." The hills all bear names:

> There's one hill called the Chicken,
> And one called Catacomb;

There's the hill of Kerosene,
And the hill of the Skeleton,
The hill of Astonishment,
And the hill of Babylon
(*CP*, 112)

And the poem is devoted to a young man of Babylon named Micuçú, "a burglar and killer, / An enemy of society," who "had escaped three times / From the worst penitentiary." In his last escape he wounded three policemen: so the soldiers are after him. "Ninety years they gave me," he says. " 'Who wants to live that long? / I'll settle for ninety hours, / On the hill of Babylon.' " Looking through binoculars, the rich people in their apartments watch the whole drama of the search, as the soldiers, nervous with their tommy guns, swarm all over the area. Meanwhile, Micuçú hides in the grasses and stares down at "the long white beaches / And people going to swim, / With towels and beach umbrellas." Through a long night he remains hidden in the hills, and the next morning, as he looks down, there again

> Women with market baskets
> Stood on the corners and talked,
> Then went on their way to market,
> Gazing up as they walked.
>
> The rich with their binoculars
> Were back again, and many
> Were standing on the rooftops,
> Among TV antennae.
> (*CP*, 116)

Now he can hear the soldiers panting in their pursuit, and, while the morning is still young, as they open fire, one gets him behind the ear— and he is dead. Soon after his burial

> . . . the little soldiers
> Are on Babylon hill again;
> Their gun barrels and helmets
> Shine in a gentle rain.
>
> Micuçú is buried already.
> They're after another two,
> But they say they aren't as dangerous
> As the poor Micuçú.

On the fair green hills of Rio
There grows a fearful stain:
The poor who come to Rio
And can't go home again.

There's the hill of Kerosene,
And the hill of the Skeleton,
The hill of Astonishment,
And the hill of Babylon.
(*CP*, 117–18)

The poem, like so many of Bishop's finest statements, asks for no "explication": its plea is unmistakable, that, whatever the particular legalities may be, we give our sympathy to this poor devil who has never had any large chance at life or liberty or the pursuit of happiness and for whom the world has always been like a wilderness. And it is a similar triumph of moral imagination and fellow feeling that one encounters again and again in poems such as "Cootchie" and "Faustina, or Rock Roses" and the beautiful poem in *Geography III*, "In the Waiting Room."

The immaculate precision of her language has led many of the commentators on her work to speak of Bishop as a "poet's poet"—which is a bit of fanciness that, prompted by however much of appropriate admiration and respect, may be more than a little questionable. For the tag "poet's poet" tends to suggest an imagination sufficient unto itself, taking its own aseity for granted and, with a royal kind of disdain for the world, making poetry out of nothing more than the idea of poetry itself. But nothing could be further from the sort of métier to which Bishop kept an absolute commitment, for she was a poet without myth—even about the poetic vocation itself. And, as she makes us feel, when she in the act of composition crossed out a word and replaced it with another, she did so not for the sake merely of the particular mosaic of language being fashioned but because the stricken word did not adequately render this or that detail of something she had *observed*. Her primary fidelity was to the Real and to Things. Although there are numerous poems—like "The Burglar of Babylon" and "Visits to St. Elizabeths," and "In the Waiting Room"—that find their space in the realm of "the interhuman," she was most principally a poet of the subject-object relationship.

So it is something like "Cape Breton"—one of the most perfect poems of our time—that presents her characteristic manner and method. Again, the setting of the poem is Nova Scotia, and the poet is standing somewhere on the Cape one quiet Sunday morning, looking out on "the high 'bird islands,' Ciboux and Hertford":

> the razorbill auks and the silly-looking puffins all stand
> with their backs to the mainland
> in solemn, uneven lines along the cliff's brown grass-frayed edge,
> while the few sheep pastured there go "Baaa, baaa."
> (Sometimes, frightened by aeroplanes, they stampede
> and fall over into the sea or onto the rocks.)
> The silken water is weaving and weaving,
> disappearing under the mist equally in all directions,
> . . . .
> and somewhere the mist incorporates the pulse,
> rapid but unurgent, of a motorboat.
> (CP, 67)

And not only is the sea overhung by mist, but so, too, are "the valleys and gorges of the mainland," a mist that seems like "the ghosts of glaciers" or like "rotting snow-ice sucked away / almost to spirit." The entire scene is enveloped by an eerie kind of chill—and everywhere there is silence, a silence so absolute it can be *heard*. A wild, abandoned road "clambers along the brink of the coast," but the yellow bulldozers scattered along its track are "without their drivers, because today is Sunday." And the little white churches in the region appear to "have been dropped into the matted hills / like lost quartz arrowheads." The poem says:

> Whatever the landscape had of meaning appears to have been
>   abandoned,
> unless the road is holding it back, in the interior,
> where we cannot see,
> where deep lakes are reputed to be,
> and disused trails and mountains of rock
> and miles of burnt forests standing in gray scratches
> like the admirable scriptures made on stones by stones—
> and these regions now have little to say for themselves
> except in thousands of light song-sparrow songs floating upward
> freely, dispassionately, through the mist, and meshing
> in brown-wet, fine, torn fish-nets.
> (CP, 67–68)

For the merest moment this silent, empty world appears perhaps at the point of coming to life. A small bus, filled with passengers, comes along, past "the closed roadside stand, [past] the closed schoolhouse," and stops to discharge "a man carrying a baby." But, after getting off, he

climbs over a stile, and goes down through a small steep meadow,
which establishes its poverty in a snowfall of daisies,
to his invisible house beside the water.

(*CP*, 68)

The human presence, when at last it appears, leads us to expect that
surely now *something* will be disclosed, that whatever this landscape had
of meaning will now be shown not *altogether* to have been abandoned.
But there is no epiphany: the man, too, disappears into the interior,
"where we cannot see." Nevertheless,

The birds keep on singing, a calf bawls, the bus starts.
The thin mist follows
the white mutations of its dream;
an ancient chill is rippling the dark brooks.

(*CP*, 68)

One interpreter offers what may well be the definitive comment on the
poem when he suggests that "'Cape Breton' is a glimpse into a heart of
darkness," that "Bishop's vision is to Conrad's as Marlow's is to
Kurtz's."[24] For this indeed is what the poem is peering into, the dark,
uncommunicative, and unknowable noumenality at the heart of the
world. The speaker is *looking* at this landscape as intently and as pierc-
ingly as she can—but it does not look back at her: whatever there is of
meaning remains "in the interior, / where we cannot see," and on this
quiet Sunday morning "the high 'bird islands'" and the weaving waters
and "the valleys and gorges of the mainland" and the road clambering
along the edge of the coast and the man carrying a baby "have little to
say for themselves." All is enveloped in mist, and the scene is overborne
by "an ancient chill."

Yet, recalcitrant though the world may be, Bishop could find nothing
else to depend upon except what she could *see* and *observe;* and thus she
seems never to have been inclined to reach what was at one point Stevens' exasperated conclusion that "reality is a cliché"[25] which the poet
had better try to do without: on the contrary, she represents a constantly
unquerulous submissiveness to the hegemony of *l'actuelle,* always taking
it for granted that (as Jacques Maritain once remarked in *The Dream of
Descartes*) "human intellection is living and fresh only when it is centered
upon the vigilance of sense perception."

Unlike Stevens, Bishop was not in the habit of discussing her poetics
in her poetry, but the endlessly absorbing and subtle poem "The Map"
conveys, for all its indirection, perhaps the best inkling to be found anywhere of how she viewed her special responsibility as a poet. She is look-

ing at a printed map, and she notices how the land that is "shadowed green" appears to lie in water. But then she wonders if indeed the land may not "lean down to lift the sea from under, / drawing it unperturbed around itself." May it not be the case that the land is "tugging at the sea from under?" And, as she gazes at this map, she marvels at the transforming perspective that the mapmaker's art casts upon the surfaces of the earth:

> The shadow of Newfoundland lies flat and still.
> Labrador's yellow, where the moony Eskimo
> has oiled it. We can stroke these lovely bays,
> under a glass as if they were expected to blossom,
> or as if to provide a clean cage for invisible fish.
> The names of seashore towns run out to sea,
> the names of cities cross the neighboring mountains
> —the printer here experiencing the same excitement
> as when emotion too far exceeds its cause.
> These peninsulas take the water between thumb and finger
> like women feeling for the smoothness of yard-goods.
>
> Mapped waters are more quiet than the land is,
> lending the land their waves' own conformation:
> and Norway's hare runs south in agitation,
> profiles investigate the sea, where land is.
> Are they assigned, or can the countries pick their colors?
> —What suits the character or the native waters best.
> Topography displays no favorites; North's as near as West.
> More delicate than the historians' are the map-makers' colors.
>
> (CP, 3)

Now, of course, the unspoken premise of the poem is that the cartographer's craft is a mode of art. And his images, like those of any true artist, practice a very radical kind of metamorphosis upon the things of earth: they make the peninsulas of the land appear "flat and still": they render the waters of the sea as calm and quiet, when actually they are roiled with agitation: they make it appear that Norway is a sort of hare running south: and—in, as it were, a spirit of frolic—they organize themselves into highly intricate patterns of figuration that belong to the order of the metonymic. Yet the cartographer's "profiles investigate" topographical actualities: he cannot allow "the countries [to] pick their colors": he is not free to rearrange at will the contours of geography: he must be faithful to the given literalities of nature. And thus he supervises a very "delicate" art indeed—an art, as Bishop may be taken to be imply-ing, not unlike that of poetry itself.

So it is *amor mundi*, never *contemptus mundi*, that one feels to be in-scribed over her entire work. Although on occasion (as she suggests in "Wading at Wellfleet") she considers the sea to be "all a case of knives," she loves it nevertheless. The "huntress of the winter air" (in "The Colder the Air") consults "not time nor circumstance," but she admires "her per-fect aim." And, as she tells us ("The Imaginary Iceberg"), she would "rather have the iceberg than the ship." Like the black boy Balthazár in "Twelfth Morning; or What You Will," she thinks "that the world's a pearl," and thus her poems want (as she says of the crude artifact being described in "The Monument") "to cherish something" and want to say "commemorate." She intends to receive the world sacramentally— though, being without myth or religious commitment, hers is a sacra-mentalism without warrant or justification. Nevertheless, she wants, as one imagines, to find a way of making something like Dylan Thomas's declaration, that her poems, with whatever of uncertainty and agnosti-cism they may contain, "are written for the love of Man and in praise of God, and I'd be a damn' fool if they weren't."[26] Hers, as Robert Mazzocco says, is "the middle range, the middle style." "History as nightmare, man as a cipher"—these "*de rigueur* subjects . . . [she] subverts."[27] And thus she has never claimed the wide popularity that is more easily won by those writers who offer some kind of existentialist *frisson*. But her deep influence is easily traced in the work of poets such as Randall Jarrell and Robert Lowell and Richard Wilbur and James Merrill. And in "The Map," "The Monument," "Roosters," "The Fish," "Cape Breton," "The Arma-dillo," and scores of other poems she appears as one of the most remark-able poets to have graced the American scene, no doubt not a major fig-ure, not one in the range of a Frost or a Stevens or a Carlos Williams but one whose legacy will long be a bench mark against which false senti-ment and specious eloquence will be severely judged.

CHAPTER SIX

Robert Penn Warren's Career in Poetry: Taking Counsel of the Heart Alone

> We must try / To love so well the world that we
> may believe, in the end, in God.
> —WARREN, "Masts at Dawn," in *Incarnations*

> I am a man of religious temperament in the modern
> world who hasn't got any religion.
> —WARREN, "Interview," in Peter Stitt, *The World's Hieroglyphic Beauty*

> So he took counsel of the heart alone. . . .
> —WARREN, "The Last Metaphor," in *Thirty-Six Poems*

J ohn L. Stewart in his book of 1965, *The Burden of Time*, which is per-haps the most penetrating of the various studies of the Nashville Fugitives, devotes two of his finest chapters to Warren, and the first of these is "Robert Penn Warren: The Long Apprenticeship"—a superbly apt formulation, when we think of Warren's career not as a novelist but as a poet. For in this range of his work his apprenticeship was indeed of long duration, spanning thirty years, from the early 1920s to the mid-point of the century. It would not, of course, have occurred to anyone in, say, the year 1950 to think of him as an apprentice-poet, for one would then, looking back to his book of 1944, *Selected Poems: 1923–1943*, have thought of poems in that volume such as "The Ballad of Billie Potts," "Original Sin: A Short Story," "Revelation," "Mexico Is a Foreign Coun-try: Five Studies in Naturalism," "Bearded Oaks," "Love's Parable," "The Return: An Elegy," "Kentucky Mountain Farm," and "Pondy Woods"—one would have thought of poems such as these as having already be-come established modern classics.

But, then, as Warren himself said (in his interview with Marshall Walker [in Walker's *Robert Penn Warren: A Vision Earned*]), "something happened about '45. I got so I could not finish a short poem. I wrote, started many over that period of years. [But] I never finished one—I lost the capacity for finishing a short poem. I'd write five lines, ten lines, twenty lines—it would die on me. I lost my sense of it."[1] And, given the subsequent course that his poetry took, one suspects that the seat of the trouble lay in the fact that, gradually, his basic sensibility had undergone a profound kind of change that made it difficult for him to continue to work within the sorts of poetic conventions that for twenty years had controlled his verse.

Early on in his undergraduate years at Vanderbilt he had been introduced (chiefly by his teacher John Crowe Ransom and his slightly older contemporary Allen Tate) to the major poets of the English seventeenth century and to the principal avatars of twentieth-century modernism (especially to Pound and Eliot). And the influence of Donne and Marvell as well as of Eliot and Ransom and Tate remained a decisive force in the shaping of his rhetoric as a poet, long after he had found his own voice and manner, so that his most characteristic poems of the 1930s and early 40s are generally marked by the highly cerebral intensity, the complex syntax, the ingenious conceits, and the intricate cacophonies belonging to the traditions that offered him his primary bench marks. But during these years he was gradually taking full possession of his gifts for story-telling, and no doubt as a result of the labors exacted by his brilliant novel of 1939, *Night Rider*, and by the equally impressive novel that followed it four years later, *At Heaven's Gate*, he found himself increasingly drawn to narrative forms. In short, the purely contemplative lyric—which indeed he had sometimes found it necessary to complicate with anecdotal material, as in poems such as "Eidolon" and "Revelation" and "Pondy Woods"—began no longer to be an adequate vehicle for his central interests: it tended to "die on him," and thus, after the appearance in 1944 of the *Selected Poems*, though his work as a fictionist was steady and proving ever more fruitful (*All the King's Men*, 1946; *The Circus in the Attic and Other Stories*, 1948; *World Enough and Time*, 1950), his poetic career appeared over a long period to have suffered some strangely unaccountable stoppage, albeit his never having ceased to consider his first calling to be toward poetry rather than prose fiction.

Fortunately, however, while holding in 1944 an appointment as Poetry Consultant at the Library of Congress, Warren began to brood over one of the most ghastly stories recorded by American history: the incident of a Negro slave's dismemberment by axe—on the night of 15 December 1811 in Livingston County in western Kentucky, near Smithland—at the hands of Lilburne and Isham Lewis, who were the sons of Thomas Jefferson's sister, Lucy Jefferson Lewis. After their mother's death, their father,

Colonel Charles Lewis, had left the family estate ("Rocky Hill") under their management and returned to his native Virginia. So, holding absolute sovereignty over Rocky Hill, on that fateful night they chose to punish the seventeen-year-old slave, a boy named George, for having broken a favorite pitcher of their mother's, and did so by hacking him to pieces in the meathouse in the presence of the other slaves, the fatal blow being struck by Lilburne, who swung the axe so deeply into George's neck that he was well-nigh decapitated. Then the two brothers forced one of the other slaves to dismember the body and to throw the pieces into a blazing stove.

Warren had heard a garbled version of the story in his Kentucky boyhood from a great-aunt, but not until he began his yearlong residence on the staff of the Library of Congress had he ever had an opportunity to track down its actual sources. It having never, though, been dislodged from his mind or lost its mesmerizing power, after a time in that year he was poking into all such contemporaneous accounts of the episode as he could locate in old newspapers and journals, and, more and more, his fascination with it deepened, until finally in the summer of 1946 he went down to Smithland to visit the site on which the Lewis house had stood and to squint at all the records that could be turned up in the county courthouse bearing on the indictment of the Lewises for murder and on the subsequent trial.

He later said in a brief memorandum prepared for the *New York Times Book Review* (23 August 1953) that "at first, I wasn't sure what caught my fancy. Then I knew: it was that this was Jefferson's family. The philosopher of our liberties and the architect of our country and the prophet of human perfectibility had this in the family blood." But he did not know immediately what he wanted to make of it. For a time he thought of basing a novel on the episode, till at last he had to say to himself that "the historical material doesn't have the structure of a novel, it doesn't fulfill itself circumstantially, it spreads out and doesn't pull in at the end." And, moreover, he believed that a novel "couldn't bear the burden of comment probably necessary to interpret the material." Then he tried to design a play in which Jefferson as a kind of choric figure would serve as a commentator brooding over the affair. "But again," as he said in the piece he prepared for the *New York Times Book Review*, "the plot problem appeared." Finally, however, a dramatic poem seemed the right form, a poem that would involve "a dialogue of all the characters, including Jefferson"—including, furthermore (in order that the thing might be given "a wider perspective than even Jefferson, or the ghost of Jefferson, would provide"), still "another character—the 'poet'—R.P.W., as a kind of interlocutor." And what developed was the magnificently in-strumentated colloquy published in 1953—*Brother to Dragons: A Tale in Verse and Voices.*

Today, as we look back on this richly imagined work, at a remove of forty years, it appears to be undoubtedly the great watershed of his ca-reer as a poet. For we can now see that it was in *Brother to Dragons* that Warren, after years of being no longer able to submit to his special pur-pose the stiff, tight formalities and decorums of the *poème bien fait,* at last won through to a new freedom and expansiveness of expression, which would in turn make possible the triumphs of his late phase, of *Promises* (1957) and *Incarnations* (1968) and *Audubon* (1969), of *Or Else* (1974) and *Now and Then* (1978), of *Being Here* (1980) and *Rumor Verified* (1981) and *Chief Joseph of the Nez Perce* (1983).

"The Ballad of Billie Potts" or "Pondy Woods" presents a typical in-stance of what had been his tendency in much of his earlier poetry to mingle high and low styles, to complicate some Parnassian pattern of elegance with the vulgar earthiness of "unpoetic" colloquialisms. But whereas in this phase of his work the two styles, the high and the low, had merely been yoked together, in *Brother to Dragons* he managed gen-uinely to roughen and simplify the rhetorical surfaces of his language, and to do so in a way that henceforth enabled his loosened lines to reckon bravely with "Reality and its insufferable intransigence." True, the new kind of language that Warren for the first time made his own in this book is one that has fed and fattened on the old traditions of pulpit and polit-ical and courthouse rhetoric coming out of the American South, and it is, therefore, a language that sometimes explodes into bombast. But over his last thirty years, as he moved from his fifties into his sixties and on be-yond the biblical three-score-and-ten into his ninth decade, his command of this language steadily (though with some bit of occasional intermit-tence) grew more and more masterful, and we can presently see the re-markable capacity of its graver modes to bear an immense freight of feel-ing and of its gayer, more comic modes to turn marvelous somersaults of vivacity. In *Brother to Dragons,* however, his control was not so secure, and the language sometimes gets out of hand and moves toward a screeching sort of stridency and hysteria. In one passage, for example, "R.P.W." is recounting his automobile trip down to Kentucky to visit the bluff overlooking the confluence of the Cumberland and Ohio Rivers whereon the Lewis house had stood, and he wants to speak of having stopped at a certain point on U.S.62 to urinate by the side of the high-way—but the tone and pitch are out of all proportion to this perform-ance:

> . . . when the road
> Was empty, [I] stopped just once to void the bladder,
> And in that stunning silence after the tire's song
> The July-fly screamed like a nerve gone wild,
> Screamed like a dentist's drill, and then a million
> Took up the job, and in that simultaneous outrage
> The sunlight screamed, while urine spattered the parched soil.[2]

Yet, as Leslie Fiedler reminded us in his review of the book in 1954 (*Partisan Review* 21, no. 2), Warren's subject is Nightmare, and thus, as Fiedler shrewdly argued, "bombast and melodrama," instead of being squeamishly regarded as hopelessly dishonorable, deserve in this instance to be thought of as having a proper place in the total design of the poem, as indeed necessary in some measure if the poem is to do justice to the enormities at which it wants to make us stare.

Now the notable fact in the historical record which undoubtedly gave Warren his point of leverage on his material is that, though nearly fifteen years intervened between the Lewises' dreadful deed and Jefferson's death in 1826, he never on any occasion made reference to the monstrosities of his nephews.[3] Which indicates how disinclined was this Enlightenment *philosophe* to consider himself a "brother to dragons" (Job 30:29), for he had seen, or thought he had seen, "brightness blaze" on all men, their "natural innocence" dancing "like sunlight over the delighted landscape." Conceiving himself and his gallant comrades among the Founding Fathers of America to be unstained by the improbities of the Old World, he had been certain (like Job) that he and his kind walked "upright and perfect . . . and eschewed evil," that there was "a fair time" ahead when all human lusts and deliriums would be shaken off. This, as he says, "was . . . the old notion that propped my heart and thewed up / My human arm." But, of course, his great "rational hope" for the unborn tomorrows had simply blinded him to the moral chaos that indwells the human soul, and, when confronted by the outrage of Rocky Hill, his last state is worse than the first, the confusion of cynicism and despair having succeeded the confusion of optimism and illusion. He who had been upborne by his confidence in the perfectibility of man now speaks (or the "ghost" of Jefferson now speaks), as the poem gets under way, of "the immitigable ferocity of [the] self," of the "unsummerable arctic of the human alienation," and he declares: "I . . . reject, cast out, repudiate, / And squeeze from my blood the blood of Lilburne."

It is, however, the intention of the poem that Jefferson should take the hand of his nephew Lilburne, that he should "take it, and the blood slick on it," and come to understand that he is indeed a brother to dragons. And, as Warren realized early on once he had tackled the project, Jefferson had to be the protagonist of the entire action, for it was he, the great champion of "the children of light" against "the children of darkness" (to use Reinhold Niebuhr's formulations), who needed to be educated by the tragedy. So, in the colloquy that the poem arranges in *"no place"* and at *"any time,"* he is gradually led to fundamentally new perceptions.

At first the dreadful news from Rocky Hill so unnerves him that his former perfectibilism gives way to a kind of Manichaean view of Lilburne's criminality as but type and example of the essential defectiveness of the human being as such—and, as he says to his sister Lucy, "There's no forgiveness of our being human. / It is the inexpugnable error." He concludes that evil belongs to the intrinsic nature of humankind:

. . . Lilburne is an absolute of our essential
Condition, and as such, would ingurgitate
All, and all you'd give, all hope, all heart,
Would only be disbursed down that rat hole of the ultimate horror.

But his fellow colloquists will not allow Jefferson simply to flounder in his newly embraced bitterness and cynicism, for certain of them understand that things are less simple than he would now make them out to be. One of his interlocutors, R.P.W., reminds him, for example, that we are not mere automatons of natural necessity, that the "transition" leading from "the unaccomplished" to "the accomplished," from "the nonexisting" to "the existing," is the freely made choice and that there is, therefore, "no way out of the responsibility / Of trying to achieve responsibility."

Again, the ghost of Meriwether Lewis is brought into the dialogue. He, Jefferson's distant cousin and protégé, had been sent westward by the president as commander of an expedition to explore the Missouri River and the Louisiana Territory, and afterward he was named governor of the Territory. But, there, with the hostilities that had grown up amongst the French and Spanish and American settlers, he found himself on every side facing anger and suspicion, much of it prompted by his connection with Jefferson. So shattering was the experience that in 1809 he took his own life, and, now, as he faces his former patron, he tells him that he was indeed "murdered" by Jefferson's lie: "I am the man you did give the bullet to. / I am the man you killed." For, as he wants to suggest, it was precisely Jefferson's lessons on the essential virtuousness and innocence of man that unfitted him, Meriwether, to cope with the moral ambiguity that belongs to the actual human condition. So, as he says, he was "sent unbuckled and unbraced" into the wilderness:

. . . I would honor more the axe in the meat-house,
As more honest at least, than your special lie
Concocted, though out of nobleness—oh, yes,
It was noble, but was concocted for your comfort
To prove yourself nobler in man's nobleness.
Yes, in man's nobleness, you'd be the noble Jefferson.
And if that is not vanity—

The severity of Meriwether Lewis's charge, that his death was brought to pass by a "vanity of virtue" and was Jefferson's own "handiwork," does elicit from his old patron the grudging admission that he may indeed have been "unprepared for the nature of the world, / And unprepared . . . for my own nature." Yet he persists in his cold and contemptuous rejection of the "butcher" of Rocky Hill: ". . . I'll accept no part of that responsibility." Which prompts his sister in turn to speak to him more sternly than she has previously done.

Earlier in the poem Lucy Jefferson Lewis had suggested that it is "the human curse . . . simply to love and sometimes to love well, / But never well enough." And she seems constantly to think of how deeply failure is inwrought into the texture of human life. She tells her brother that, much as she loved her son Lilburne, she "Would have seen him die in the direst pain, rather / Than know he had come to do the thing he did," and she acknowledges her fear that her very love must itself have been "infected with failure." As she thinks of how fond she was of her spoons and her cups, she wonders if Lilburne's deed may not in part have been a matter of his feeling required to defend "the vanities . . . [she'd] loved." And when Jefferson brusquely dismisses her "female fondness," suggesting that it is now by way merely of compounding the crime, her quick rejoinder is that, on the contrary, this is what he himself is doing—out of "fear." He impatiently replies that he has never feared any man—to which Lucy quietly answers, "Yes, one." Jefferson asks, "Who?" And she says:

His name is Jefferson.
I mean yourself. I mean the deepest fear.
Yes, when you had learned in that report from Kentucky
What evil was possible even in the familial blood,
Your fear began, the fear you had always denied, the fear
That you—even you—were capable of all.
And so in that consanguinity, still to deny
The possibilities of self,
Even in the moment when you claimed that Lilburne
Had robbed you of your hope of human good,

In vanity and virtue and your fear,
You struck. You struck Lilburne down—and yet strike
Poor Lilburne down, and over and over again, the axe
Falls. The axe falls, and you cast him forth in the fire,
And the fire flares red on your face where the sweat is.
And as George was to Lilburne, so Lilburne is to you,
And as innocence was all Lilburne wanted, it is all
You yourself want, or have wanted. But, Brother,
If you would assume the burden of innocence . . .
. . . . you must take
His hand. . . .

And then at last Lucy truly catches the conscience of her brother, and she says:

> We had hoped to escape complicity,
> You and I, dear Brother. But we have seen the unfolding
> Of Time and complicity, and I, even in my love,
> And in the milk of my breast, was in guilty involvement,
> And my son died. And you, even in your aspiration,
> Could prime the charge for our poor Meriwether.
> And this is why in our best gifts we could give
> Only the worst. It is because my love and your aspiration
> Could not help but carry some burden of ourselves,
> And to be innocent of that burden, at last,
> You must take his hand, and recognize, at last,
> That his face is only a mirror of your possibilities,
> And recognize that you
> Have deeper need of him than he of you,
> For whatever hope we have is not by repudiation,
> And whatever health we have is not by denial,
> But in confronting the terror of our condition.
> All else is a lie.

Lucy, whose very name means "light," does indeed bring clarity and discernment to Jefferson, so that in the end she succeeds in cross-questioning him into a new humility that enables him wearily to make a crucial confession:

> Yes, Meriwether said I lied,
> But long since I had lost the strength for that lie,
> But cannot yet find the strength to endure without it,
> But can affirm my need only in the curse and rejection
> Of him who had robbed me of the comfort of the lie.

His sister does not, however, want him to conclude that his old dream, that his old hope, was merely "a reflex of . . . [his] vanity." "If," she says, "there was vanity, fear, and deceit, in its condition, / What of that? For we are human, and must work / In the shade of our human condition." Which prompts Jefferson's last great declaration:

> Now I should hope to find the courage to say
> That the dream of the future is not
> Better than the fact of the past, no matter how terrible.
> For without the fact of the past we cannot dream the future.
> I think I begin to see the forging of the future.
> It will be forged beneath the hammer of truth
> On the anvil of our anguish. . . .
> We must strike the steel of wrath on the stone of guilt,
> And hope to provoke, thus, in the midst of our coiling darkness
> The incandescence of the heart's great flare.

So Jefferson does at last repossess the unity of his own life, for he discovers that there is no separating himself from the minotaur—"our brother, our darling brother"—at the last turn of his life's labyrinth. Moreover, in discovering that he is indeed a brother to dragons, he also repossesses a sense of the unity of humankind. And it is this "central illumination" to which he is brought that forms a major theme of the poem's great coda, which, in being devoted to R.P.W.'s concluding reflections on the entire drama, indicates how deeply this "red-headed [fellow], freckled, lean, a little stooped," has himself been rehabilitated by the action of the whole colloquy. Here, the poet is brooding on "the human bond" and "the necessity of virtue," and the leitmotif of his meditation is most concisely set forth in this passage:

> Fulfillment is only in the degree of recognition
> Of the common lot of our kind. And that is the death of vanity,
> And that is the beginning of virtue.

> The recognition of complicity is the beginning of innocence.

·

In the five or six years that Warren was working on this poem, it absorbed "all the juice." Then, as he said (in his interview with Marshall Walker), "some little time after I had finished *Brother to Dragons* I felt a whole new sense of poetry. I felt freer than I had felt before. The narrative sense began to enter the short-poem—as a germ, that is. So in the summer of '54, when [my wife] Eleanor and I and a then-baby daughter were living in . . . [a] ruined fortress in Italy, there was suddenly just this new sense of *release*—so the short poems began to come [again] in that year."[4] But, though *Brother to Dragons* looks toward his later poetry in the way he suggests, it also reaches toward his subsequent work in its formulation of what was to be the glowing yet sober "trophy of truth" being exhibited in so much of the poetry that followed in the wake of his book of 1953. And, in taking hold of this trophy, which is close to the center of his work over the last thirty years of his career, we would do well to have in mind a phase of the argument in his brilliant essay on Coleridge's *The Ancient Mariner* ("A Poem of Pure Imagination: An Experiment in Reading," *Selected Essays*).

The essay is firmly poised against the notion (as articulated by such a scholar as John Livingston Lowes) that "the poem is nothing more than a pleasant but meaningless dream," even as it is also poised against the judgment expressed by that estimable Presbyterian lady, Mrs. Barbauld, who, as Coleridge reports in *Table Talk*, "once told me that she admired *The Ancient Mariner* very much, but that there were two faults in it—it was improbable, and had no moral." Warren wants to resist just as strenuously as he can the notion that the poem merely presents "an agreeable but scarcely meaningful effusion" that makes no significant contact with reality. But the question as to what kind of statement he finds the poem lining itself up behind is not easily answered, for his argument, as it runs through nearly seventy-five pages, is too complex and too subtle to allow any swift rehearsal even of this or that part of it. Suffice it to say that he wants to insist that the poem is a highly integrated structure that concerns primarily that *One Life* within which all the creatures of earth are caught up—"the one Life" (as Coleridge speaks of it in "The Eolian Harp")

> . . . within us and abroad
> Which meets all motion and becomes its soul,
> A light in sound, a sound-like power in light,
> Rhythm in all thought, and joyance every where.

It is this One Life that the Mariner sins against in the act of motiveless malignity he commits when he takes up his crossbow and fatally wounds the kindly and beneficent albatross that has accompanied his ship through those treacherous waters in the vicinity of the South Pole. And his burden of remorse and shame—so heavy that he but vainly tries to pray—does not lift until the day comes when, as he looks down at water snakes frolicking in the ship's shadow, he begins to bless them:

> Beyond the shadow of the ship,
> I watched the water-snakes:

They moved in tracks of shining white,
And when they reared, the elfish light
Fell off in hoary flakes.

Within the shadow of the ship
I watched their rich attire:
Blue, glossy green, and velvet black,
They coiled and swam; and every track
Was a flash of golden fire.

O happy living things! no tongue
Their beauty might declare:
A spring of love gushed from my heart,
And I blessed them unaware:
Sure my kind saint took pity on me,
And I blessed them unaware.

The self-same moment I could pray;
And from my neck so free
The Albatross fell off, and sank
Like lead into the sea.

At an earlier time the Mariner, when he looked down upon the sea, had descried only "a thousand slimy things," but, once he consents to behold the world by the light (as Warren phrases it) of "the imagination in its value-creating capacity," the water snakes cease to be merely so many slimy things of the deep, for, noticing now "their rich attire," he sees them with what Coleridge in volume 1 of *The Notebooks* (entry No. 921) calls "the deep power of Joy." And the special kind of receptivity which Coleridge calls "Joy" is, as he says in the Ode on "Dejection,"

> . . . the spirit and the power,
> Which wedding Nature to us gives in dower
> A new Earth and new Heaven,
> Undreamt of by the sensual and the proud.

In short, this skinny little seaman begins to be aware of what Warren nominates as "the chain of love which binds human society and the universe." And, in the moment in which the Mariner recognizes that he and these water snakes are both caught up within *One Life* and cries out, "O happy living things," in that moment, as he blesses them, he finds himself also blessed as well. So, as Warren argues, the poem is not only about the One Life that unites all the world's creatures but also about the imagination.

What gives this essay its special interest is not only the clarity with which it illuminates a persisting theme of Coleridge's thought but also the evocativeness with which, perhaps by a happy accident, it strikes one of the great ground notes of Warren's own testimony as a poet. In the particular case presented, for example, by *Brother to Dragons*, what makes its protagonist, Thomas Jefferson, initially so problematic a figure is precisely his stubborn reluctance to acknowledge any consanguinity with Lilburne, his unwillingness to take his nephew's hand, with "the blood slick on it." And he does not improve or become a better man until he has "eaten the bitter bread" of self-confrontation: nothing is redeemed until others cross-question him out of his old vanity into a recognition that he himself has "devised evil in the heart" and is therefore not outside the human condition, the One Life that embraces all, dragons as well as those who would be angels. Nor does Warren ever quite cease to urge upon us the essential unity of existence. Personal life is a unity that we sunder only at our peril, as when we try to separate ourselves from our respective pasts. And so too is it also with the collective life. St. Luke's Gospel, in chapter 10, speaks of a dialogue between Christ and "a certain lawyer," who says: "Master, what shall I do to inherit eternal life?" But when the catechumen is reminded of "what is written in the law"— "Thou shalt love the Lord thy God with all thy heart, and with all thy soul, and with all thy strength, and with all thy mind; and thy neighbor as thyself"—he asks, very much in the manner of a lawyer, "But who is my neighbor?" Which would no doubt prompt from Warren the charge that this finicky little scribe, in spinning out his rigmarole, proves his bad faith, since, being as we are irrefragably members one of another, there is none who may not be one's neighbor. Our collective life, in other words, is *One Life*, the life (to use Charles Williams' term) of *Coinherence*— which unites us with *all* our contemporaries, as well as with all the generations that have gone before. Nor does Warren want merely to insist upon the unity of humankind, for he is also reminding us over and again of our weddedness to Nature and to all its diverse things and creatures. One Life: this is, indeed, his great theme.

This is not, of course, to say that Warren's poetry is hagridden by a single idea: nothing could be further from the truth: his work explores and tests many different interests and emotions and values, and it does by no means present any sort of uncompounded, monolithic structure of thought. But, like all major poets—and he is surely one of the chief American examples of our period—he has his center of gravity. Or, to change the figure, we may say that, keeping an allegiance to (in Dr. Johnson's old phrase) his "ruling passion," in whatever direction his meditations move, they tend recurringly to come back to what he took to be the bedrock reality of the human situation, that we are, *nolens volens*, committed to One Life.

.

In 1952, after a divorce that followed some years of unhappiness in his relation with his first wife, Warren was married to the writer Eleanor Clark, and two years later they spent their summer with their little daughter, Rosanna, on the Italian coast, about ninety or a hundred miles north of Rome, at Pòrto Ercole, the site of a ruined sixteenth-century fortress built in the period when King Philip II of Spain held sovereignty in the area. The months there proved an enormously fruitful time for Warren, and many of the poems constituting his book of 1957, *Promises*, were written or begun in this Mediterranean setting. The book presents a powerfully moving body of work characterized by a suppleness of language which, as it advances beyond the taut strictness of meter and rhyme marking the early poetry, appears wonderfully appropriate to the kind of hospitality to large ranges of human experience that distinguishes these poems. The cycle with which the volume begins—"To a Little Girl, One Year Old, in a Ruined Fortress"—comprises five poems that are dedicated to the poet's daughter, Rosanna, and they are filled with the adoring delight that the father takes in the imperious vivaciousness of this golden little beauty. Yet a certain pathos enters the poems, for their setting is the Mediterranean coast at Pòrto Ercole in the summer of 1954—which means that the background against which this child runs and laughs and dances is an old, old world scarred by "the malfeasance of nature" and "the filth of fate." Adjacent to their residence, for example, is a hovel occupied by a *gobbo* (hunchback) and his family, the youngest child being

> . . . defective because the mother,
> Seven brats already in that purlieu of dirt,
> Took a pill, or did something to herself she thought would not hurt.
> But it did, and no good, for there came this monstrous other.

But the defective child's twelve-year-old sister, who watches over her throughout each day and who is "beautiful like a saint," attends to her "with pure love, calm eyes" ("The Child Next Door"). And it is with a similar gladness that little Rosanna atop a certain bluff late in the summer, in a "thinned out" season ("The Flower"), accepts a tattered, "sea-salt browned" blossom with the same satisfaction with which earlier in the summer she had grown accustomed to plucking on that bluff a lovely blue blossom for her yellow hair: it is "as though human need / Were not for perfection." But flaws there are in nature and in the human heart—which prompts the poet, as he looks at his darling, to pronounce a kind of benediction ("Colder Fire"):

> You will live your own life, and contrive
> The language of your own heart, but let that conversation,
> In the last analysis, be always of whatever truth you would live.

> For fire flames but in the heart of a colder fire.
> All voice is but echo caught from a soundless voice.
> Height is not deprivation of valley, nor defect of desire,
> But defines, for the fortunate, that joy in which all joys should
>   rejoice.

By far the greater part of *Promises* is devoted to a long cycle of poems dedicated to the poet's son, Gabriel. At a certain point in *Brother to Dragons* "R.P.W." recalls one Sunday afternoon many years earlier when, "after the chicken dinner and ice cream," he watched his own father "with grave patience" attempting to teach some bit of Latin to his little granddaughter, the child of R.P.W.'s brother—

> . . . and she would say
> The crazy words, and laugh, they were so crazy.
> There's worse, I guess, than in the end to offer
> Your last bright keepsake, some fragment of the vase
> That held your hopes, to offer it to a child.

And the poems dedicated to Gabriel may be regarded as such an offering of this sort as Warren himself wanted to tender to his own little son more than thirty years ago. Unlike the poems dedicated to Rosanna, most of these poems have not a European but an American setting, many of them indeed harking back to Warren's Kentucky boyhood. In poem after poem, as his memory captures some person or event or scene from that time long past, he is struggling to retrieve the significance of what is being recalled, for he wants to hand it on as a "bright keepsake" to his son, since, given the interdependence that binds the present to the past, the One Life that embraces us all, Gabriel will need to know the roots from which his father is sprung.

For Gabriel's eventual enlightenment he records, for example, in more than one poem moments out of his own boyhood in which he lost something of his early innocence. In "Court-martial" he remembers a summer day at the farm of his grandfather, when, as the old man—shrunken and gray in his "pale-washed" blue jeans—sat quietly smoking his pipe in the shade, he chanced to ask the meaning of the word *guerrilla*. "'Bushwhackers, we called 'em,'" replied his grandfather, plunged immediately into recollections of his experience as a Confederate cavalry officer in the Civil War and of how the Yankees were "'just out to plunder and ride / And hell-rake the pore countryside.'" The old man went on to describe so vividly the kind of summary justice meted out to them that the boy was able to see in his mind's eye his grandfather as a young man searching for the right tree and reaching for the rope, as he was able also to see the victim's outraged face, with the tongue out and "the spittle not yet dry," as the last cry was uttered. And, in this moment that brought a kind of end to his childhood, the speaker remembers how, as the air appeared to darken, he realized that "The world is real. It is there."

Or, again, in "School Lesson Based on Word of Tragic Death of Entire Gillum Family" the poet remembers the Gillum children—Dollie-May, Susie-May, Forrest, Sam, and Brother—who, with their "milky blue eyes" and adenoids big enough to make you choke, each day tramped six miles into school from the back country. And he remembers the day on which, after they failed to appear, word came that their dim father, Old Slat Gillum—who used to stop people in town to say: "'Say, mister, / I'll name you what's true fer folks, ever-one'"—had stabbed to death with an ice pick the entire family. So the Gillum children's schoolmates were left to study "the arithmetic of losses, / To be prepared when the next one, / By fire, flood, foe, cancer, thrombosis, / Or Time's slow malediction, came to be undone." As we are told, however, *"There was another lesson, but we were too young to take up that one."*

There are many other strong narrative poems in this mode among the keepsakes Warren was preserving for Gabriel, poems that, in taking him back to the people of an earlier generation, will (as the poet hopes) at some late hour in the future help him to bend an ear to what those who have gone before "are trying to say" and "to forgive them their defects, even their greatness"—poems that will assist him in realizing that (as it is put in "Ballad of a Sweet Dream of Peace") "we're all one Flesh."

Still other poems in the collection for Gabriel want to speak not so much of particular people in the past as of certain scenes that form that "landscape lost in the heart's homely deep." One thinks, for example, of the beautiful poem "Gold Glade," which takes us into some lovely cleared space in "the woods of boyhood" into which the poet stumbled one autumn evening. And there "in gold light" stood a stately old hickory tree, "absolute and bold," "the great shagbark" itself giving forth a golden light. One can virtually *hear* the silence that filled this enchanted vale:

No breathing of air, no leaf now gold-falling,
No tooth-stitch of squirrel, or any far fox bark,
No woodpecker coding, or late jay calling.
Silence: gray-shagged, the great shagbark
Gave forth gold light. There could be no dark.

But of course dark came, and I can't recall
What county it was, for the life of me.
Montgomery, Todd, Christian—I know them all.
Was it even Kentucky or Tennessee?
Perhaps just an image that keeps haunting me.

No, no! in no mansion under earth,
Nor imagination's doman of bright air,
But solid in soil that gave it its birth,
It stands, wherever it is, but somewhere.
I shall set my foot, and go there.

Or, among the poems devoted to celebration of place, one thinks of "Country Burying (1919)" as a fine example of the crisp, simple eloquence of which Warren by the mid-1950s had become a master. "A thousand times you've seen that scene: / Oak grove, bare ground, little white church there, / Bone-white in that light, and through dust-pale green / Of oak leaf, the steeple pokes up in the bright air." To such a place he remembers accompanying his mother one summer day for the funeral of a woman she had barely known but of whom she said, "'I respect her.'" After the burial, they departed down a red clay road, and he has never returned. "But," he says,

. . . should I come back, and come back where that place is,
    Oak grove, white church, in day-glare a-daze, I might enter.

For what? But enter, and find what I'd guess:
    The odor of varnish, hymnals stacked on a chair,
Light religiously dim by painted paper on window glass,
    And the insistent buzz of a fly lost in shadow, somewhere.

Of the poems devoted to a *genius loci*, surely the finest is the short sequence "Boy's Will, Joyful Labor without Pay, and Harvest Home (1918)," which marvelously evokes what a threshing day was like on a Kentucky farm. The boy is ever so eager to play his part in the farm's great annual collective effort, and, as he bolts his oatmeal at breakfast, "the dogs are barking, mad as hatters": it seems that "the world won't wait." His hand simply "aches for the pitchfork heft," and, once he gets into the fields, his exertions are so strenuous that one of the hired men is led to say, "'Boy, save yore strength, 'fore you got none left.'" All through this day of hard, constant labor "light, gold, leans on the land," and, as "the thresher's gap-toothed maw" moves across the grounds, field mice and rabbits flee its approach. But one black snake does not escape its doom:

> Defiant, tall in that blast of day,
> Now eye for eye, he swaps his stare.
> His outrage glitters on the air.
> Men shout, ring around. He can't get away.
> Yes, they are men, and a stone is there.
> . . . .
> An old man, standing stooped, detached,
> Spits once, says, "Hell, just another snake."

Yet for the boy, at the end of the day, now that the thresher "has stopped its racket" and "the work is done," the *evening* is "wounded": we are all one flesh. . . . And, as Warren looks back across the years, he says:

> . . . all history lives in the head again,
> And I shut my eyes and I see that scene
> And name each item, but cannot think
> What, in their urgency, they must mean,
>
> But know, even now, on this foreign shore,
> In blaze of sun and the sea's stare,
> A heart-stab blessed past joy or despair,
> As I see, in the mind's dark, once more,
> That field, pale, under starlit air.

Nor must one forget the "Lullabies" among the poems dedicated to Gabriel, for they are triumphs, the first and the third being, indeed, among Warren's greatest poems. The first ("Lullaby: Smile in Sleep") anticipates the child dreaming of "Reality"—whereby he may be forearmed to deal with "The world's brute ox-heel wrong, and shrewd hand-harm." But it bids him also to dream of grace, for "Grace undreamed is grace forgone." The second ("Lullaby: Moonlight Lingers")—as it murmurs reiteratively, "Sleep, son, past grief"—does, by the progress of its song, put the father in mind of one who "died long ago" and whose face this sleeping child "will never know," whose voice he "will never hear": it is the voice of his own father: "I can hear / That utterance as if tongue-rustle of pale tide in moonlight: / *Sleep, son. Good night.*" And the third ("Lullaby: A Motion Like Sleep")—as it quietly sings, "So, son, now sleep"—expectantly looks toward the child's being wakened by "clang of cock-crow, and dawn's rays," when he shall "know, in excitement of day-blaze, / How like a wound, and deep, / Is Time's irremediable joy."

Over a long period, Warren suffered no lack of bilious detractors, and *Promises* did not escape their captiousness; but by far the greater number of his more discerning readers found themselves gratefully marveling at the mastery represented by this remarkable book, marveling at the depth and delicacy of feeling behind it, at the richness of the experience it organizes, and at the eloquence consequent upon a new ease and directness of expression that here bespoke the last sophistication of technical virtuosity. So it was generally felt to be an act of justice that, in the field of poetry, it should have been awarded both the Pulitzer Prize and the National Book Award.

The volume that followed *Promises—You, Emperors, and Others* (1960)—is a far less distinguished collection in which many of Warren's efforts are marked by one or another kind of false start or uncertain stop or failure of rhetoric, and it is significant that he reissued only six of its seventy-nine pages in his *New and Selected Poems: 1923–1985*. This act of rescission does no doubt reflect a somewhat excessive severity of judgment, for it is by no means difficult to find here and there poems in *Emperors* which are marked by various local felicities—such as "The Letter about Money, Love, or Other Comfort, If Any," "In Moonlight, Somewhere, They Are Singing" and "Debate: Question, Quarry, Dream" (in the sequence "Some Quiet, Plain Poems"), the cycle of poems called "Ballad: Between the Boxcars (1923)," and "So You Agree with What I Say." But, clearly, the one major poem in the book of 1960 is "Mortmain."

By the end of the 50s Warren was becoming habituated to the writing of sequences of poems rather than isolated lyrics, and "Mortmain" presents a cycle of five poems devoted to meditations on his dead father. The opening poem recounts his being flung by his plane "through dark and / The abstract flight-grid of sky" to his dying father's bedside in 1955, to "ruck of bedclothes ritualistically / Reordered by the paid hand / Of mercy." And, as he stands there, "travel-shaken," his father manages for the merest moment to lift his hand "but cannot / Make contact":

> Like an eyelid the hand sunk, strove
> Downward, and in that darkening roar,
> All things. . . . .
> Were snatched from me, and I could not move,
> Naked in that black blast of his love.

The second poem takes us back to the time of his father's adolescence in Trigg County, Kentucky, circa 1885, when, at the age of sixteen, he was "cutting crossties for the first railroad in the region" and learning *koinē* Greek. The poem also recalls a morning, much later, when, as a grown man, his father, while shaving, recited to his son (the poet) in Greek the opening sentence of the Fourth Gospel—and then, "laughing from the deep of a dark conquest and joy, / Said: 'Greek—but it wasn't for me. Let's get to breakfast, boy.'"

The third poem, "Fox-Fire: 1956," moves forward seventy-one years to an evening when the poet, as he holds his father's old grammar in his hand, tries to understand "that sound, / Like wind, that fills the enormous dark of my head." And, in that moment, he hears his own little son in another room laughing:

> I know he sits there and laughs among his toys,
> Teddy bear, letter blocks, yellow dumptruck, derrick, choo-choo—
> Bright images, all, of Life's significance.
> So I put the book on the shelf, beside my own grammar,
> Unopened these thirty years, and leave the dark room,
> And know that all night, while the constellations grind,
> Beings with folded wings brood above that shelf,
> Awe-struck and imbecile, and in the dark,
> Amid History's vice and velleity, that poor book burns
> Like fox-fire in the black swamp of the world's error.

The fourth poem, "In the Turpitude of Time: N.D.," meditates on

> How cause flows backward from effect
> To bless the past occasion, and
> How Time's tongue lifts only to tell,
> Minute by minute, what truth the brave heart will fulfill.

And in the final poem, "A Vision: Circa 1880," the poet, now himself in late middle age, again looks back to his father's youth, to a time even earlier than that of the second poem, and sees his father as a boy "poised between woods and the pasture, sun-green and green shadow"—"lips / Parted in some near-smile of boyhood bemusement." Suddenly he strives to cry across the years: "*Listen!* . . . *Listen! I know—oh, I know—let me tell you!*" He wants to give the boy the benefit of his own knowledge, his own experience. But the young figure—"in patched britches and [with] that idleness of boyhood / Which asks nothing and is its own fulfillment"—turns "with imperial calm" and "rejoins / The shadow of woods" with a grin on his face.

Warren is, of course, often to be found brooding on the mystery of filiation: it is to the fore in the fine early poem on his mother's death, "The Return: An Elegy," as it also is in the beautiful poem that opens the

sequence dedicated to Gabriel in *Promises*, in which, as he thinks of his
mother and father, Ruth and Robert, lying side by side in the cemetery
that holds their bones bathed "in a phosphorus of glory," he hears them
murmuring to him, "'Child . . . / We died only that every promise might
be fulfilled.'" And "Mortmain" found an equally great companion piece
in the long sequence of six poems—again, on his dead mother—entitled
"Tale of Time," which was published in his *Selected Poems, New and Old:
1923–1966*. Here, as the poet remembers his mother's dying on an October day in the 1930s when "the last oak leaf of autumn" was not yet
fallen, he is distressed by the realization that, in no longer being able "to
remember the faces she saw every day," he has "therefore lost that
much / Of her." But now, "far from Kentucky," he does most poignantly
remember his black nurse who held him as a child in her arms, as he
"cried out in the wide / Day-blaze of the world." And he recalls the day
on which, as she was dying, he, long since a grown man, went with his
father to visit her, as she sat "propped in a chair," being unable to breathe
in a prone position. He remembers how, as he leaned over her, her hand
feebly rose to touch his cheek, the voice only able to say "*you*," and he
remembers how first he and then his father kissed the old woman's dry,
hot cheek. And, as he thinks of these three, his parents and this beloved
old woman, he wonders what he and they would talk about now. He has
not forgotten the time when, as a child, he "lay lost in the long grass,
sun setting," and when his mother appeared, saying, "'Your hand— /
Give it here, for it's dark and, my dear, / You should never have come in
the woods when it's dark. . . .'" But, as he reminds himself, he is now in
his sixties, much older than his mother was at the time of her death: so
what would she say to "a balding stranger"? In such wise does his meditation proceed, as he turns over and over in his mind this fabric of life—
his mother and his father and his black nurse—by which long ago he was
so deeply formed and nourished. Then at last comes the sudden realization that, if he would live aright, there is but "one solution":

> You
> Must eat the dead.
> You must eat them completely, bone, blood, flesh, gristle, even
> Such hair as can be forced. You
> Must undertake this in the dark of the moon, but
> At your plenilune of anguish.

It is, to be sure, a metaphor so violently macabre as to be unnecessarily
distracting. Yet its meaning can hardly be mistaken. The fourth poem in
the sequence tells us that "we must learn / The nature of being, in order /
In the end to be. . . ." And Warren intends, furthermore, to tell us that

we learn the nature of our being and give it a chance at fulfillment only as we eat the dead, only as we so ingest the past as to make the heart alive to the Oneness of life, to the unsunderable unity of past and present: in this way only can we win through to fullness of identity.

Moreover, Warren also feels it necessary to say most especially to his fellow Americans that, despite the degree to which his lengthened shadow falls across their heritage, Emerson will be found of little help, as they try to reckon with the human condition. Over and again Harold Bloom has laid it down that Warren's genius is Emersonian, and just as regularly this is an attribution that Warren himself firmly refused, nowhere perhaps more emphatically than in the quirkily humorous sequence "Homage to Emerson, On Night Flight to New York," which he included in his *Selected Poems: 1923–1966* and which, unhappily, he excluded from *New and Selected Poems: 1923–1985*. As his plane zooms across the blackened skies, the poet holds a volume of Emerson's essays on his lap, a "finger of light" in the "pressurized gloom" striking down "to poke the page." And he ruminates about this man for whom there was "no sin," "not even error," and who "thought that significance shines through everything." Well, he says to himself, "At 38,000 feet Emerson / Is dead right." But then it occurs to him that, even at such a distance from the quotidian realities of the earth, "you had better / Try to remember something specific, if / You yourself want to be something specific." At this moment he suddenly remembers from his boyhood "the old colored man" who once said to him, *"You is got white skin and hair red as a termater, but / You is human-kind"*—which, true enough, is a fact that it may be "hard to remember" at "38,000 feet" but which, nevertheless, is a fact more solid than anything to which the Sage of Concord ever beckoned our attention. As "the nose of the DC-8 dips" in its approach to the shining city below, he thinks of the friends he has there, people whose "lives have strange shapes" which Emerson's essays in no way illumine, and his meditation finds then its focus—on "the human bond," "the human fabric," and on how "the process of living can become Truth." "Let us move," he says, "toward the city," which is left much too far behind by Emerson's vague kind of loftiness. Yes, says Warren (in his interview with Marshall Walker), "when it comes down to Hawthorne and Emerson meeting on the wood paths of Concord, I'm strictly for Hawthorne. I really have something that's almost a pathological flinch from Emersonianism, from Thoreauism, from these oversimplifications . . . of the grinding problems of life and of personality."

Incarnations, the collection of new poems which he published in 1968, showed Warren by then to be steadily in full command of the kind of

passionate, commodious, relaxed, but penetrative style of which he began to take possession in *Promises,* and the book, for all the variousness
of its human material, expresses a remarkable integrity of import. Its
title, however, is no doubt misleading in its Christian resonance, for the
"incarnations" being exhibited make no reference to any disclosure of
Transcendence through Immanence. Or, if these terms are to be used at
all, it would be necessary to say something to the effect that Warren is by
way of wholly relocating the dimension of Transcendence within the dimension of Immanence. One of the book's two epigraphs is a sentence
from the Old Testament's Book of Nehemiah which avers: "Yet now our
flesh is as the flesh of our brethren." And this maxim suggests the kind
of incarnation which is at issue: the embodiment or manifestation in any
particular life of the One Life that embraces all. In the seven-poem sequence, "Penological Study: Southern Exposure," a convict who cut his
wife's throat is dying of cancer in a southern penitentiary: "deep . . .
inside his gut, / The pumpkin grows and grows." And when the warden
stops outside his cell to say, " 'Jake— / You know we're pulling for you,"
Jake's inward and unarticulated response is simply, "Oh, Warden, / Keep
that morphine moving, for we are all / One flesh"—which, in its echo of
"Ballad of a Sweet Dream of Peace" in *Promises* ("we're all one flesh"),
serves to emphasize how central in this book is Warren's vision of the
organic cohesiveness of human existence, of the communion that unites
all human flesh. This, as he wants to say, "We must try / To love so well
. . . that we may believe, in the end, in God."

Which is, for example, in a way what the long sequence "Internal In-
juries" comes to at last. The first of the eight poems fully sets forth the
dramatic situation:

> *Nigger:* as if it were not
> Enough to be old, and a woman, to be
> Poor, having a sizeable hole (as
> I can plainly see, you being flat on the ground) in
> The sole of a shoe (the right one), enough to be
>
> Alone (your daughter off in
> Detroit, in three years no letter, your son
> Upriver, at least now you know
> Where he is, and no friends), enough to be
>
> Fired (as you have just today
> Been, and unfair to boot, for
> That durn Jew-lady—there wasn't no way

To know it was you that opened that there durn
Purse, just picking on you on account of
Your complexion), enough to be

Yourself (yes, after sixty-eight
Years, just to have to be
What you are, yeah, look
In the mirror, that
Is you, and when did you
Pray last), enough to be,

Merely to be—Jesus,
Wouldn't just *being* be enough without
Having to have the pee (quite
Literally) knocked out of
You by a 1957 yellow Cadillac driven by
A spic, and him
From New Jersey?

Why couldn't it of at least been a white man?

Here, then, is the scene: after being hit by a car driven by "a spic," this poor Negro domestic, her hat caught under the wheel of a truck and her screams sounding with the regularity of a metronome, lies in a New York street, surrounded by the merely curious. The accident has occurred in the neighborhood of the old Penn Station, which is being torn down, the pneumatic jack-hammers speaking in their code—*tat-tat-tat*. The poet is watching the little drama from his taxi, and, just at the point when the ambulance at last arrives and when he can no longer bear the sight of the victim's violated flesh, as he bids his driver to move on, he puts to him his question: "Driver, do you truly, truly / Know what flesh is, and if it is, as some people say, really sacred?" May it be the case, in other words, that a proper reverence or a casual contempt for human flesh is in some sense proof of our belief in God or of our allegiance to Absurdity?

But the poems in *Incarnations* are not about human flesh alone: many of them are about the flesh of figs or plums or fish. The "only human" (as it is spoken of in the poem "Skiers") is but one thread in the larger fabric of the world—and *all* of it is in view, as *One Flesh*, when Warren says (in "Masts at Dawn"), "We must try / To love so well the world that we may believe, in the end, in God."

·

In the year following that in which *Incarnations* appeared, Warren published, in 1969, what is perhaps the central masterpiece of his career in poetry or, at least, the work that absolutely convinced many readers of the veritable lordship he had won of his art: it was his *Audubon: A Vision*, which he had been meditating for a quarter-century. When he was handling, as he frequently was, historical figures and incidents, his primary allegiance was never to Clio but to the imperatives of his own imagination, and thus he was inclined to respond with utter impatience to the pedantry that prompted some of his critics to remark disapprovingly his various redactions of what appears to be the factual record of this distinguished nineteenth-century artist-ornithologist, John James Audubon. It needs to be remembered, however, that the man who produced *The Birds of America* had indeed been a sort of folk hero in American culture long before it ever occurred to Warren to write about him, so that it is difficult to see wherein there was anything illicit in this poet's undertaking to reimagine and re-create an already legendary figure.

The sequence of poems Warren devoted to Audubon is very largely based on an incident that Audubon himself recounted in one of the "Episodes" (or "Delineations of American Scenery and Manners") with which he intercalated his descriptions of birds in the five-volume *Ornithological Biography*, the "Episode" entitled "The Prairie"; but, in several details, Warren's reconstruction of the incident considerably modifies Audubon's own account. While traveling alone on the prairie somewhere near the Missouri-Kentucky border, Audubon, at the "shank-end of day," as he emerges one wintry evening from a densely wooded tract, stumbles on a squalid, primitive little settlement:

> . . . sudden
> The clearing: among stumps, ruined cornstalks yet standing, the spot
> Like a wound rubbed raw in the vast pelt of the forest. There
> Is the cabin, a huddle of logs with no calculation or craft:
> The human filth, the human hope.
>
> Smoke,
> From the mud-and-stick chimney, in that air, greasily
> Brims, cannot lift, bellies the ridgepole, ravels
> White, thin, down the shakes, like sputum.
>
> He stands,
> Leans on his gun, stares at the smoke, thinks: "Punk-wood."
> Thinks: "Dead-fall half rotten." Too sloven,
> That is, to even set axe to clean wood.

"He halloos." And from within the cabin comes an old crone, "tall, taller than he," with a fierce, rough-hewn face and a great "tumble and tangle / Of dark hair . . . and under the coarse eyebrows, / The eyes, dark, glint as from the unspecifiable / Darkness of a cave." She says: "'Ye wants to spend the night? Kin ye pay? / Well, mought as well stay then, done got one a-ready, / And leastwise, ye don't stink like no Injun.'"

On entering the dark, malodorous hovel Audubon finds the other guest, an Indian, who, "Hunched by the hearth, lifts his head, looks up, but / From one eye only, the other / An aperture below which blood and mucus hang, thickening slow"—and this the result of his having that day accidentally destroyed his eye when an "arrow jounced back off his bowstring." After propping his gun in a corner, Audubon reaches under his hunter's frock and takes out his gold watch, which the woman immediately grabs, hanging it about her neck on its thong loop. "And near it the great hands hover delicately / As though it might fall":

> The time comes to take back the watch. He takes it.
> And as she, sullen and sunken, fixes the food, he becomes aware
> That the live eye of the Indian is secretly on him, and soundlessly
> The lips move, and when her back is turned, the Indian
> Draws a finger, in delicious retardation, across his own throat.

> After food, and scraps for his dog, he lies down:
> In the corner, on bearskins, which are not well cured,
> And stink, the gun by his side, primed and cooked.

> Under his hand he feels the breathing of the dog.

> The woman hulks by the fire. He hears the jug slosh.

After Audubon beds down, the woman's two sons "come in from the night," and he, with the Indian's warning in mind, "Thinks: 'Now.'" Although he and the Indian pretend to be sleeping soundly, he never ceases to watch "through slit lids":

> The sons
> Hunker down by the fire, block the firelight, cram food
> Into their large mouths, where teeth
> Grind in hot darkness, their breathing
> Is heavy like sleep, he wants to sleep, but
> The head of the woman leans at them. The heads
> Are together in firelight.

Then, "like the whisper and *whish* of silk," he hears the woman sharpening a knife on fine-grained stone, and, when she rises, she is holding the knife in her hand. "He thinks: 'Now.'" But, though he "knows / What he must do, do soon," a strange kind of "lassitude / Sweetens his limbs." "'Now, now' the voice in his head cries out," but, to his own bafflement, he finds himself unable to spring into action, though his gun is "primed and cocked" and though he is certain that the crone is at the point of plunging the knife into his body. In this instant, however, the door bursts open, and three travelers—"alert, strong, armed"—enter the cabin. Immediately, "the Indian / Is on his feet, pointing." And the travelers, in the way of frontier vigilantes, truss up the woman and her sons till the bestially murderous threesome can be hanged at dawn.

In the gray light of daybreak the woman and her men are taken out to a great oak tree, and, after their legs are bound with thongs, they are asked if they want to pray, whereupon the woman says: "'If'n it's God made folks, then who's to pray to? / . . . Or fer.'" And she bursts into laughter. As they stand there, Audubon for the first time is able clearly to see her face:

> Under
> The tumbled darkness of hair, the face
> Is white. Out of that whiteness
> The dark eyes stare at nothing, or at
> The nothingness that the gray sky, like Time, is, for
> There is no Time, and the face
> Is, he suddenly sees, beautiful as stone, and
>
> So becomes aware that he is in the manly state.

As he confronts the coarse yet furiously vital self-affirmation of this frontier woman who believes in nothing but her own life-force, he—who for a brief moment had been at the point of perversely opting for oblivion—is suddenly seized with a paroxysm of pleasure and joy at being still alive, and his erection is the sign of this abrupt upsurge of ecstasy. Meanwhile, the vigilante-travelers (referred to by Audubon in "The Prairie" as "Regulators") proceed with their business:

> The affair was not tidy: bough low, no drop, with the clients
> Simply hung up, feet not much clear of the ground, but not
> Quite close enough to permit any dancing.
> The affair was not quick: both sons long jerking and farting, but she,
> From the first, without motion, frozen
> In a rage of will, an ecstasy of iron, as though
> This was the dream that, lifelong, she had dreamed toward.
>
> The face,
> Eyes a-glare, jaws clenched, now glowing black with congestion
> Like a plum, had achieved,
> It seemed to him, a new dimension of beauty.

After the hanging, the travelers soon disappear into the forest, "and the Indian, / Now bearing the gift of a gun that had belonged to the hanged-ones, / Was long since gone, like smoke fading into the forest." But for a long while Audubon is unable to stir, as he stands "staring / At the face . . . / . . . in idiotic benignity"—in such a benignity as is visited upon him by his at last finding it po. ;ible now to accept his fate as explorer and artist, as a result of the example offered by this fierce old woman's unimpassioned acceptance of her own fate. Hitherto, anterior to that period of time covered by the poem itself, as Warren reminds us in his interview with Peter Stitt,[5] Audubon's tendency had been to resist his fate, as he recurrently told himself that he ought not to wander through the world hunting birds, that he ought to elect some stable occupation that would enable him decently to support his family. But now, as the poem says, "We are only ourselves, and that promise"—and, henceforth, "He continued to walk in the world": as the fourth section of the poem puts it,

> His life, at the end, seemed—even the anguish—simple.
> Simple, at least, in that it had to be
> Simply, what it was, as he was,
> In the end, himself and not what
> He had known ought to be. The blessedness!—

As he looked at the woman hanging from the tree, he yearned "to be able to frame a definition of joy," and the poem suggests that in time he did indeed achieve that definition through nothing other than the resoluteness of his dedication to his calling as artist and naturalist. True, he did not "Keep store, dandle babies, and at night nuzzle / The hazelnut-shaped sweet tits of Lucy." Yet, as Warren suggests,

> The definition of love being, as we know, complex,
> We may say that he, after all, loved his wife.

> The letter, from campfire, keelboat, or slum room in New Orleans,
> Always ended, "God bless you, dear Lucy."

Audubon's life, of course, was not without difficulty. Often, "Below the salt, in rich houses, he sat, and knew insult," as he sought the necessary patronage that would enable him to get on with his work. Yet, though he "was not unacquainted with contumely," his life was far from being destitute of dignity and joy. "He walked in the world. Knew the lust of the eye." "He saw the Indian, and felt the splendor of God." To be sure, strange it doubtless is that one who so loved the world nevertheless murdered more birds than any other man who ever lived, but, as Warren says (in the interview with Peter Stitt), in his hunt for models for his drawings "he destroyed beauty in order to create beauty":

> He slew them, at surprising distances, with his gun.
> Over a body held in his hand, his head was bowed low,
> But not in grief.

> He put them where they are, and there we see them:
> In our imagination.

Which is Warren's way of indicating that his final intention is to exhibit Audubon as type and example of the artist.

The poem's coda says:

> Tell me a story.

> In this century, and moment, of mania,
> Tell me a story.

> Make it a story of great distances, and starlight.

> The name of the story will be Time,
> But you must not pronounce its name.

> Tell me a story of deep delight.

And, if we are right in feeling this to be the story that is here related, we may surely say that *Audubon*, in telling this story, proves itself the great poem in the literature of this century on the character and vocation of the artist.

·

Calvin Bedient says (in his book *In the Heart's Last Kingdom*) that "*Audubon* rose above . . . [Warren's] previous volumes like a curiously abrupt, grand escarpment" and that he did not subsequently "write anything to equal it"[6]—whereas Harold Bloom's various discussions of Warren appear to suggest that virtually *all* the poetry after *Incarnations* partakes of a greatness indisputable and overwhelming.[7] And these verdicts are perhaps significant primarily for the examples they offer of the need so frequently observable in the criticism of Warren's work for vastly greater modulation of judgment. After the appearance of *Audubon*—in his sixty-seventh year—he published a body of work that might well be the achievement of a lifetime: *Or Else* in 1974, a third volume of *Selected Poems* in 1976 (carrying a major sequence ["Can I See Arcturus from Where I Stand?"] not previously collected), *Now and Then* in 1978, *Being Here* in 1980, *Rumor Verified* in 1981, *Chief Joseph of the Nez Perce* in 1983, and the

New and Selected Poems of 1985. Though, apart from Eliot and Auden, there is perhaps no other poet using the English language in this century who has claimed so immense a literary and critical sophistication as Warren commanded, he was capable of failures in taste that are shocking in one of his breadth of culture and assured self-consciousness, and he no doubt published far more in the last decade or so of his career than unfailingly scrupulous circumspection would have allowed. Yet, for all his occasional garrulity and historical nostalgia and his perhaps too constant commitment to a limited number of themes (the nature of identity, the nature of time) and his fondness for the persona of (as Paul Mariani calls it) the "redneck shit-kicker,"[8] when he died at the age of eighty-four in September 1989, he held a very special position of eminence on the Anglo-American scene, for he alone, in his fealty to the Romantic sublime, required to be thought of as having won the grandeur of a Yeats or a Frost or a Stevens.

The work in *Or Else,* the volume that followed the triumph of *Audubon,* is occasionally spoiled by a sententious kind of abstractness and banality (as in "I Know a Place Where All Is Real," "Bad Year, Bad War: A New Year's Card, 1969," "What You Sometimes Feel on Your Face at Night," "News Photo"), but this collection presents some of Warren's finest poems—and one of the great love poems of the age, the poem "Birth of Love." Early one late summer evening, "sun just down," the poet and his wife are swimming, and he is several strokes out when she rises to leave the water. Then, as she stands on the bank of the pond and draws a "towel grasped in each hand, / . . . back and forth across back and buttocks, . . . / With face lifted toward the high sky," he is suddenly transfixed by the sight of her lean, erect body "marked by his use, and Time's":

> This moment is non-sequential and absolute, and admits
> Of no definition, for it
> Subsumes all other, and sequential, moments, by which
> Definition might be possible. The woman,
>
> Face yet raised, wraps,
> With a motion as though standing in sleep,
> The towel about her body, under the breasts, and,
> Holding it there, hieratic, as lost Egypt and erect,
> Moves up the path that, stair-steep, winds
> Into the clamber and tangle of growth. Beyond
> The lattice of dusk-dripping leaves, whiteness
> Dimly glimmers, goes. Glimmers and is gone, and the man,

Suspended in his darkling medium, stares
Upward where, though not visible, he knows
She moves, and in his heart he cries out that, if only
He had such strength, he would put his hand forth
And maintain it over her to guard, in all
Her out-goings and in-comings, from whatever
Inclemency of sky or slur of the world's weather
Might ever be. In his heart
He cries out.

It is indeed an "absolute" moment, this moment in which there is wrested from the man a *cri de coeur* that is beyond all speech, as he, in looking from a distance at his wife, is suddenly so overborne by her preciousness and her vulnerability before the capricious weathers of the world that he is moved wordlessly to beseech the heavens to watch over and protect her.

There are many other poems of a comparable distinction in the book of 1974—including "I Am Dreaming of a White Christmas: The Natural History of a Vision," "Rattlesnake Country," "There's a Grandfather's Clock in the Hall," "Reading Late at Night, Thermometer Falling," and "Folly on Royal Street before the Raw Face of God," which, like his poems of the later 70s in *Now and Then* (1978) and *Being Here* (1980), are exploring the various continuities of flesh and time that constitute that One Life which constantly focalizes Warren's meditation. To be sure, as he says at one point in *Or Else* ("Interjection #2: Caveat"), "on- / ly, in discontinuity, do we know that we exist, or that, in the deep- / est sense, the existence of anything / signifies more than the fact that it is / continuous with the world"—but, nevertheless, as he also insists, "we must think of the / world as continuous, for . . . / . . . if it were not so, you wouldn't know / you are in the world, or even that the / world exists at all." And it is with the cohesions and permanencies that give unity to life that he tends generally to be concerned, most especially with the continuity between *was* and *is,* as in "I Am Dreaming of a White Christmas," one of the major poems in *Or Else.*

Here, the poet again brings before us his mother and father, who are set, as it were, in a faded, brown daguerreotype of the old family parlor, his father seated in his Morris chair and his mother in her rocker. They sit rigidly, as mummies, before a cold hearth on Christmas morning, the Christmas tree now "un-greened" and brown, and beneath it three packages. There are three chairs in the room for the children in the family, but they are empty; the speaker thinks: *"They're empty, they're empty, but me—*

oh, I'm here!" The parents and everything in the room are covered with "That silken and yellow perfection of Time that / Dust is." Then the scene abruptly shifts to the present: it is a late-summer afternoon, and the narrator stands in New York City's Times Square, amidst "the blunt crowd [that] thrusts, nudges, jerks, jostles." The working day now over, clerks are going home, night watchmen waking up, old men leaving the hardcore movie houses. "A mounted policeman sits a bay gelding." Surrounded by "the first hysteria of neon," the poet thinks of the snow that is no doubt already falling on the mountains of West Montana and wonders if he will ever know "What present there was in that package for me, / Under the Christmas tree." And the concluding lines might well be taken as the epilogue for much of Warren's poetry of the 70s:

> All items listed above belong in the world
> In which all things are continuous,
> And are parts of the original dream which
> I am now trying to discover the logic of. This
> Is the process whereby pain of the past in its pastness
> May be converted into the future tense.

·

After the appearance of *Being Here* in 1980 very nearly everybody was sounding hosannas of praise for Warren, even many who in an earlier period had resisted his poetic manner and message. Then, of course, in 1980, he was already seventy-five years of age, and that he so late in his life should have been committed to so passionate a love affair with the world as is recorded in this great sequence of fifty poems makes a profoundly moving example of a rare kind of vibrancy of mind and heart. Indeed, to read through the entire cycle is to feel that the very title of the book is hymnic and celebratory. The final stanza of the long poem "Synonyms" says:

> There are many things in the world, and I have seen some.
> Some things in the world are beautiful, and I
> Have seen some. But more things are to come,
> And in the world's tangled variety,
> It is hard sometimes to remember that beauty is one word for reality.

And this testimony about beauty being but another word for reality Warren was prepared to make even though much of the reality he confronted was an affair of "unworded revelation" ("Aspen Leaf in Windless World"), taking him with "The merciless grasp of unwordable grace / Which has no truth to tell of future or past— / But only life's instancy"

("Youthful Truth-Seeker, Half-Naked, At Night, Running Down Beach South of San Francisco"). In some mountainous district, for example, he stares at a "white alabaster" blanket of snow ("Snowshoeing Back to Camp in Gloaming"), as he stands "on that knife-edge frontier / Of Time-lessness, knowing that yonder / Ahead was the life I might live / Could I but move / Into the terror of unmarred whiteness under / The be-numbed and frozen sun." But, as he looks "starward," he confronts "the unnamed void where Space and God / Flinch to come, and where / Un-Time roars like a wind that only / The dead, unweeping, hear." Or in the poem "Preternaturally Early Snowfall in Mating Season" he is again in a mountainous region, in a "world of glitter and dawn-snow whiteness," where he notices signs of a buck having "wrestled and struggled to mount" a doe on the spot she "had made her huddle." And, as he moves through this "white world" with nothing in his "skull but the simple awareness of Being," he can see naught but "the guessed-at glory." In 1977, in his interview with Peter Stitt, Warren said: "More and more for me the germ of a poem is an event in the natural world."[9] And it is on such events that the poems in *Being Here* focus. Moreover, these are events that (as the poem "Code Book Lost" in *Now and Then* says) carry an "undeclared timbre." They are events, whether involving an encoun-ter with some remote waterfall or cave or deserted beach, that carry a strange surplusage of meaning unimposed by the poet himself: things appear to "lean" toward the human spectator. And, when they seem most filled with numinousness, with the *Mysterium tremendum*, they are imaged forth in terms of distance or brightness or whiteness. But just such things at last, almost unfailingly, prove elusive and leave you won-dering if "there [is] a message there for you to decipher" ("Aspen Leaf . . ."): "the guessed-at glory" seems never to be apprehensible, so that one is left marveling at a world whose "language we cannot utter" ("Lan-guage Barrier").

Yet, as the beautiful poem "Night Walking" suggests, Warren has no intention of concluding that the quest for some immediate contact with the Sublime is mistaken. Here, the poet is wakened in the course of a night by what he thinks to be

> . . . the first bear this year
> Come down off the mountain to rip
> Apples from trees near my window—but no,
> It's the creak of the door of the shop my son stays in.
> Now booted and breeched but bare
> From waist, he now stands
> Motionless, silent, face up

> To the moon, tonight full, now late and zenithward high
> Over forests as black as old blood
> And the crags bone-white.

Immediately the father is captivated by his son's restlessness, and he throws on levis and boots to go out into the dark "guiltily" to watch, from behind a parked car, the young man's movements. The son slowly follows a track leading up into the bordering mountain range

> Where from blackness of spruces great birches
> Stand monitory, stand white—
> Moving upward, and on, face upward as though
> By stars in an old sea he steered.

On and on the son clambers upward from one ridge crest to another, the father "with laggard cunning" following, with a "mixture of shame, guilt, and joy." At last, now knowing how far his son intends to go, he decides to make his way on back to his bed, but, in the very moment in which he turns about, he finds himself "paralyzed" by a recollection from his own young manhood: he remembers a night long ago when he, too, went "moon-walking on sea-cliffs" and dreamed of that which he could barely name. And he also remembers a kind of failure that was a part of that night, for he, as he reminds himself, "heard no voice in the heart." But, even so, he would not have his son desist, and the final words of the poem he addresses from a distance to the son:

> At any rate, you must swear never,
> Not even in secret, the utmost, to be ashamed
> To have lifted bare arms to that icy
> Blaze and redeeming white light of the world.

He wants to say to his son something like what is said in "Interjection #7: Remarks of Soul to Body" (*Or Else*):

> Keep doing your duty, yes, and some fine day
> You'll get full pension, with your every need
> Taken care of, and not a dime out of your own pocket—
> Or anybody's pocket, for that matter—for you won't have
> Any needs, not with the rent paid up in perpetuity.

True, from Warren's perspective the various landmarks we encounter in our journeyings, all seem enigmatical, ambiguous, of uncertain import—and the world's beauty appears "tangled and hieroglyphic" ("The Mission," *Now and Then*). Indeed, in the poems collected in *Being Here*, as in large ranges of Warren's other poetry, what one feels over and again is, to speak paradoxically, the *presence* of the *Deus absconditus:* that is, the ultimate ground of meaning and value is veiled and unsearchable. Yet the world is represented (in Hopkins' term) as instressed with splendor, charged with grandeur: for Warren, its marrow and elixir can be conceived to be nothing other than Glory. Glory, however, in its radical transcendence—and, in this, Warren is deeply akin to a poet so greatly different as A. R. Ammons—is not to be taken by direct assault: perilous indeed is it even to attempt to do so: as he says in "What Day Is" (*Incarnations*),

> Do not
> Look too long at the sea, for
> That brightness will rinse out your eyeballs.

In short, a proper *pietas* will carefully respect the essential hiddenness of the Numinous. And it is the rigor with which this is insisted upon in *Being Here* that makes one think of it, of all Warren's books, as the one that, in most relentlessly pressing the religious issue, proves itself the indispensable text for taking the measure of his late vision—most especially when one thinks of poems such as "Boyhood in Tobacco Country," "The Moonlight's Dream," "Youthful Truth-Seeker," "August Moon," "Preternaturally Early Snowfall in Mating Season," "Sila," "On into the Night," "Language Barrier," "The Cross," and "Night Walking."

·

In the work of his last years this great master moved from strength to strength, as his talent, with a miraculous effortlessness, scanned and rescanned a world about which he had been writing for more than sixty years. And in *Rumor Verified: Poems 1979–1980* (1981), in the book-length poem *Chief Joseph of the Nez Perce* (1983), and in the large body of previously uncollected poems in *New and Selected Poems: 1923–1985* (1985) he was at the top of his form, representing such an astonishing vitality as did Hardy and Yeats and Stevens in their own great age. Moreover, even in his ninth decade he could yet see Arcturus. True, he knows (as he says in the poem "Waiting" [*Now and Then*]) that for anything like full comprehension one may have to wait—"Until / The last owl hoot has quivered to a / Vibrant silence." But Ursa Major and all the other constellations will still be there—not easily to be deciphered but, nevertheless, imaging forth the Transcendence that we uncertainly and darkly descry. The "rumor verified" in his book of 1981 is, to be sure, "That you are simply a man, with a man's dead reckoning, nothing more." But that which most deeply belongs to the essential nature of his humanity drives him on not only to the instancies of his life in this world but also to those distant, narrow, mountainous ledges from which we glimpse "Beyond the last flamed escarpment of mountain cloud" the white radiance of Eternity.

In the wonderful group of poems from the early 1980s—"Altitudes and Extensions"—with which Warren opened his *New and Selected Poems: 1923–1985*, "Arizona Midnight" and "Last Walk of Season" convey, as concisely perhaps as any of his late poems, the hard-won autumnal equanimity that at the end formed his controlling perspective. In the former poem he speaks of lying in his sleeping bag and of listening to "The grief of the coyote [which] seems to make / Stars quiver whiter over the blackness which / Is Arizona at midnight." As he lies on his back staring upward, he thinks to himself:

> I know
> Nothing to tell the stars, who go,
> Age on age, along tracks they understand, and
> The only answer I have for the coyote would be
> My own grief, for which I have no
> Tongue—indeed, scarcely understand.

Amidst the absolute darkness he can descry, eastward, no hint of dawn: the one thing he can dimly see, as he listens to the coyote's wail, is a "single great cactus" that "has / Its own necessary beauty." And, similarly, in "Last Walk of Season," as he speaks of climbing up a "mountain trail / To see the last light," he is struck by the necessary beauty that belongs to the landscape just before the onset of autumn. Everything has just been washed with rain:

> How bright,
> Rain-washed the pebbles shine! A few high leaves
> Of birch have golden gone. Ah, the heart leaps
> That soon all earth will be of gold:
> Gold birch, gold beech, gold maple. That
> Is its own delight. Later, nothing visible
> Except black conifers will clamber
> Up the first white of ridge, then the crag's blank sun-blaze of snow.
> Can it be that the world is but the great word
> That speaks the meaning of our joy?

In this "westward hour" at summer's end this man who has been walking a long time has come "where . . . [he] had meant to come." And, having found in something like the way of Dr. Johnson that reality is "the lake . . . left by a glacier older than God," is "the sun. / . . . flamehuddled in mist," and having found that rain-washed pebbles and golden birches and black conifers all have their "necessary beauty," he wants

"Not to exist, except as part of that one / Existence. . . ." And, loving the world with such a fierceness as amounts in the end to believing in God, he wanted, moreover, simply to sing of the Glory that indwells every nook and cranny of the *One Life* to which all creatures belong, bringing (in Coleridge's phrase) "joyance every where." Which is to say that there is an *o altitudo!* underlying all his final words. And it is the unillusioned eloquence with which Warren in poem after poem over his last years uttered this cry of grateful reverence and jubilation before the world at hand that does in part give him the special kind of majesty that he commands among American poets as the century approaches its close.

~~~~~~

CHAPTER SEVEN

The Poetry of Richard Wilbur—
"The Splendor of Mere Being"

Even when death has taken
An exceptional man,
It is common things which touch us,
   gathered
In the house that proved a hostel.

. . . .

It is the straight back
Of a good woman
Which now we notice. For her guests' hunger
She sets the polished table.

And now the quick sun,
Rounding the gable,
Picks out a chair, a vase of flowers,
Which had stood till then in shadow.

It is the light of which
Achilles spoke,
Himself a shadow then, recalling
The splendor of mere being.

. . . .

—RICHARD WILBUR, "For Dudley"

Toward the end of an essay on his own poetry (*Responses—Prose Pieces: 1953–1976*) Richard Wilbur proposes a point of vantage for its appraisal, when he says: "A good part of my work could, I suppose, be understood as a public quarrel with the aesthetics of Edgar Allan Poe."[1] And the frequency with which he emphatically expresses in other essays, as well as in many of his poems, his distaste for Poe's general project as a poet and thinker suggests that his quarrel with his nineteenth-century predecessor may indeed deserve to be thought of as playing an executive role in his own enterprise. "Poe's aesthetic, Poe's theory of the nature of art," he says, "seems to me insane."[2] And its insanity for Wilbur is consequent upon what he takes to be its underlying assumption, that, given the essential mediocrity and dishevelment of the world at hand, *real* life is *elsewhere*. What is posited in Poe's homemade metaphysics is the emergence of the world out of God's self-diffusion into space, this disintegration of the original divine unity having had the result of the deity's existing now only in what Poe speaks of as the "infinite individualizations of Himself." But though every finite reality, whether it be a creature of the sea or of the land, carries within itself a fragment of the divine, it is a divinity corrupted and defiled and awaiting its being ultimately gathered back into the reassembled unity of the Godhead.

Since, of all the fragments of God that are scattered about the world, it is the spark of the divine within the imagination of the poet that burns most brightly, it is therefore the duty of the poet to reconstitute the *Ur-grund* through the fusing power of visionary thought. The poet's high calling is to retreat from the tainted materiality of time and space and—in his quest of the supernal beauty that will prevail once God has again been (if we may say so) ingodded—to "live continually," as Poe phrased it, "in a reverie of the future."[3] The poet must disengage himself from all earthly things and undertake to dwell entirely within the universe of the dream. Thus it is no wonder that Poe's own poetry, in the manner of his stories, abstains from any profound moral involvement with the life of the human community, for it wants, as Wilbur says, to "throw overboard that factuality, and that narrative or logical clarity, which would render it compassable by the mundane intellect: and it must eschew all human emotions, since, when compared to the sense of beauty, they are . . . 'vapid and insignificant' and 'trammel the soul in its flight' "[4] to the Empyrean.

Now it was inevitable that such an aesthetic as Poe's should strike such a poet as Wilbur as simply insane, for, whereas Poe's patron saint might be said to have been Dionysius the Areopagite, Wilbur's appears to be St. Athanasius. Which is to say that the poet of *The Beautiful Changes* and *Ceremony* and *Things of This World* and *The Mind-Reader* is one whose Way in his dealings with the body of this world is not the Way of Rejection but rather the Way of Affirmation. His is the vigilance of one upon whom the natural order of common things is pressing all the time, and he wants to translate into the images and meters of poetry not the light that never was on land or sea but, rather, the light of ordinary day, for, above all else, he is convinced that it is in the order of common things that (as

Charles Williams says in his fine book on Dante, *The Figure of Beatrice*) "the great diagrams are perceived; [that it is] from them [that] the great myths open; [and that it is] by them [that we understand] the final end."[5]

In recent years Quentin Anderson, Harold Bloom, Irving Howe, and Richard Poirier have been only the most prominent among various others who have sought to persuade us that Emerson (for all his vatic windiness and the tenuousness of his actual hold on cultivated readers of our period [apart, that is, from scholars in "American studies"]) remains the great decisive strategist of the American literary imagination. If one does not look for any line of simple genetic relationship between the Sage of Concord and his presumed heirs, so in some sense he may well be. Yet it is strange that the peremptoriness with which Emerson's priority is urged has not prompted any counterclaim, at least among professional Americanists in literary studies, in behalf of Jonathan Edwards. True, it often seems beyond possibility to redeem Edwards from the image clung to by ignoramuses, of a "sulphurous, ranting revivalist" bent on bullying his congregants into docility by the specter of Sinners in the hands of an Angry God. But, in relation to his career as the great minister of the Church at Northampton, Massachusetts (1729–50), the old stereotype is absurdly incongruous, for his Northampton sermons generally represent a bold attempt in a chaste and meticulous language to reckon with (as he termed it) the "decay of vital piety" brought by the moldering of the tradition of Cotton Mather into a sort of muscular moralism. And his formal theological treatises—say, the *Treatise Concerning Religious Affections*, the *Essay on the Trinity*, the *Images of Divine Things*, and *The End for Which God Created the World*—present incontestable evidence of his being, before Reinhold Niebuhr, the one truly great and original theologian in the American tradition.

But, when one thinks of such a paradigmatic status as Edwards may be considered as having for the American literary imagination, one will have him in mind not so much in his capacity as theologian as in his vocation as philosopher—in which, again, until the advent of the generation of Peirce and James and Royce, his supremacy in our native tradition was unmatched. Here, of course, his claim upon us is not that of a philosopher of language or of literary art but is rather that of one specializing in metaphysical and moral philosophy. And what is of the highest importance for discerning the special character of his thought in this regard is that the organizing principle of Edwards' entire philosophic meditation is a doctrine of Being, since for him Being is that than which there is nothing of higher ontological status: it is that without which every particular being would be destitute of any reality at all. Edwards did not conceive Being to be any sort of *thing* or *entity* which we may confront as we confront a gazelle or a person, since it is that which is constantly present in all the things of this world, enabling them to be whatever it is for which they are destined by their inner constitution. He would have delighted in Meister Eckhart's formulation of it as the *Is-ness* of everything that exists or in Gerard Manley Hopkins' formulation of it as "the dearest freshness deep down things." As he said in his early essay "Notes on the Mind," "men are wont to content themselves in saying merely that it is Something, [but] that Something is He, by whom all things consist":[6] that is, as a Christian theist, he chose to call this "Something" that is nearer to us than we are to ourselves, that flows out toward the farthest peripheries of the universe and that invades the most intimate neighborhood of our experience—he chose to call it *God*. And because God is nothing other than Being itself, "Closer is He than breathing," as Tennyson was later to say, "and nearer than hands and feet."

Edwards' great stress falls, in other words, on the immediacy of the Divine Presence: true, we do not behold it nakedly and without mediation, since our contact with it comes always by way of our contact with His creatures, but it is available to the heart's intuition in, with, and under our encounter with every aspect of Creation. Admittedly, Edwards sometimes appears to have recourse to the monarchical language of primitive supernaturalism, which was, of course, the idiom most familiar to his contemporaries, but for him the "transcendence" of God was explicable not in terms of the "higher" or "outer" reaches of the stratosphere but rather in terms of His penetration of every nook and corner of reality. This may suggest a penchant for a sort of crypto-pantheism, and, indeed, Edwards' method of thought is close enough to pantheism for a pantheistic echo to be heard in its proper name, which is *panentheism*. But to maintain, as he does, that the Divine is in everything and that everything is in the Divine is by no means to assert, in the manner of pantheism, that the world and God are coterminous and that the multiplicity of finite existence is wholly absorbed in some impersonal Absolute. In short, he stands in the Augustianian mystical-realist line of Christian thought that, in its emphasis on the immediacy of the Divine Presence in every dimension and on every level of reality, says in effect that (as Edwards puts it in the "Miscellanies") "all things are in Him, and He in all."

Through the various themes forming this elaborate vision of Being, Edwards built a complex counterpoint that led Perry Miller in his pioneering book of 1949 (*Jonathan Edwards*) to speak of him as "one of America's five or six major artists, who happened to work with ideas instead of with poems or novels."[7] It was a counterpoint calculated to say in effect what Elizabeth Barrett Browning's "Aurora Leigh" says, that "Earth's crammed with heaven, / And every common bush afire with God." Indeed, perhaps even more regularly than American poetry has followed the injunction of Emerson's Orphic poet to "Build therefore your own world" it has decided, from the time of Whitman to that of William Carlos Williams, that, the world at hand being already refulgent with the plenitude of Being, it need not move *elsewhere* for *real* life (in the manner of Poe) but need only take its recourse to the quotidian scene of the everyday hour. And it is to this Edwardsean line of thought and vision that Richard Wilbur is most deeply committed—though, of course, when I speak in this way of Edwards as the fountainhead of a certain mode of American poetry, I have in mind (as Irving Howe says, when he speaks of the relation of "the Emersonian moment" to the early Melville and Mark Twain [in *The American Newness*]) "something more consequential than influence. I have in mind 'cultural fit,' the way seemingly disparate or contrary elements of a culture can end in subterranean, even mysterious, connections."[8]

The reveling in the sheer ontological amplitude of the world which shapes much of Wilbur's most characteristic utterance was already being sounded in his brilliant first book of 1947, *The Beautiful Changes*, in such a poem as the sonnet "Praise in Summer":

> Obscurely yet most surely called to praise,
> As sometimes summer calls us all, I said
> The hills are heavens full of branching ways
> Where star-nosed moles fly overhead the dead;
> I said the trees are mines in air, I said
> See how the sparrow burrows in the sky!
> And then I wondered why this mad *instead*
> Perverts our praise to uncreation, why
> Such savor's in this wrenching things awry.
> Does sense so stale that it must needs derange
> The world to know it? To a praiseful eye
> Should it not be enough of fresh and strange
> That trees grow green, and moles can course in clay,
> And sparrows sweep the ceiling of our day?

The poet admits to the attack of embarrassment he suffers when, after feeling "called to praise, / As sometimes summer calls us all," he suddenly realizes that the very performance of the poetic act, since it involves metaphoric transformations of things, ordains that his shall be a "mad *instead*" that, in "wrenching things" into patterns of his own invention, commits him to a kind of *uncreation*: candor requires him to remind himself that the hills are *not* "heavens full of branching ways," that the trees are *not* "mines in air." So he must confront the question as to whether it may not be the case that poetry, in submitting the world to its own conceits, "perverts" doxology. Given the fullness with which the things of earth are already invested with the *integritas*, the *consonantia*, and the *claritas* of Being, ought it not be enough "To a praiseful eye . . . / That trees grow green, and moles can course in clay, / And sparrows sweep the ceiling of our day?" And though the dilemma posed by this very radical interrogation of the poetic act as such is not resolved—is it imagination or reality that deserves to claim the primacy?— his way of raising the dilemma hints at the primacy that Wilbur's conscience prompts him to accord to trees and sparrows, which, given their radiant haecceity, do not *need* poetic transfiguration (though the concluding line, in what it says of sparrows, slyly suggests that, in the final analysis, metaphor is, willy-nilly, inescapable).

The sort of *pietas* toward the richness of the created world adumbrated in "Praise in Summer" is a constantly recurrent leitmotif in the logic of Wilbur's poetry, for we are invited over and again to forswear any ascetical denial of "the spirit's right / Oasis"—as in the great poem "'A World without Objects Is a Sensible Emptiness'" (*Ceremony*, 1950):

> The tall camels of the spirit
> Steer for their deserts, passing the last groves loud
> With the sawmill shrill of the locust, to the whole honey of the arid
> Sun. They are slow, proud,
>
> And move with a stilted stride
> To the land of sheer horizon, hunting Traherne's
> *Sensible emptiness.* . . .

In their perversity, these "beasts" within us are "connoisseurs of thirst" who strain to move out beyond the regions of our common habitation, so drawn are they to what from a distance appear to be the "prosperous islands" of refreshment that dot a desert country—but these islands "That shimmer on the brink / Of absence" are "accurst," for, as we discover, they are "pure mirage." So, as the poem counsels,

> Turn, O turn
> From the fine sleights of the sand, from the long empty oven
> Where flames in flamings burn
>
> Back to the trees arrayed
> In bursts of glare, to the halo-dialing run
> Of the country creeks, and the hills' bracken tiaras made
> Gold in the sunken sun,

> Wisely watch for the sight
> Of the supernova burgeoning over the barn,
> Lampshine blurred in the stream of beasts, the spirit's right
> Oasis, light incarnate.

What we are being reminded of is that, when we are tempted by some *deceptio visus* to head for the false light of "prosperous islands" beyond the world's strand, a certain *metanoia* is required, a turning back to the common things of "the ordinary universe," for, having been stout and good enough to form the environment within which Glory could enter the world by way of a simple barn at Bethlehem, it is in these common things that "light incarnate" shall be found: *they,* in other words, are "the spirit's right / Oasis." In short, the locus of grace and truth is none other than this "opulent bric-a-brac earth" (as it is spoken of in "On the Eyes of an SS Officer" [*The Beautiful Changes*]).

A similar emphasis is felt in what is perhaps Wilbur's most famous poem, "Love Calls Us to the Things of This World," the title poem of his book of 1956 (*Things of This World*). The mood here, however, is sunny and playful, as the poem in its opening lines recounts the protagonist's reentering the world of daylight and consciousness after a night's sleep: in the moment of waking,

> The eyes open to a cry of pulleys,
> And spirited from sleep, the astounded soul
> Hangs for a moment bodiless and simple
> As false dawn.
> > Outside the open window
> The morning air is all awash with angels.

And one will smile perhaps at the whimsey with which the newly wakened man confounds a morning's laundry hung out to dry with angels. But he, after all, having just been "spirited from sleep, . . . / Hangs for a moment bodiless and simple / As false dawn," and thus the optical illusion is understandable, for indeed, as the wind makes the bed sheets and blouses and smocks fly first in one direction and then in another, the morning air does seem "awash with angels":

> Now they are flying in place, conveying
> The terrible speed of their omnipresence, moving
> And staying like white water. . . .

It is a charming scene, and the "cry of pulleys" and the angels in the air just outside the bedroom window invest this early-morning hour with that which makes the day ahead so cheerful a prospect as to invite jubilation and exultancy.

Then the festive air suddenly lifts, for, with the ebb of the winds, the blouses and smocks "swoon down into so rapt a quiet / That nobody seems to be there," and "The soul shrinks / From all that it is about to remember, / From the punctual rape of every blessed day":

> Yet, as the sun acknowledges
> With a warm look the world's hunks and colors,
> The soul descends once more in bitter love
> To accept the waking body, saying now
> In a changed voice as the man yawns and rises,
>
> "Bring them down from their ruddy gallows;
> Let there be clean linen for the backs of thieves;
> Let lovers go fresh and sweet to be undone,
> And the heaviest nuns walk in a pure floating
> Of dark habits,
>   keeping their difficult balance."

The recollection of all the ambiguous transactions with which our days are filled does, undoubtedly, prompt us to shrink from remembering our improbities and to feel, once one has begun clearheadedly to face how sorry is the use we make of our granted hours, that the day ahead will most certainly be "raped." Yet, as the poem wants to enjoin, let us not be more fastidious than the sun itself, which unhesitantly "acknowledges / With a warm look the world's hunks and colors": it knows far more surely than do we ourselves how imperfect things are amongst us: nevertheless, in its generosity, it consents to "clean linen" being reserved not merely for the righteous and for "lovers" but also "for the backs of thieves," as well as for "the heaviest nuns [who] walk in a pure floating / Of dark habits." In the light of the incalculable possibilities thrown up by a world that, throughout all its various tracts and byways, is infused with the grace of Being, no creatures are to be adjudged irredeemable from the standpoint of any presumed hierarchical polity, not even thieves. For the world that God, or Being-itself, indwells is *radically*, essentially, good. And, if we respond with large-heartedness to love's call "to the things of this world," we shall, like the heaviest nuns, keep our "difficult balance."

The urbane serenity with which Wilbur appears to accede to the proposition that the world, as it is most fundamentally constituted, is our true home has had a strangely nettling effect on his more captious critics.

"Holding up the things of this world . . . as a solution to the dilemmas of human existence," said Theodore Holmes (*Poetry* Magazine, April 1962), "can only be satisfactory for the privileged and unthinking."[9] No, as his detractors like to assert, Wilbur seems not to bear the stigmata of any great suffering or of what popular existentialism in the 1950s and 60s called "the human condition." And they declare that the ceremonious formality of his elegant rhymes and complex meters represents the self-indulgence of a *dandysme* incapable of any sort of prophetic relevance to our own late, bad time. Nor do they fail to tax him with a relentless cheerfulness that regularly avoids the tribulations brought by devils and demons. Long ago the late Randall Jarrell wrote (*Poetry and the Age*) that "Richard Wilbur is a delicate, charming, and skillful poet" who specializes in "a sugar-coated-slap-in-the-face rhetoric" that offers "a real though rather mild pleasure" of the kind that leads one to think, with some bit of surprise, 'Why would anybody want to write like that?'" And Jarrell's animadversions about the "academic, tea-party"[10] ethos of Wilbur's poetry, as well as his resolute nastiness of tone, have been parroted off and on ever since by commentators whose numerousness is astonishing when one considers that he is, for all his many distinguished competitors, our finest living American poet.

To think, for example, of the austere and exigent strictness of vision controlling the great poem "Giacometti" *(Ceremony)* is immediately to be reminded of how radically misconceived is this bilious estimate of Wilbur's achievement which is frequently bruited about. The poem begins by speaking of how rock so "insults us" by its very hardness and its unvoiced threat of striking us that "its buried glare begets a like / Anger in us, and finds our hardness." So, in our pride

> . . . and armed, and with a patient rage
> We carve cliff, shear stone to blocks,
> And down to the image of man
> Batter and shape the rock's
> Fierce composure, closing its veins within
> That outside man, itself its captive cage.
>
> So we can baffle rock, and in our will
> Can clothe and keep it.

In this way, by carving rock into human images, a kind of triumph over its intractability may be won. But, as the poem argues, the passage of time will prove such a triumph to be illusory, for, as we change, we will find ourselves "strange / To what we were" and thus "much worse mocked / Than cliffs can do." And, as it is suggested, most especially in our own time amidst all the declensions of a secular age must we feel the unlikelihood of a rendering of the human image achieving any sort of permanent validity, for

> . . . we on every side
> Random as shells the sea drops down ashore,
> Are walking, walking, many and alone.
>
> What stony shape could hold us now, what hard
> Bent can we bulk in air, where shall our feet
> Come to a common stand?

Then the poet thinks of the distinguished Italian sculptor Alberto Giacometti, who, in the period in which the poem was written, was producing in Paris in his Montparnasse atelier those tall, emaciated human figures that his name most immediately today puts us in mind of, and it occurs to him that

> . . . Giacometti in a room
> Dim as a cave of the sea, has built the man
> We are, and made him walk:
> Towering like a thin
> Coral, out of a reef of plaster chalk,
> This is the single form we can assume.
>
> We are this man unspeakably alone
> Yet stripped of the singular utterly, shaved and scraped
> Of all but being there,
> Whose fullness is escaped
> Like a burst balloon's: no nakedness so bare
> As flesh gone in inquiring of the bone.
>
> He is pruned of every gesture, saving only
> The habit of coming and going. Every pace
> Shuffles a million feet.
> The faces in this face
> Are all forgotten faces of the street
> Gathered to one anonymous and lonely.

It is the sternest possible judgment that Wilbur proposes, that

> . . . never more
> Diminished, nonetheless
> Embodied here, we are
> This starless walker, one who cannot guess
> His will, his keel his nose's bony blade.

Indeed, it is a judgment that, in its severity, is of a piece with Eliot's account of the "Unreal city, / Under the brown fog of a winter dawn," whose crowds flow across London Bridge, exhaling "Sighs, short and infrequent," with each man's eyes "fixed . . . before his feet." And, like *The Waste Land*, "Giacometti" wants to utter something like Baudelaire's apostrophe to his reader: *Hypocrite lecteur,—mon semblable,—mon frère!* So, quite to the contrary of Theodore Holmes's charge of 1962, the discourse carried on by this poet is hardly that of one who sees things "from the Parnassian heights of wealth, privilege, ease, refinement, and education" and who looks "down on the . . . sufferings of humankind without being part of them."[11]

Or, again, in the spring of 1976 a review of *The Mind-Reader* appeared in *The New Republic* in which it was said of Wilbur: "He is a bell too conscious of its clapper, clapper-happy. Pert but proper, always safe rather than sorry, his poetry is completely without risks, a prize pupil's performance. His ideas are always cut exactly to the size of his poems; he is never puzzled. And the ideas are all sentiments, aware of their potential high-minded emotional value and determined to snuggle into it."[12] Although this vulgar nonsense might not seem incredible if it came from a fool, one finds it simply stupefying that so cultivated a man as Calvin Bedient could have committed himself to so silly an estimate of one who in this book had presented poems such as "The Eye," "A Wedding Toast," "In Limbo," "Cottage Street, 1953," "The Fourth of July," "A Black Birch in Winter," "For the Student Strikers," and "Children of Darkness"—and the masterpiece forming the title poem of the book.

"The Mind-Reader" is a deeply affecting dramatic monologue spoken by an old Italian who spends his days drinking at a table in a café, where, for a small price, he offers the clairvoyance of a fortuneteller:

> I give them
> Paper and pencil, turn away and light
> A cigarette, as you have seen me do;
> They write their questions; fold them up; I lay
> My hand on theirs and go into my frenzy,
> Raising my eyes to heaven, snorting smoke,
> Lolling my head as in the fumes of Delphi,
> And then, with shaken, spirit-guided fingers,
> Set down the oracle.

"I have no answers," he says, and he admits to fobbing off his suppliants with stock replies that he scribbles down in response to their written questions:

It makes no difference that my lies are bald
And my evasions casual. It contents them
Not to have spoken, yet to have been heard.
What more do they deserve, if I could give it,
Mute breathers as they are of selfish hopes
And small anxieties, Faith, justice, valor,
All those reputed rarities of soul
Confirmed in marble by our public statues—
You may be sure that they are rare indeed
Where the soul mopes in private, and I listen.

Then, in one of the great moments of the poem, he addresses a poignant question to his silent auditor:

Is there some huge attention, do you think,
Which suffers us and is inviolate,
To which all hearts are open, which remarks
The sparrow's weighty fall, and overhears
In the worst rancor a deflected sweetness?
I should be glad to know it.

And the quotation from the opening collect of the Anglican Eucharistic office—"all hearts are open"—leaves us in no doubt regarding whose attention it is about the possibility of which the old man wistfully ponders.

The length of this great poem deters me from undertaking here to scan the full range of feeling and reflection it embraces, but the profundity of the pathos with which it renders the anguish of this old charlatan—which he himself expresses with the most extraordinary grace and scrupulousness—ought to convince most thoughtful readers of the breadth of sympathy and moral seriousness which Wilbur brings to the human scene. Indeed, the suggestion that he is merely a "clever" and an "elegant" gentleman-versifier who, in his clapper-happiness, is "never puzzled" is nothing more than a piece of absurdity—the negotiability of which in the currency of critical discourse today asks for an explanation in terms of a "phenomenology" of the literary life and its politics of the present time which cannot be attempted on this occasion.

Robert Frost tells us in "Birches" that "Earth's the right place for love," and Wilbur, believing this indeed to be so, takes it for granted that we are called to praise the things of this world. But, still again, to charge him with an insensitive acquiescence in the actualities of whatever happens to be prevailing circumstance is egregiously to misconstrue his real intention, and of this we should be reminded by the fine but complex poem "A Voice from under the Table" (*Things*). "The calves of waitresses parade about / My helpless head upon this sodden floor," says the drunken speaker, for he is in truth *under the table*: "I swallowed all the phosphorus of the seas / Before I fell into this low distress"—which is for him to admit that he has thoroughly fired himself up in overindulgence. So his initial question is in part, "How shall the wine be drunk . . . ?" But he toasts "the birds in the burning trees / That chant their holy lucid drunkenness," for his thirst "conceives a fierier universe," a more lustrous and resplendent world of value and gratification, than that which the product of the grape confers. And because he takes this yearning for another universe to be not only his but also that of all people, as he thinks of his table companions who have managed to remain more sober than he, he says, "You upright people all remember how / Love drove you first to the woods. . . ."

In the mythology of the poem "love," the search for the perfect woman, is something like a charade whereby he who is incomplete enacts the quest for completeness and fulfillment. But, though "Helen was no such high discarnate thought / As men in dry symposia pursue," she "was as bitterly fugitive, not to be caught / By what men's arms in love or fight could do." And thus it is that, as the poem says, "The end of thirst exceeds experience": one's reach forever surpasses one's grasping powers. Yet, as the speaker prays with a wonderfully Yeatsian kind of bravado, "God keep me a damned fool, nor charitably / Receive me into his shapely resignations." There is to be no retreat from restlessness or from strenuous enterprise in quest of the Good Place, the New Jerusalem; and the dream of a more perfect order of life shall be sustained by the confidence that there is (as one of the great lines of the poem puts it) "a South to all our flights of love." It is hardly the testimony of one who is prepared passively to say that whatever is is right and sufficient.

But, though the depth of Wilbur's commitment to "the world's body" does not preclude idealistic sentiment seeking melioristic transformations, he does, as numerous poems indicate, despise all programs presupposing the unlimited manipulability of the created order. And, in this connection, one thinks immediately of "Beasts" (*Things*):

> Beasts in their major freedom
> Slumber in peace tonight. The gull on his ledge
> Dreams in the guts of himself the moon-plucked waves below,
> And the sunfish leans on a stone, slept
> By the lyric water,

> In which the spotless feet
> Of deer make dulcet splashes, and to which
> The ripped mouse, safe in the owl's talon, cries
> Concordance.
> . . . .
> Meantime, at high windows
> Far from thicket and pad-full, suitors of excellence
> Sigh and turn from their work to construe again the painful
> Beauty of heaven, the lucid moon
> And the risen hunter,
>
> Making such dreams for men
> As told will break their hearts as always, bringing
> Monsters into the city, crows on the public statues,
> Navies fed to the fish in the dark
> Unbridled waters.

And who are the "suitors of excellence"? We may say perhaps that they are those of whom Auden is speaking in his poem "The Managers," which tells us that we are ruled today by overzealous

> Men, working too hard in rooms that are too big,
> Reducing to figures
> What is the matter, what is to be done.
> A neat little luncheon
> Of sandwiches is brought to each on a tray,
> Nourishment they are able
> To take with one hand without looking up
> From papers a couple
> Of secretaries are needed to file,
> From problems no smiling
> Can dismiss. . . .
> . . . . Far into the night
> Their windows burn brightly. . . .

Of these master spirits "For whom . . . / . . . there will be places on the last / Plane out of disaster," Auden says: "No; no one is really sorry for their / Heavy gait and careworn / Look, nor would they thank you if you said you were." They, as Wilbur remarks, are "Far from thicket and pad-fall." Which is to say that, amidst their graphs and charts and protocols, they are at a great distance from all the harmonies of nature with which even the cries of a "ripped mouse, safe in the owl's talon," voice "concordance."

For them, "the painful / Beauty of heaven" is merely something "construed," and thus, representing as they do unbridled intellect, it is no wonder that they bring monsters into the *polis* and make such dreams as break the human heart.

Yet, deeply repelled as Wilbur is by the kind of rationalistic managerialism that in our time—with the collapse of *Gemeinschaft* into *Gesellschaft*—has "the last word on how we may live or die," it is for him but type and example of our larger affliction by that imperialism of intellect which would read out of the world everything but itself, leaving us then in a desert of its own contrivance. And it is against the impiety of this dereliction that he is warning over and again—as, for example, in the wonderful poem "The Aspen and the Stream" in his book of 1961, *Advice to a Prophet*. The poem takes the form of a dialogue between the Stream and the Aspen on its shore. With great respect, the Aspen wants to express the admiration it feels for the Stream and for the apparent selflessness with which it reflects its environment:

> Beholding element, in whose pure eye
> My boughs upon a ground of heaven lie—
> O deep surrendered mind, where cloud and stone
> Compose their beings and efface your own,
> Teach me, like you, to drink creation whole
> And, casting out my self, become a soul.

But the elaborate punctiliousness of the Aspen elicits only a very brusque and disdainful response from the Stream:

> Why should the water drink,
> Blithering little tree?
> Think what you choose to think,
> But lisp no more at me.
>
> I seek an empty mind.
> Reflection is my curse.
> Oh, never have I been blind
> To the damned universe,
>
> Save when I rose in flood
> And in my lathered flight
> So fouled myself with mud
> As to be purged of sight.

Thus it becomes apparent that, though the Aspen wants nothing so much as to be happily related to its fellow creatures, the Stream wants to be utterly "purged" of "the damned universe." And the Aspen is aghast:

Your water livens me, but not your word,
If what you spoke was what I thought I heard.
But likely I mistook you. What with the claims
Of crow and cricket teaching me their names,
And all this flap and shifting in my head,
I must have lost the drift of what you said.

But, of course, the Aspen has not mistaken the drift of the Stream's testimony, and the latter remains adamant in its hatred of the things of
earth: as it says, it wants to "shake the daylight off / And repossess my
soul." To which the Aspen replies:

Out of your sullen flux I shall distil
A gayer spirit and a clambering will,
And reach toward all about me, and ensnare
With roots the earth, with branches all the air—
Even if that blind groping but achieves
A darker head, a few more aspen-leaves.

The sober, good-natured sanity of the Aspen makes for a perceptiveness
that, though unillusioned, is surely more inspiriting than the sour super-
ciliousness of the Stream. It knows that the soil in which its own roots
are infixed is nourished by the Stream: "Your water livens me." But, as it
says, "Out of your sullen flux I shall distil / A gayer spirit." It claims no
great heroic intention, acknowledging that its life may well entail little
more than a sort of "blind groping"; but its spirit is upborne by the
knowledge that at least its groping will involve a reaching out "toward
all about me," toward the earth below and the air above: in its sense of
things, in other words, Love is the unfamiliar Name behind the design
of the world, and to dedicate oneself to Love is to be blessed, even if
one's gropings achieve only "a few more aspen-leaves." Conceiving its
universe to be "damned," the Stream can think of but one happy time,
"when I rose in flood / And in my lathered flight / So fouled myself with
mud / As to be purged of sight." But the Aspen, in seeking to learn how
"to drink creation whole," appears touched by the charismata of grace.

So, when the Sublime is sought in the manner of the Stream, it will be
missed—and this is being hinted at in "The Undead," "Still, Citizen Sparrow," "Conjuration," "Merlin Enthralled," "The Juggler," "Beowulf,"
"The Beautiful Changes," and ever so many other poems. But, again, it
must be insisted upon that Wilbur's habit of reminding us that the route
toward the *mysterium tremendum* leads through the quotidian realities of
the everyday world betokens no failure on his part to recognize how fearful these realities may be. He has been declared to be comfortably un-

aware of "the devils and trolls" that indwell the commonplace, diurnal scene. But how could any reader give his suffrage to this judgment after an encounter with the title poem in the book he published in 1969, *Walking to Sleep*, which is made haunting by its horrific account of the ordinary landscape of the soul?

Like "The Mind-Reader," "Walking to Sleep" is a powerful dramatic monologue, and the conceit on which it is reared requires it to offer to the insomniac a recipe for curing sleeplessness. One's attention is immediately arrested by the opening lines:

> As a queen sits down, knowing that a chair will be there,
> Or a general raises his hand and is given the field-glasses,
> Step off assuredly into the blank of your mind.
> Something will come to you.

"Something will come to you," that is, if, as you lie sleepless on your bed, you undertake an imaginary walk. But the landscape for this promenade must be chosen carefully, lest the journey simply make you more wakeful. If, for example, your walk is to be past an old farm, let it not be too "shady-linteled," for out of its barn may come a "trotting cat whose head is but a skull." And on the road you are taking

> . . . permit no roadside thickets
> Which, as you pass, might shake with worse than wind;
> Revoke all trees and other cover; blast
> The upstart boulder which a flicking shape
> Has stepped behind; above all, put a stop
> To the known stranger up ahead, whose face
> Half turns to mark you with a creased expression.

And, if your "steady trudging" brings you to a house that you decide to enter,

> Detach some portion of your thought to guard
> The outside of the building; as you wind
> From room to room, leave nothing at your back. . . .

The speaker says:

> Your concern
> Is not to be detained by dread . . .
> But to pursue an ever-dimming course
> Of pure transition, treading as in water
> Past crumbling tufa, down cloacal halls
> Of boarded-up hotels, through attics full

Of glassy taxidermy, moping on
Like a drugged fire-inspector. What you hope for
Is that at some point of the pointless journey,
Indoors or out, and when you least expect it,
Right in the middle of your stride, like that,
So neatly that you never feel a thing,
The kind assassin Sleep will draw a bead
And blow your brains out.

And, as the insomniac walker journeys toward "the strong dream" by which he will eventually be chosen, the poem, in an intensely surrealistic idiom, sets forth much else by way of exploring the labyrinthine complexity of the human heart that, with "the claws of nightmare," murders sleep. Which is to say that the devils and trolls that pursue us are not ignored.

.

Now a further observation remains to be made about the kind of vision at work in Wilbur's poetry, and it concerns the underlying poetic controlling his work. Or, we may speak of the issue more concretely by posing the question as to the view of the proper role of the imagination that guides his poetry. And no sooner does this question begin to be raised than we feel ourselves facing something like a paradox. For, on the one hand, given the frequency with which he is inviting us to offer a kind of Amen to the things and creatures of earth because they are themselves instinct with Being, can any room at all be made within the logic of his thought for the imagination's having any metamorphic or transformative role? Does he not express by implication a commitment to a doctrine of *mimesis* so radical as to disallow any claim being made for *poiesis* as the essential act of literary art? But then, on the other hand, the poems themselves are, in all their salient particulars, the achievement of one of the great master tropists in modern poetry, whose utterance is constantly drenched in metaphor and synecdoche, in metonymy and irony. So, as the reader may ask, what, after all, is the theory of imagination that informs and controls Wilbur's whole project?

The answer to this question is not easily come by. We did, of course, remark at the outset his suggestion in the sonnet "Praise in Summer" that the sort of reconstitution of the world that poetic metaphor entails represents a betrayal of the world. But, clearly, the notion that the poetic imagination does in some sense represent a principle of error is hardly one in which the working poet can comfortably rest, and thus it is not surprising that Wilbur recurrently takes up afresh the issue as to what indeed the true mission of the imagination really is in relation to a world before whose richness and amplitude the appropriate attitude of mind is one of gratitude. It is a theme that appears to be for him as inexhaustible as it was for Stevens, and in poem after poem he tackles it from one or another angle, the whole body of his testimony having by now become so multifarious as to preclude any simple summary or schematization.

Frequently, his meditation takes an allegorical turn—in the sense, that is, of reflecting on the imagination in the terms not of poetry but of painting and sculpture. But it may be taken for granted that what he says in this connection does in the end for him bear most importantly on the poetic enterprise. One will think, for example, of "A Dutch Courtyard" and "My Father Paints the Summer" and "L'Etoile" from *The Beautiful Changes*, or of "Ceremony" and "Giacometti" from *Ceremony*, or of "A Baroque Wall-Fountain in the Villa Sciarra" from *Things of This World*, and there are various others. But, among these poems, what one will perhaps be most struck by are the concluding five stanzas of "Objects" (*The Beautiful Changes*).

Wilbur is deeply devoted to the paintings of the seventeenth-century Dutch master Pieter de Hooch, and the following lines in "Objects" record the reflections elicited in him by de Hooch's *Courtyard with Two Officers and a Woman Drinking* (in the National Gallery of Art in Washington):

> Guard and gild what's common, and forget
> Uses and prices and names; have objects speak.
>
> There's classic and there's quaint,
> And then there is that devout intransitive eye
> Of Pieter de Hooch: see feinting from his plot of paint
> The trench of light on boards, the much-mended dry
>
> Courtyard wall of brick,
> And sun submerged in beer, and streaming in glasses,
> The weave of a sleeve, the careful and undulant tile. A quick
> Change of the eye and all this calmly passes
>
> Into a day, into magic.
> For is there any end to true textures, to true
> Integuments; do they ever desist from tacit, tragic
> Fading away? Oh maculate, cracked, askew,
>
> Gay-pocked and potsherd world
> I voyage, where in every tangible tree
> I see afloat among the leaves, all calm and curled,
> The Cheshire smile which sets me fearfully free.

One feels that what Wilbur is most captivated by is the "intransitiveness" of this painter's eye. He does not seize a particular object merely for the sake of moving through it or around it to something *else:* on the contrary he invites us to gaze upon and pay heed to *this* courtyard wall, to *these* streaming glasses, to the weave of *this* sleeve, and it is the intransitiveness of his eye that makes it devout: it "guards" and "gilds." This is why, when we have departed from the museum and left this painting behind, we find that by a kind of "magic" we are newly alive to the *true* textures, to the *true* integuments, of the things wherewith our world is furnished: they do not simply fade away. Indeed, when we voyage back into the "Gay-pocked and potsherd world," "objects speak." And this may be taken to be the first thing that Wilbur wants to say about the poetic imagination, that by guarding and gilding "what's common" it gives a tongue, a voice, to the things of earth.

But, then, if the notion of guarding and gilding may be thought to be little more than a reiteration of the mimeticist doctrine of eighteenth-century English neoclassicism (in the manner, say, of Addison), we will find it very greatly radicalized in the penultimate and the final stanzas of "All These Birds" (*Things of This World*):

> Let us, with glass or gun,
> Watch (from our clever blinds) the monsters of the sky
>   Dwindle to habit, habitat, and song,
>   And tell the imagination it is wrong
>   Till, lest it be undone,
>   it spin a lie
>   So fresh, so pure, so rare
>   As to possess the air.
>
> Why should it be more shy
> Than chimney-nesting storks, or sparrows on a wall?
>   Oh, let it climb wherever it can cling
>   Like some great trumpet-vine, a natural thing
>   To which all birds that fly
>   come natural.
>   Come, stranger, sister, dove:
>   Put on the reins of love.

And the crucial passage here is, of course, that which speaks of the imagination being wrong till it shall "spin a lie / So fresh, so pure, so rare / As to possess the air." But the poem makes it clear that it is not lining itself up behind anything like Poe's Gnostic rejection of the natural order, for it bids the imagination to be like "some great trumpet-vine, a natural thing / To which all birds that fly / come natural"—constrained only by "the reins of love."

Or, again, "The Beacon," one of the great poems in *Things of This World*, is also casting a searchlight on, among other things, the nature of the imagination. "Founded on rock and facing the night-fouled sea," as one looks up at it flashing its light first on and then off, a beacon may appear to be simply blinking "at its own brilliance." But to turn one's gaze from the beacon itself to "the Gordian waters" beyond the shoreline is to realize that, in those moments when its light is on, it is indeed "making the sea-roads out . . . / . . . and the buxom, lavish / Romp of the ocean-daughters." "Then in the flashes of darkness it is all gone, / . . . and the dark of the eye / Dives for the black pearl / Of the sea-in-itself":

> Watching the blinded waves
> Compounding their eclipse, we hear their
> Booms, rumors and guttural sucks
> Warn of the pitchy whirl
>
> At the mind's end. All of the sense of the sea
> Is veiled as voices nearly heard
> In morning sleep; nor shall we wake
> At the sea's heart.

The noumenon or *Ding an sich*, "the sea-in-itself," is, of course, beyond our reach, though, could it be apprehended, it would be a metaphysical gem beyond price, a "black pearl." Amidst the pitch-black obscurity of the night, however, we can only hear the "booms" and "guttural sucks" of the waves: "All of the sense of the sea / Is veiled. . . ." But, once the beacon's light flashes on again, then it

> . . . with one grand chop gives clearance to
> Our human visions, which assume
> The waves again, fresh and the same.
> Let us assume that we
>
> See most of darkness by our plainest light.
> It is the Nereid's kick endears
> The tossing spray; a sighted ship
> Assembles all the sea.

A careful reading of these lines will lead one to feel that at some point in the poem it is difficult exactly to locate the beacon, though it does not cease to be itself, becomes also a simulacrum of the imagination, so that when, after a moment of darkness, its luminosity is restored and the poem suggests then that we "see most of darkness by our plainest light," what is being spoken of is at once the beacon's illumination of "the night-fouled sea" *and* all the various tropes and myths whereby the swirling, chaotic waters of this sea are being ordered within Wilbur's discourse. The waters are being spoken of as "Gordian" and as reflecting the "romp of the ocean-daughters"—and it is, we are told, "the Nereid's kick endears / The tossing spray." In other words, that "plainest light" through which we "see most of darkness" is the light of the imagination. Indeed, the final clause of the poem, in reminding us that "a sighted ship / Assembles all the sea," puts us in mind of Stevens's "Anecdote of the Jar," a jar that he placed amidst "the slovenly wilderness" of a desolate Tennessee landscape: "The wilderness rose up to it, / And sprawled around, no longer wild," the jar having taken "dominion everywhere"—by dint of its being a work of artifice, a work of the imagination, which, as such, substantializes a form round which the formlessness of this wilderness can assemble itself. And so it is with a ship when "sighted," when it is at once lit up by the beacon's light and grasped by the imagination: it can then assemble "all the sea." Which is to say that it belongs to the capacity of the imagination to be able to give a human form and meaning to the various recalcitrancies that are a part of the created order.

Now the kinds of reflections on the special office of the imagination that are shaping "Objects" and "All These Birds" and "The Beacon" we encounter in many of Wilbur's major poems—in "Cicadas," "In a Bird Sanctuary," and "Poplar, Sycamore" (*The Beautiful Changes*); in "Merlin Enthralled," "An Event," "Looking into History," and "Digging for China" (*Ceremony*); in "Ballade for the Duke of Orléans" and "A Hole in the Floor" (*Advice to a Prophet*); in "The Eye" (*The Mind-Reader*); and in still others too numerous to mention here. True, he speaks of the imagination as he speaks of everything else, never discursively or didactically but always indirectly and with the inflections distinctive of poetic language, so that the poems setting forth his conception of *poiesis* may at first appear to have quite a different subject. And again and again he is to be found suggesting ever so delicately that the imagination, when it is healthy and when it truly understands its real mission, will seek not any heterocosmic alternative to the world we inherit from nature and history but will seek rather to celebrate the radical holiness and the indelible beauty that indwell the things of this world, imperfect as they may be (and he is sometimes very insistent indeed on how imperfect is the world with which we must reckon).

So, in a way, Wilbur bears a certain resemblance to American poets of our period with whom it would not at first occur to us to think of him as bearing any affinity at all. For he, with his commitment to a poetry of elaborate artifice, to a poetry hospitable to dissentient ideas and countervailing images and antithetical feelings, is thought of as inseparably a part of that generation of poets—Elizabeth Bishop, the early Robert Lowell, Howard Nemerov, Anthony Hecht, William Meredith—who were initially responsive to the seventeenth-century English Metaphysicals and to the modern tradition of Hopkins, Eliot, Stevens, Tate, Ransom, and Marianne Moore. And between these people and those of their contemporaries who have been most responsive to the "open forms" and "deep images" of William Carlos Williams and Charles Olson—poets such as George Oppen, Robert Duncan, Robert Creeley, Gary Snyder, and Robert Bly—there is thought to be a very great divide indeed, as there no doubt is with respect to fundamental matters of poetic stratagem and style. Yet, in the case of Wilbur at least, we may notice in one important particular this divide being surmounted, in the degree to which he appears to be seeking a kind of metaphysical ground not unlike that at which, say, a poet like Robert Duncan aims.

Against the sort of triumphalist constructivism that was deeply a part of classically modernist poetics a poet such as Duncan, like others in his circle, wants very much to assert that poets cannot legitimately claim the right to create a world *ex nihilo*, because whatever it is that is truly worth celebration is already immanent within the primary structures of the world we face: as he says (in an essay he contributed to a volume of 1966 edited by Howard Nemerov [*Poets on Poetry*]), "Central to and defining the poetics I am trying to suggest . . . is the conviction that the order man may contrive or impose upon the things about him . . . is trivial beside the . . . natural order he may discover in them."[13] Or, again, as he says even more emphatically in the same essay, "It is not that poetry imitates, but enacts in its order the order of first things." What he clearly intends to imply is that, however much metamorphic freedom may be granted to poetic art, it may not claim the right to transmogrify reality into whatever it chooses to make of it, since the world does already sustain an order of meaning and value which we ignore at our peril.

This is, essentially, the testimony Wordsworth was making when, in his preface to the second edition of *Lyrical Ballads*, he spoke of his "deep impression of certain inherent and indestructible qualities of the human mind, and likewise of certain powers in the great and permanent objects that act upon it, which are equally inherent and indestructible. . . ." He was asserting, in other words—against the Coleridgean view of the imagination as free to impose its forms on the world and then to respond to its own inventions—that there is a fundamental coincidence between mind and nature and that the primary duty of the poetic imagination, therefore, is to respect and to venerate the antecedence of those values and meanings with which the world is primordially laden. It is no doubt an unfashionable sort of doctrine in these poststructuralist days of our misery in which we face, as it were, on every side a Kantianism gone wild. But, paradoxical as it may seem, it is such a doctrine that many "post-modernists" in American poetry like Robert Duncan have wanted to espouse.

Now it is on precisely such a metaphysical ground as this that Wilbur takes his stand. He, too, takes it for granted that the rock of reality is that with which all poetic statement must finally reckon, that the imagination must sublimate its own apprehensions before the assertiveness of "the things of this world," for they are "crammed with heaven." And it is just this posture of mind that lends a profoundly religious cast to his general testimony. It is only occasionally that he has recourse to a distinctively Christian idiom, as he does in "A World without Objects" or in "A Christmas Hymn" (*Advice to a Prophet*), but the whole emphasis of his thought might be said to be incarnationalist—in the sense that the fundamental norm of consciousness is located in a powerful Presence beyond the mind (Being-itself, as we have nominated it), which, however much it may transcend the things of nature and history, is nevertheless pervasively immanent within the ordinary and the commonplace, in that dimension of their depth that forever eludes and withstands all the conceptual nets of our devising. And thus he consistently keeps a sense of the human order as "isled" in a world that is everywhere radiant of mystery and wonder and glory, since the Ineffable is equally to be encountered in all the blessings as well as in all the defeats of our earthly pilgrimage.

·

To have in hand Wilbur's magnificent volume of 1988, *New and Collected Poems*, which brings within one big book virtually his entire accomplishment as a poet (excepting chiefly his remarkable translations of the plays of Molière and Racine), is to be able clearly to see how various and wonderful his achievement is. Although he has now entered the eighth decade of his life, the *Collected Poems* of 1988 documents a career by no means so long as that which is traversed by the *Collected Poems* of Hardy and Frost and Stevens and Warren, but it has been a career marked by a steadiness of work over more than forty years that, in its consistent brilliance, is truly extraordinary.

Usually, of course, when a poet produces a body of writing so large as Wilbur's, even when he or she is endowed with exceptional gifts, one will find areas of it that are gray and flat and without any sort of high vitality. But his *oeuvre* is singularly unmarked by such failure: it embraces, to be sure, various degrees of success, and some of his poems are far more distinguished than others, but I find none representing the kind of botch, the kind of deadness, that we may come upon here and there in the work even of many of those—one will think, say, of Stevens—who command an unquestioned lordship of the medium.

In his essay "On My Own Work" (*Responses*), Wilbur says: "My own position on poetry, if I have to have one, is that it should include every resource which can be made to work. . . . As a poet . . . I am the grateful inheritor of all that my talent can employ. . . . So far as possible, I try to play the whole instrument." And one suspects, indeed, that his determination "to play the whole instrument" is that which accounts for some of his early poems having the air of a performance. But everywhere we find cogency of thought, precision of grammar and clarity of syntax, amazing adeptness in the management of meter and rhyme, a mastery of poetic forms amounting to sheer wizardry, unbroken integrity of basic point of view, great breadth of human interest and variety of subject, a capacity for passionate yet always controlled eloquence, and a splendor of metaphor well-nigh overwhelming.

Increasingly, however, through the 1960s and 70s his speech became more personal and direct, more forthright and less elaborate, though no less rigorous and exact. As he said in a *Paris Review* interview in 1977, "When I was putting down those simple lines—lines like 'It is always a matter, my darling, of life or death, as I had forgotten'—I was excited by their very simplicity."[14] And this late simplicity and straightforwardness are particularly evident in the "New Poems" in his volume of 1988—in, for example, the beautiful text of the cantata "On Freedom's Ground" (done in collaboration with the composer William Schuman), in "The Ride," in "Leaving," in "Trolling for Blues," in "Advice from the Muse," and in various others. Among these poems the finest perhaps is the meditation in blank verse on "Lying," which begins:

> To claim, at a dead party, to have spotted a grackle,
> When in fact you haven't of late, can do no harm.
> Your reputation for saying things of interest
> Will not be marred, if you hasten to other topics,
> Nor will the delicate web of human trust
> Be ruptured by that airy fabrication.

When we thus varnish and alter and misrepresent small matters of fact—for the sake perhaps of adding some bit of spice to the masque in which we are actors "at a dead party"—it can hardly, of course, be claimed that our intentions are harmful or truly vicious: we may be simply bored, moved by "a dull / Impatience or a fierce velleity, / A champing wish, stalled by our lassitude, / To make or do." Nevertheless, "th' Apostate Angel," "in Heav'n call'd Satan," is the Prince of Lies, and small wonder

it is that he soon enters the poem whose atmosphere begins then noticeably to darken—to the point, indeed, of prompting the poem to ponder
the question as to whether poetry itself may not be a form of lying not
wholly unrelated to the casual taradiddles making up the small change
of conversation at a dead party:

> Odd that a thing is most itself when likened:
> The eye mists over, basil hints of clove,
> The river glazes toward the dam and spills
> To the drubbed rocks below its crashing cullet,
> And in the barnyard near the sawdust-pile
> Some great thing is tormented. Either it is
> A tarp torn loose and in the groaning wind
> Now puffed, now flattened, or a hip-shot beast
> Which tries again, and once again, to rise.
> What, though for pain there is no other word,
> Finds pleasure in the cruellest simile?
> It is something in us like the catbird's song. . . .

Poetry, in other words, in its commitment to *mimesis*, to "likening," to
trope, is, in a way, a sort of lying. And the pleasure the poet takes in
simile, even when it is cruel or rehearsing some cruelty, makes him something like a catbird whose song, in the manner of a mockingbird's, also
strikes us as a kind of mimicry. But it is a mimicry that, "harsh or sweet,
and of its own accord, / Proclaims its many kin," and it may therefore be
thought to be "tributary / To the great lies told with the eyes half-shut /
That have the truth in view"—as, in the examples offered, in the ancient
Greek tale of the centaur Chiron "Who . . . / Instructed brute Achilles in
the lyre," the biblical tale "of the garden where we first mislaid / Simplicity of wish and will," and the old Norman tale of Roland "who to Charles
his king / And to the dove that hatched the dove-tailed world / Was faithful unto death, and shamed the Devil." It is a poem that makes a splendid
example of the richness we face when Wilbur is at full stretch.

To attempt, however, in a single essay to review Wilbur's achievement
is inevitably to feel the chagrin occasioned by one's inability in brief compass to speak of a vast number of marvelous poems that cry out for comment and praise, and one is strongly tempted to permit oneself the in-
dulgence that Randall Jarrell did not hesitate to claim in a great essay on
Frost, of making long lists of poems he would have liked to discuss. The
temptation is so very strong that (though without approaching the
lengths to which Jarrell went) I cannot resist saying that to have ventured
to speak at all about Richard Wilbur without having spoken of "Sunlight
Is Imagination," "Water Walker," "The Giaour and the Pacha," "Light-

ness," "Caserta Garden," "Castles and Distances," "La Rose des Vents," "Juggler," "Driftwood," "A Black November Turkey," "Merlin Enthralled," "Looking into History," "An Event," "A Baroque Wall-Fountain in the Villa Sciarra," "For Dudley," "Seed Leaves," "The Eye," and "The Ride" is indeed to feel a very great chagrin. For these poems are among the many masterpieces this writer has *added* to the literature of our time. Nor has it been possible to speak of his many brilliant translations of poems by Valéry, Baudelaire, Nerval, Borges, Villon, Voznesensky, and others. But, as I have said, he is, now that Robert Penn Warren has passed from the scene, our greatest living American poet. And it makes for me more than a small amazement that this judgment has not been more regularly recorded than it has been.

CHAPTER EIGHT

The Poetry of A. R. Ammons

A definite limitation of human rationality . . . was recognized in the
West until the 17th century; in this view the intellect cannot have direct
knowledge of essences. The only created mind that has this knowledge
is the angelic mind. . . . The angelic mind suffers none of the limitations
of sense; it has immediate knowledge of essences. . . . Imagination in an
angel is thus inconceivable, for the angelic mind transcends the
mediation of both image and discourse. I call that human imagination
angelic which tries to disintegrate or to circumvent the image in the
illusory pursuit of essence.
—ALLEN TATE, "The Symbolic Imagination," in *The Forlorn Demon*

It was, however high the phrases, the common thing from which Dante
always started, as it was certainly the greatest and most common to
which he came. His images were the natural inevitable images—a girl in
the street, the people he knew, the language he learned as a child. In
them the great diagrams are perceived; from them the great myths open;
by them he understands the final end.
—CHARLES WILLIAMS, *The Figure of Beatrice*

Shall we call this the Poetic Way? It is at any rate the way of the poet,
who has got to do his work with the body of this world, whatever that
body may look like to him, in his time and place.
—ALLEN TATE, "The Symbolic Imagination"

*I*t has been a privilege over the past twenty-five years or so to watch
the steadiness with which A. R. Ammons has gradually consolidated
his position as one of the major poets of our period—such a privilege,
indeed, as one takes the people of an earlier generation to have enjoyed
as they watched the progress of a Frost or an Eliot or a Stevens or an
Auden. There may be those, however, who feel their present sense of
Ammons's distinction to be somewhat remarkable in the light of the various mannerisms and idiosyncrasies wherewith he can so much try the

patience of even his most lenient readers. At a certain point in his book-length poem of 1965, *Tape for the Turn of the Year*, he says, offhandedly, "maybe I write / too much," and so he does: the logorrhea can be released by his glancing at a weed or by his being touched by the merest breath of wind. Very little is required for his loquaciousness to be set going: as he says in the long poem "Summer Session 1968,"

> in my yard's more wordage than I
> can read:
> the jaybird gives a shit:
> the earthworm hoe-split bleeds
> against a damp black clump:
>
> the problem is
> how
> to keep shape and flow. . . .

And sometimes, as his talk profusely and aimlessly maunders along, the shape and flow not being kept, he cannot resist self-mockery—as when, for example, at a certain point in "Summer Session" he jocularly tosses off the admission "I scribble, baby, I mean / I breeze on. . . ."

Again, one is frequently brought close to utter exasperation by his penchant for clogging his discourse with the scientific jargon of the autodidact who is devoted to *Science*, as in the poem called "Mechanism," which bids us to

> honor the chemistries, platelets, hemoglobin kinetics,
> the light-sensitive iris, the enzymic intricacies
> of control
>
> the gastric transformations, seed
> dissolved to acrid liquors, synthesized into
> chirp, vitreous humor, knowledge,
>
> blood compulsion, instinct: honor the
> unique genes,
> molecules that reproduce themselves. . . .

Although he makes large room in his meditations for "the / violence, grief, guilt, / despair, absurdity" of the world, Ammons seems regularly to be a cheerful, happy poet—one for whom it is not at all out of character at the end of a poem to sign off by saying "toodleoo" (as in "Cold Didn't Keep the Stuff" [*The Snow Poems*]). So it strikes us as a little odd when he permits himself such a querulousness as he expresses when he remarks in canto 122 of his long poem *Sphere*: "I can't understand my readers: / they complain of my abstractions. . . ." But even odder than the uncharacteristic petulance is the unconsciousness it conveys of what is so much a part of his own distinctive signature, for, if there is anything for which his readers must indeed make generous allowance, it is precisely his frequent recourse to a strange kind of rough, windy rhetoric of high (too high) generality that thins out and diminishes the experiential force of his witness—as when, again and again, his tone is that of the following passage from his "Essay on Poetics":

> I am seeking the
> mechanisms physical, physiological, epistemological, electrical,
>
> chemical, esthetic, social, religious by which many, kept
> discrete as many, expresses itself into the
> manageable rafters of salience, lofts to comprehension, breaks
>
> out in hard, highly informed suasions, the "gathering
> in the sky" so to speak, the trove of mind, tested
> experience, the only place there is to stay, where the saints
>
> are known to share accord and wine, and magical humor floats
> upon the ambient sorrow: much is nearly stable there,
> residencies perpetual. . . .

Indeed, so infixed is his bias toward abstractions that on some he confers a recondite kind of tenor and prestige—terms such as "nucleation," "periphery," "curvature," "surround" (used as a noun), "salience," "node," "molecule," "suasion"—and they pop up on page after page, forming a language that simply will not linger in the mind.

Nor does one find particularly engaging his special sort of heartiness—about, say, how nice it is to "eat a pig dinner sometimes and sit / down in a deep chair that rightangles / your uplumping belly out / [and] cuts off the avenues of circulation," so that "boluses of air / form promoting gastric / distress." And the ribaldry—of which there is a good deal—never seems unforced and is never invigorating, being regularly marked by the grossness of the locker room, as in the following anecdote tacked on at the end of the poem "Poetry Is the Smallest" (*The Snow Poems*):

poet friend of mine's	still his fat wife's
dick's so short	radiant every morning:
he can't pull it long enough	he humps well, probably,
to pee straight with:	stringing her out far and
not to pee on	loose on the frail hook:
anybody by surprise	and, too, I notice she
sideways, he hunkers	follows his words

into the urinal so far   closely like one who
he looks like, to achieve,   knows what a tongue can do.
relief:

So, in approaching the massive body of work which Ammons has now produced, captiousness has much to batten on. But our great good fortune is the man's fluency, for, despite all the dross, there are, literally, dozens and dozens of poems whose splendor will make one want to shout, breathlessly (in something like the terms with which the late Delmore Schwartz greeted Ralph Ellison's novel in 1952): Reality (hear! hear!) is not mocked as long as such poems can be written.[1] And I begin by offering but one poem in evidence, "Triphammer Bridge":

> I wonder what to mean by *sanctuary*, if a real or
> apprehended place, as of a bell rung in a gold
> surround, or as of silver roads along the beaches
>
> of clouds seas don't break or black mountains
> overspill; jail: ice here's shapelier than anything,
> on the eaves massive, jawed along gorge ledges, solid
>
> in the plastic blue boat fall left water in: if I
> think the bitterest thing I can think of that seems like
> reality, slickened back, hard, shocked by rip-high wind:
>
> *sanctuary, sanctuary,* I say it over and over and the
> word's sound is the one place to dwell: that's it, just
> the sound, and the imagination of the sound—a place.

So it is that Ammons rejoices in and savors the very word "sanctuary" and finds the meaning of the word in "the / word's sound," in "just / the sound, and the imagination of the sound"—a kind of "jail," yes, for it shuts out and shelters us against the bitterer shocks of rain and "rip-high wind," yet a place like "a bell rung in a gold / surround," indeed "the one place to dwell," this place that we are granted by the munificence of nothing other than the imagination itself. Before a poem such as this, which talks not about itself but about its subject and which refuses to say all that it means, yet presenting an absolutely perfect transparency—before such a poem criticism must simply be struck dumb, for it can do nothing but admire the mastery with which the parts of the whole have been selected and so joined together that the whole seems not to have any parts at all. And it is with this kind of mastery that we are confronted throughout large tracts of Ammons's poetry.

Harold Bloom and various others have insisted on the necessity of our regarding Ammons as standing in a line of descent that leads directly back to the great original avatars of American Romanticism, Emerson and Whitman—and so he does. Which is perhaps to say that, beyond all else, he is a poet of the sublime. For the most fundamental premise of all his principal meditations is that the sheer ontological weight and depth of the world are such as to invest all the finite things of earth with an incalculable complexity and inexhaustibility, so much so indeed that really to savor the full-fledged otherness of the immediate givens of experience is to find them testifying to their own finitude by their silent allusions to a transfinite dimension within themselves.

The English philosopher G. E. Moore was greatly charmed by the old saying of Bishop Butler's to the effect that "everything is what it is and not another thing"—so charmed indeed that Moore found in this proposition the central motto of his own philosophy. But for Ammons— for the poet who says that "if a squash blossom dies, I feel withered as a stained / zucchini and blame my nature"—such a proposition must seem only a kind of stupid claptrap, because he knows (like Theodore Roethke) that to perform an act of true attention before a worm or a vine or a blade of grass is in turn to know that not even the humblest creature of earth can be platitudinized into being merely what it is rather than another thing. Indeed, he is a poet who convinces us that he believes that, through indolence of spirit, to refuse to be radically amazed by that surplusage of meaning that may be found in a garden slug or a spider weaving its web is to reduce the world to a sort of lackluster slum.

The seventeenth-century Chinese treatise on the art of painting *The Mustard Seed Garden Manual* suggests (as has been noted earlier) that a painter, if picturing a man in the presence of a mountain, should render the man as slightly bent in an attitude of reverent homage to the majesty of the mountain, just as the mountain should be made to appear as if it, too, is saluting its visitor. Or, if a lutist is being pictured beneath the moon, he, as he plucks his instrument, should seem to be listening to the moon, and the moon should appear to be listening to his music. And, Emersonian that he is, Ammons would, I suspect, be quick to approve of such instructions, for, like the sage of Concord, he, too, considers the world to be an affair of reciprocities and affinities and profound "correspondences" between matter and spirit. Which is to say that, in his sense of things, we dwell in a universe that requires us to be in commerce with that which transcends the human, with that which Longinus called the Sublime. True, given the evidence presented by his poetry, it would appear that, at least for Ammons qua poet, the traditional apparatus of the Sublime, the apparatus of the Christian mythos, represents a structure of thought to which he is generally disinclined to have recourse. Yet the whole drift of his poetic arguments clearly reveals it to be his intention to make such a testimony as Wordsworth voices in "Tintern Abbey":

> . . . I have felt
> A presence that disturbs me with the joy
> Of elevated thoughts; a sense sublime
> Of something far more deeply interfused,
> Whose dwelling is the light of setting suns,
> And the round ocean and the living air,
> And the blue sky, and in the mind of man:
> A motion and a spirit, that impels
> All thinking things, all objects of all thought,
> And rolls through all things.

Here, for example, in the great poem "The City Limits" is one of Ammons's purest and most beautiful accounts of the Glory that indwells the world:

> When you consider the radiance, that it does not withhold
> itself but pours its abundance without selection into every
> nook and cranny not overhung or hidden; when you consider
>
> that birds' bones make no awful noise against the light but
> lie low in the light as in a high testimony; when you consider
> the radiance, that it will look into the guiltiest
>
> swervings of the weaving heart and bear itself upon them,
> not flinching into disguise or darkening; when you consider
> the abundance of such resource as illuminates the glow-blue
>
> bodies and gold-skeined wings of flies swarming the dumped
> guts of a natural slaughter or the coil of shit and in no
> way winces from its storms of generosity; when you consider
>
> that air of vacuum, snow or shale, squid or wolf, rose or lichen
> each is accepted into as much light as it will take, then
> the heart moves roomier, the man stands and looks about, the
>
> leaf does not increase itself above the grass, and the dark
> work of the deepest cells is of a tune with May bushes
> and fear lit by the breadth of such calmly turns to praise.

This light, this radiance, that "does not withhold / itself" is what Wallace Stevens (in "Notes toward a Supreme Fiction") calls the "candor" in things, that munificence which leads them to unveil themselves, so that they may be shown forth as what they most essentially are. Or, another equivalent is what Hopkins (in "God's Grandeur") speaks of as "the dearest freshness deep down things"—which is that informing *élan* or power that enables all things to be what their inner entelechies intend them to be. This freshness, this candor, this radiance, is something temperate and gentle: though it "pours its abundance" everywhere, it does not by force invade that which is "overhung or hidden" or which chooses to refuse it. Nor can one see it as one sees a rose or a gazelle: it is not *here* or *there*, because it is, as Stevens says, the "insolid billowing of the solid" ("Reality Is an Activity of the Most August Imagination," *Opus Posthumous*), that ontological energy wherewith "the glow-blue / bodies and gold-skeined wings of flies" are given their special kind of presence. "When you consider the radiance," when it is truly considered—*then*, "then / the heart moves roomier," and fear is turned to praise. So if, when you look at violets, you consider the radiance, you do not then dismiss them with a shrug, saying that they are simply what they are and not another thing: instead, you exclaim (with Walter Savage Landor): "Good God, the violets!" Which is a response elicited by some obscure recognition that the violets are an outward and visible sign of an inward and spiritual grace.

True, the radiance is *within* the violets, or they are "accepted into" it. But, then, as Emerson, Ammons's great master, says in volume 3 of his *Journals*, "Blessed is the day when the youth discovers that Within and Above are synonyms." And, indeed, Ammons's poetry frequently envisages the numinous and the sublime as Above. Yet he is constantly expressing his discomfort with and his mistrust of great heights. The Emerson of *Nature* is convinced that, when one is high and lifted up, "all mean egotism vanishes": in the loftiest and most exalted regions, he says, "I become a transparent eyeball; I am nothing; I see all; the currents of the Universal Being circulate through me." But the quite different testimony made by Ammons's fine early poem "Hymn" strikes a note that one hears again and again in "The Unmirroring Peak," in "Choice" and "Kind" and "High and Low" and "Convergence" and "Offset" and countless other poems. He says in "Hymn":

> I know if I find you I will have to leave the earth
> and go on out
>   over the sea marshes and the brant in bays
> and over the hills of tall hickory
> and over the crater lakes and canyons
> and on up through the spheres of diminishing air
> past the blackset noctilucent clouds
>   where one wants to stop and look

way past all the light diffusions and bombardments
up farther than the loss of sight
  into the unseasonal undifferentiated empty stark

And I know if I find you I will have to stay with the earth
inspecting with thin tools and ground eyes
trusting the microvilli sporangia and simplest
  coelenterates
and praying for a nerve cell
with all the soul of my chemical reactions
and going right on down where the eye sees only traces

You are everywhere partial and entire
You are on the inside of everything and on the outside

I walk down the path down the hill where the sweetgum
has begun to ooze spring sap at the cut
and I see how the bark cracks and winds like no other bark
chasmal to my ant-soul running up and down
and if I find you I must go out deep into your
  far resolutions
and if I find you I must stay here with the separate leaves.

The "you" being addressed in the "Hymn" is the ultimate source of all the plenitude with which the world is furnished: it is Being itself, the aboriginal reality from which everything else springs, what Stevens speaks of in "Notes toward a Supreme Fiction" as "the whole, / The Complicate, the amassing harmony." And Ammons's choice of an anthropomorphic idiom for his salute to this aboriginal reality is merely a conceit. He knows, of course, that a conventional wisdom says that, in order to find it, one "will have to leave the earth / and go on out" beyond the earth. Yet he finds himself most deeply nourished by the natural order of common things, by "the sea marshes" and "the hills of tall hickory" and the sweetgum when it begins "to ooze spring sap at the cut." He does not want to be any sort of aviator or angel, flying off into the "diminishing air" of the world beyond, for, amidst that "unseasonal undifferentiated empty stark," he fears that there is nothing to be beheld but a kind of blind glitter of nothingness. He does not, in other words, propose to take the Absolute by direct assault, believing as he does that, as a poet, he (as Allen Tate puts it) "has got to do his work with the body of this world." As he says, "I know if I find you I will have to stay with the earth," and he has no intention of searching after the eternity of Platonic heavens, since he suspects that such heavens will be found to be merely what he speaks of in the poem "Convergence" as "the peak of /

illusion's pyramid." So his is the vigilance of a man on whom the things of this world are pressing all the time, and he believes that it is in them that (as Charles Williams says) "the great diagrams are [to be] perceived; [that] from them the great myths open." Whether or not he knows it, Ammons's patron saint (as with Richard Wilbur) is not Dionysus the Areopagite but St. Athanasius, for, in his dealings with the things of earth, his Way is not the Way of Rejection but rather the Way of Affirmation.

In its reflections on the relation of the Sublime to the mundane order Ammons's poetry resorts, however, far more frequently to the polarity between the One and the Many or between unity and multiplicity than it does to the polarity between the heights and the lowlands of the world. But his mistrust of any sort of mystical angelism is in no way altered by the change in figure. The poem "Early Morning in Early April" (*Briefings,* 1971) pictures, for example, a landscape overhung with a rainy mist that has "hung baubles" on the trees, underlacing the maple branches "with glaring beadwork," and the poem says:

> . . . what to make of it:
> what to make of a mist whose characteristic
>
> is a fine manyness coming dull in a wide
> oneness: what to make of the glass
> erasures, glass: the yew's partly lost.

The unstated assumption is that the diversity, the variety, the multifariousness, belonging to all the concrete particularities with which our world is furnished offers the human spirit an essential kind of delight and nourishment—whereas the staircase leading to unity takes us (as the poem "Staking Claim" says)

> all the way to the final vacant core
> that brings
> things together and turns them away
>
> all the way
> to stirless bliss!

And *Tape for the Turn of the Year* registers an even more emphatic reprobation of unity: it says (in the entry for 9 December):

> . . . we can approach
> unity only by the loss
> of things—
> a loss we're unwilling

> to take—
> since the gain of unity
>   would be a vision
> of something in the
> continuum of nothingness:
> we already have things:
>   why fool around:
>   beer, milk,
> mushroom cream sauce,
> eggs, books, bags,
> telephones & rugs:
>   pleasure to perceive
> correspondences, facts
> that experience is
> holding together, that
> what mind grew out of
> is also holding together:
> otherwise? how could we
> perceive similarities?
>   but all
> the way to unity is
> too far off . . .

Sometimes (as in "Left," the penultimate piece in the *Collected Poems*) the image of the "center" connotes the same range of meaning over which the notion of "unity" presides, as the image of "periphery" replaces that of "multiplicity." And this lexicon of height and unity and center makes a strangely cryptic language, but one that, for all its enigmaticalness, intends to warn us away from that black mysticism or magical gnosis which seeks some kind of unmediated contact with the Sublime. We are not angels, and, as Ammons often wants to remind us, the path, the narrow and direct path, that we must take into felicity and wisdom is one that leads *through* the immediate, concrete, finite things of this world in which the Sublime is incarnate. As he says in canto 86 of his extraordinary long poem "Hibernaculum,"

> the sum of everything's nothing: very nice: that
> turns the world back in on itself: such as right
> when you possess everything, you'd give everything
>
> up for a sickle pear: I hope my philosophy will turn
> out all right and turn out to be a philosophy so as
> to free people (any who are trapped, as I have been)

from seeking any image in the absolute or seeking
any absolute whatsoever. . . .

In short, what we confront is (as Jean Cocteau once phrased it) *le mystère laic*, the "lay mystery" or the secular mystery of Transcendence within Immanence.

Ammons's profound reverence for this secular mystery is expressed in a vast number of his poems, and it forms one of the principal strands of his work. Here, for example, is the testimony he makes in the opening part of the beautiful poem entitled simply "Still":

> I said I will find what is lowly
> and put the roots of my identity
> down there:
> each day I'll wake up
> and find the lowly nearby,
> a handy focus and reminder,
> a ready measure of my significance,
> the voice by which I would be heard,
> the wills, the kinds of selfishness
> I could
> freely adopt as my own:
>
> but though I have looked everywhere,
> I can find nothing
> to give myself to:
> everything is
>
> magnificent with existence, is in
> surfeit of glory:
> nothing is diminished,
> nothing has been diminished for me. . . .

This devotion to what is "lowly," to the "lovely diminutives" of the world (as Roethke called them—snails and weeds and cockroaches), this sense of "everything" as "in surfeit of glory," as "magnificent with existence"— it is precisely this that attests to Ammons's fidelity to a vision such as Blake's that wants to declare that there is nothing so paltry, so inglorious, as not to be indwelt by holiness and capable of being a means of grace— not even wind-swept grasses and "dry-burnt moss": "nothing is diminished, / nothing has been diminished for me."

So it is (as the poet and critic Richard Howard has suggested) a "littoral" range through which Ammons's poetry moves: he gives his allegiance to the coastal regions of the world. As Melville's *Moby Dick* reminds us, the sea is "the region of the strange Untried": it is "the immense Remote, the Wild, the Watery, the Unshored." And he who seeks a complete and final vision of reality, who desires a direct and un-mediated encounter with the Sublime, will risk what Melville calls "ocean-perishing," amidst "the heartless voids and immensities" of the Unshored. But, regarding as misguided all schemes for scorning or smashing the quotidian in the illusory quest of some immediate contact with the *Mysterium Tremendum* (since they yield only "the unseasonal un-differentiated empty stark"), and with his sharp sense—as he says in the long poem "Extremes and Moderations"—that "the / lofted's precari-ous," Ammons conceives the only possibility for commerce with the Transcendent to be by way of its incarnateness within Immanence. So he elects not "the region of the strange Untried" but, as he indicates in his relatively early (1965) and most famous deliverance, "Corsons Inlet," the shoreline, an inlet into "the immense Remote." As he says in this re-markable poem, "Overall is beyond me: is the sum of these events / I cannot draw, the ledger I cannot keep, the accounting beyond the ac-count."

What needs, then, to be recognized, if Ammons's poetry is to be deeply taken hold of, is that the metaphysical vision constantly at work in this poetry is one whose controlling idea is that of analogy. The clas-sical exponents of the analogical method of predication—whereby no-tions derived from what is already known are made applicable to that which is relatively unknown in virtue of some similarity between the two otherwise dissimilar "analogues"—are, of course, figures such as Alber-tus Magnus and Aquinas and Cajetan and Suarez. But, without plunging into the thickets of their speculations, we may simply say that the meta-physical principle of analogy asserts a kind of co-inherence between *es-sentia* and *esse*: it asserts, as it were, that Reality is *in* things and yet also *beyond* them, that God is at once like and unlike his creation. Between Him and His creatures there is an analogy of *being (analogia entis):* which is to say that the transient existence belonging to the creature may be a significant image or reflection of the being of God. Yet the doctrine of the *analogia entis* also posits a certain *via negationis*, since, by reason of the incommensurability between God and all things belonging to the crea-turely order, it intends to "negate" in the divine Cause all the finite and imperfect properties that belong to the effect. In short, though we may behold God not in His naked glory but only in and through the world of His creation, the *ordo creationis* does itself afford but a limited kind of vision: we only "know in part," for, as St. Paul says, "now we see through a glass, darkly." But, even if seeing darkly, what we see may not be dismissed as merely illusory, given the *analogia entis ad Deum et crea-turam.*

It is such a structure of thought that is over and again to be found shaping Ammons's poetic utterance, and nowhere more emphatically than in one of the central poems of his career, the extraordinary title poem of *Expressions of Sea Level* (1963). The place at which the meditation it records occurs is a littoral place: it is the shoreline, the land's edge, from which he looks out toward the ocean, the region of the Wholly Other, of the Numinous, of the *Mysterium Tremendum*—toward that which "is hard to name." And because "there is no way to know / the ocean's speech," the poem fixes its attention on the way "the ocean / marks itself / against the gauging land / it erodes and / builds." Since "the sea speaks far from its core, / far from its center," Ammons turns for "expressions" and "hints" of what is purported by the Deep to "broken, surf things," and he notices the evidence they give to "keen watchers on the shore" of how they have been touched by the sea and of how high its tides have risen. He says:

> how do you know the moon
> is moving: see the dry
> casting of the beach worm
>   dissolve at the
> delicate rising touch:
>
> that is the
>   expression of sea level.
> the talk of giants,
> of ocean, moon, sun, of everything,
> spoken in a dampened grain of sand.

Since the ocean's speech is "speech without words," since it is "only in the meeting of rock and sea . . . [that] / hard relevance [is] shattered into light," for "a / statement perfect in its speech" one must turn to the things of earth, to littoral things, for signs or "expressions of sea level": one must turn to the "tide-held slant of grasses," to "the / skin of back, bay-eddy reeds." As he says in "Identity," another of the poems in *Expressions of Sea Level,*

> I will show you
> the underlying that takes no image to itself,
>   cannot be shown or said,
> but weaves in and out of moons and bladderweeds,
>   is all and

> beyond destruction
> because created fully in no
> particular form. . . .

So, given the radical otherness of that which is most truly foundational or ultimate and given the necessity of its being caught, as it were, on the wing, it is not surprising that Ammons should be obsessively preoccupied with "saliences." The term has talismanic status in his lexicon, and the frequency of its recurrence belongs to his distinctive stylistic signature. He is always searching for whatever may be descried as protuberant, conspicuous, noteworthy instances of "statement" that disclose something of Ultimacy. "Consistencies," he says in the poem "Saliences,"

> . . . rise;
> and ride
> the mind down
> hard routes
> walled
> with no outlet and so
> to open a variable geography
> proliferate
> possibility. . . .

And he is on the lookout for

> fields of order in disorder,
> where choice
> can make beginnings,
> turns,
> reversals. . . .

It is the saliences, he says, that "spread firmingly across my sight" and that give him "summations of permanence."

In many of the remarkable books which Martin Heidegger was issuing in the 1940s and 50s—in *Erläuterungen zu Hölderlins Dichtung*, in *Über den Humanismus*, in *Holzwege*, and in various others—he was deeply brooding on how "withdrawn" and "distant" and "hidden" Being is, distant because it is never to be encountered nakedly and in itself but only in and through the things of earth which it "assembles" and supports. Yet at the same time, with an equal intensity, Heidegger was also meditating on how Being, as he liked to say, "hails" us, this hailing an affair of nothing other than the generosity with which Being permits the things of earth to "come-to-presence." And, were Ammons familiar with Heidegger's late phase, one would expect him to feel prompted to salute this difficult German thinker as one offering a powerful confirmation of his own basic sense of reality, for it is precisely such a dialectic as Heidegger's between absence and presence that most centrally organizes much of Ammons's poetry. For him, too, "the underlying that takes no image to itself, / cannot be shown or said": for him, too, it is hidden and distant. Nevertheless, his poetry is frequently breaking into the language of doxology (as in the poem "Cut the Grass," which gratefully marvels at "the wonderful workings of the world"), for, after all, there are saliences: there are epiphanies, there are revelations *enough* to make us feel bidden to "consider the radiance." So the poet of "This Bright Day" is, indeed, a happy poet:

> Earth, earth!
> day, this bright day
> again—once more
> showers of dry spruce gold,
> the poppy flopped broad open and delicate
> from its pod—once more,
> all this again: I've had many
> days here with these stones and leaves:
> like the sky, I've taken on a color
> and am still:
> the grief of leaves,
> summer worms, huge blackant
> queens bulging
> from weatherboarding, all that
> will pass
> away from me that I will pass into,
> none of the grief
> cuts less now than ever—only I
> have learned the
> sky, the day sky, the blue
> obliteration of radiance. . . .

The disclosures that come by way of "saliences" never carry such finality, though, as to permit us in any rigid way to schematize the world at hand, and for Ammons nothing is more iniquitous than the mind's arrogant reification of its own designs of reality. In the strange language he employs, the term "line" stands for the abstraction that wants to bring the world to heel by substantializing itself, and the passionate rejection of any and all forms of hypostasis that "Corsons Inlet" expresses strikes a note that is to be heard over and again throughout Ammons's poetry:

> I went for a walk over the dunes again this morning . . .

> the walk liberating, I was released from forms,
> from the perpendiculars,
>   straight lines, blocks, boxes, binds
> of thought
> into the hues, shadings, rises, flowing bends and blends
>   of sight:

>   I allow myself eddies of meaning:
> yield to a direction of significance
> running
> like a stream through the geography of my work:
>   you can find
> in my sayings
>   swerves of action
>   like the inlet's cutting edge . . .

> in nature there are few sharp lines: there are areas of
> primrose
>   more or less dispersed;
> disorderly orders of bayberry; between the rows
> of dunes,
> irregular swamps of reeds,
> though not reeds alone, but grass, bayberry, yarrow, all . . .
> predominantly reeds:

> I have reached no conclusions, have erected no boundaries
> shutting out and shutting in, separating inside
>   from outside: I have
>   drawn no lines. . . .

Ammons wants us, in short, as he says in *Tape for the Turn of the Year* (in the entry for 7 January), to "get out of boxes, hard / forms of mind: / go deep: / penetrate / to the true spring."

Indeed, so fearful is he of intoxication with false closures and reified postulations that in one of his early poems, "This Black Rich Country," he prays: "Dispossess me of belief: / between life and me obtrude / no symbolic forms." His assumption is that the world with which we must reckon is so mobile, so dynamic, so restless, that in the degree to which we are overly charmed by the Idea, by the mind's fabulations, we may well be to that extent rendered incompetent at coping "with this / world as it is." So he wonders in *Tape for the Turn of the Year* (in the entry for 10 January) if "our minds [have] taken us too / far, out of nature, out of / complete acceptance," and he suggests (in the entry for 9 December) that

> those who rely on any shore
> foolishly haven't faced
> it that
> only the stream is reliable:

It is his sense of the restless transiency in things that prompts him to think of the wind as his "guide," his tutor, and that leads him in scores and scores of his poems to make gales and tempests the prime movers in the drama of life. In no other body of lyric poetry in the English language is the landscape so abidingly windswept: sometimes the winds are hard and steady, and sometimes they are soft and gentle, but the air is constantly astir—and Ammons keeps it so, because the wind overruns and brushes aside "lines" and fences and boundaries, taking everything (as he says in "Saliences") "out of calculation's reach." The wind reminds us (says the poem "Guide") that "you have to . . . break / off from *is* to *flowing*": as it scuds across the terrains we occupy, sweeping in its wake whatever it comes upon, it makes us know how utterly provisional every moment is and how specious therefore all our reified concepts and intellections are. Indeed, Ammons as poet finds himself required to acknowledge that not even language may be reified: as he says in the poem "Motion,"

> The word is
> not the thing:
> is
> a construction of,
> a tag for,
> the thing: the
> word in
> no way
> resembles
> the thing, except
> as sound
> resembles,
> as in *whirr*,
> sound:
> the relation

> between what this
> as words
> is
> and what is
> is tenuous: we
> agree upon
> this as the net to
> cast on what
> is: the finger
> to
> point with: the
> method of
> distinguishing,
> defining, limiting. . . .

And thus poems themselves

> are fingers, methods,
> nets,
> not what is or was:
> but the music
> in poems
> is different,
> points to nothing,
> traps no
> realities, takes
> no game, but
> by the motion of
> its motion
> resembles
> what, moving, is—
> the wind
> underleaf white against
> the tree.

The fine simplicity of this statement about the kind of simulacrum of reality that the poem may proffer wants to be completed only by the great passage in "Hibernaculum" which speaks of that wherein the poetic word finds its best nourishment:

> if the night is to be
> habitable, if dawn is to come out of it, if day is ever
> to grow brilliant on delivered populations, the word

must have its way by the brook, lie out cold all night
along the snow limb, spell by yearning's wilted reed till
the wilted reed rises, know the patience and smallness

of stones. . . .

It is just his great success in *Tape for the Turn of the Year* in getting "out
of boxes, hard / forms of mind," in breaking "off from *is* to *flowing*," that
makes this poem of more than two hundred pages so exemplary a case
of Ammons's art and one of his more impressive accomplishments in the
medium of the long poem. It originated during the closing weeks of 1963
in a curious kind of stunt. Eight years earlier his first book, *Ommateum*,
had been published by an obscure vanity press in Philadelphia and had
been generally ignored—but the brilliant second book, *Expressions of Sea
Level*, was to be published by the Ohio State University Press in 1964. He
is, of course, today the Goldwin Smith Professor of Poetry at Cornell
University, but at the end of 1963 he was without academic honors or
preferments of any other sort. True, he had at that point recently appeared at Cornell to present a reading of his poems—the result of which,
as it seemed, might be the offer of some kind of tenuous teaching appointment. And, as the year drew to a close and as he (in the rural flat-
lands of New Jersey near Philadelphia) awaited at once the delivery of
his copies of the new book and some word about his prospect at Cornell,
it occurred to him one day to purchase a roll of adding-machine tape and
to run the entire tape through his typewriter by way of producing a
"long / thin / poem," a skinny poem "plain as / day, exact and bright!"
The poem took the form of a diary, with entries extending from 6 December 1963 through the tenth day of the following January. And it is a
great bucket that catches everything his days bring: the smells of his
wife's cooking, what "the checker at / the A & P said," weather forecasts
heard on his radio, shopping in Philadelphia at Wanamaker's, the dis-
mantling of the Christmas tree, his attempts at throwing off a bad cold,
what he and his wife have for dinner of a certain evening over at "Som-
pers Point / at Mac's" (fried shrimp for himself and crab for her)—all this
being accompanied by such asides as "just went to take a leak" and "(I
had / lunch after / 'who cannot love')." And he offers frequent interstitial
reports on the progress of his writing, as the tape slowly winds down
from his typewriter into the wastebasket over the five weeks that this
"serious novelty" is being composed. The poem is simply drenched in
the reality of the quotidian: its language is that of one who has given
himself up to the world and who has no regrets about his surrender. Yet,
for all the commitment to "the ordinary universe," Ammons in no way

relinquishes here his contemplative vocation, and, as day follows day, he is constantly engaged in a labor of reflection on how all the good things each day brings may "be managed, / received and loved / in their passing." Indeed, in his grateful acceptance of the *claritas*, the radiance, that belongs to the quiddities and haecceities of the world, he puts us in mind of the Williams of *Paterson*, especially when he (in the entry for 23 December) recites his Morning Office:

> release us from mental
> prisons into the actual
> fact, the mere
> occurrence—the touched,
> tasted, heard, seen:
> in the simple event is
> the scope of life:
> let's not make up
> categories to toss ourselves
> around with:
> look: it's snowing:
> without theory
> & beyond help:
> I accept:
> I can react with
> restlessness & quiet
> terror, or with
> fascination &
> delight: I choose the
> side of possibility.

In the entry in *Tape for the Turn of the Year* for 31 December Ammons says: "after this, / this long poem, I hope I / can do short rich hard / lyrics: lines / that   can   incubate / slowly / then   fall   into / symmetrical tangles." And, indeed, the books that followed—*Northfield Poems* (1966), the *Selected Poems* (1968), *Uplands* (1970), and *Briefings: Poems Small and Easy* (1971)—presented a large and brilliant achievement in this mode: one will think of "Reflective," "One:Many," "Saliences," "Peak," "Sphere," "Upland," "Periphery," "Cascadilla Falls," "This Black Rich Country," "This Bright Day," "He Held Radical Light," "Early Morning in Early April," and a vast number of other poems as exemplifying the kind of mastery that Ammons was regularly demonstrating in his work of the late 60s and early 70s. But already in the *Tape* and in "Summer Session 1968" (in *Uplands*) he had shown that, despite his respect for the short, hard lyric, he had the sort of sensibility that liked the chance for expatiation, for the leisurely exploration of a large theme; and this penchant he submitted to again and again in the mid- and late-70s, for it was during this period that he issued a major series of long poems—the book-length poem, *Sphere: The Form of a Motion* (1974), the cycle of *The Snow Poems* (1977), and those that were collected in the *Selected Longer Poems* of 1980 ("Pray without Ceasing," "Essay on Poetics," "Extremes and Moderations," "Hibernaculum," and, again, "Summer Session").

These big poems disclose, of course, the extraordinary *ambitiousness* by which Ammons's career has been driven, and there are those, on the one hand, who have a great enthusiasm for them and those, on the other, who regard them as merely facile and as evidencing no capacity for the kind of systematic "argument" that the long poem needs to sustain. Toward the end of "Hibernaculum" he says of his own poetic procedures:

> if there is to be
> no principle of inclusion, then, at least, there ought
>
> to be a principle of exclusion, for to go with a maw at
> the world as if to chew it up and spit
> it out again as one's own is to trifle with terrible
>
> affairs. . . .

But, if there is any principle of exclusion operative in the long poems that followed *Tape for the Turn of the Year*, it has the effect only of shutting *people* out, the whole realm of transaction with the neighbor, with (as it might be said in Ammons's slang) "the human surround." Everywhere we hear only of I, I, I—"I went to the summit and stood in the high nakedness"; "I find I am able to say / only what is in my head"; "I really do not want to convince anyone of anything"; "still I am not high on the bestseller lists, the Wonderful / Award is gradually being given to someone else." Hardly at all do these poems admit into themselves the concrete, palpable circumstantiality of our human togetherness. Indeed, "Hibernaculum" breezily acknowledges (in canto 109) that, "if the population of the earth is four billion people, / then [it has excluded] nearly four billion people." But the poems are open to whatever else happens to cross Ammons's mind. "I don't want shape," he says in *Sphere*; and he speaks there also of being "sick of good poems, all those little rondures / splendidly brought off, painted gourds on a shelf." Which is an aversion that most assuredly appears to be controlling poems such as the "Essay on Poetics" and "Extremes and Moderations" and "Pray without Ceasing," and they have not, therefore, despite their numerous local felicities, succeeded in claiming the sympathy of many readers who have found their shapelessness to be alienating.

Ammons is clearly committed to a radically open kind of form in these long poems. Already by the mid-60s the colon had become a special hallmark of his compositional method, for he had chosen consistently to use it instead of the period for a full stop. And, when the colon is separating two independent clauses, its function is nowhere more exactly defined than in Fowler's *Dictionary of Modern English Usage*, where it is said to be "that of delivering [in the clause that follows the colon] the goods that have been invoiced in the preceding words." The grammatical function of the colon is that of propelling us forward, of inducing advance, of generating movement, *motion*. Indeed, in poem after poem ("What This Mode of Motion Said," "Motion for Motion," "Four Motions for the Pea Vines," "Two Motions") Ammons is meditating on motion, and we have already noticed his saying in the poem "Motion" that "by the motion of /its motion / [the music / in poems] resembles / what, moving, is." In other words, in his sense of things reality is not primarily an affair of neatly contoured forms: on the contrary, it *is* effluence, something flexuous and cursive. And thus the poem (as he says in "The Swan Ritual") needs to be "a going concern . . . beyond all binds and terminals," not something neatly shaped like a painted gourd on a shelf but something (as "Corsons Inlet" puts it) "willing to go along, to accept / the becoming / thought, to stake off no beginnings or ends, establish / no walls. . . ." So he aims in his long poems at such an inclusiveness and such a variety as will in some measure be commensurate with the breadth and heterogeneousness of a world without circumference.

Yet, despite the indeterminate, inorganic kind of form that these poems embrace, a certain consistency is observable in the relentlessness with which he holds fast to a few governing preoccupations. He is, for example, in the "Essay on Poetics" and in "Extremes and Moderations" brooding as always on the nature of the poetic enterprise. Or, again, for all its *disjecta membra*, "Pray without Ceasing" appears to be an uncharacteristically melancholy rumination on "terror, pity, grief, death," on the "falling back and away / of time-sunk persons and places." "Hibernaculum," on the other hand, is quintessentially an Ammons poem, in its beautiful reiterations of the kind of reverence for the vast alterity and magnificence of the created universe that so much of the poetry expresses. And *Sphere* brilliantly and movingly rehearses another theme that is deeply a part of Ammons's thought, that "the categorizing mind" must so "come to know / the works of the Most High as to assent to them" and to "celebrate Him and offer Him not our / flight but our cor diality and gratitude":

> if we are small
> can we be great by going away from the Most High into our own
> makings, thus despising what He has given: or can we, accepting
>
> our smallness, bend to cherish the greatness that rolls through
> our sharp days, that spends us on its measureless currents: and
> so, for a moment, if only for a moment, participate in those means
>
> that provide the brief bloom in the eternal presence: is this
> our saving: is this our perishable thought that imperishably
> bears us through the final loss: then sufficient thanks for that:

True, these long poems of Ammons's middle period are, in their pro-
lixity and diffuseness, sometimes flawed, and some of his readers have,
therefore, accorded them a very imperfect sympathy. But they are all
filled with his special kind of eloquence, and they all belong to what he
speaks of in *Sphere* (in canto 16) as that "anthology [which] is the moving,
changing definition of the / imaginative life of the people" of our time.

In his more recent work, however—in the poems collected in *A Coast
of Trees* (1981), *Worldly Hopes* (1982), and *Lake Effect Country* (1983)—he has
returned to the short, hard lyric, and the song is simply stunning in its
purity and grace. In the "Essay on Poetics," at a certain point he playfully
turns inside-out and upside-down William Carlos Williams's notion that
there are "no ideas but in things," inviting us to consider various alter-
natives—"'no things but in ideas,' / 'no ideas but in ideas,' and 'no
things but in things.'" Yet in the same poem he avows, very much in the
accent of Williams, "I think what I see." And, indeed, in his late work he
wants to put aside all "engines of declaration" and to do nothing other
than present what he beholds: he wants to "turn / to the cleared particular" and to elicit in us the realization (as he says in the title poem in *A
Coast of Trees*) "that whatever it is it is in the Way and / the Way in it, as
in us, emptied full."

Nor can one fail to be reminded by the drift of Ammons's testimony in
the poems of the 80s of how deeply religious his basic sensibility is. Midway through the "Essay on Poetics" he says, "I am just going to take it
for granted / that the tree is in the backyard: / it's necessary to be quiet
in the hands of the marvelous." And it is in an attitude of such admiring
gratitude and veneration that he faces the manifold things of this
world—which, as he says ("Vehicle," *A Coast of Trees*), "praise themselves
seen in / my praising sight." Moreover, when he suggests that a spruce
bough in winter and a running brook and a squirrel bunching branches
"praise themselves seen in / my praising sight," he intends to be taken

not as merely turning a phrase but as speaking in full seriousness—which is surely made evident in the great poem "Singing & Doubling Together" (in *Lake Effect Country*):

My nature singing in me is your nature singing:
you have means to veer down, filter through,
and, coming in,
harden into vines that break back with leaves,
so that when the wind stirs
I know you are there and I hear you in leafspeech,

though of course back into your heightenings I
can never follow: you are there beyond
tracings flesh can take,
and farther away surrounding and informing the systems,
you are as if nothing, and
where you are least knowable I celebrate you most

or here most when near dusk the pheasant squawks and
lofts at a sharp angle to the roost cedar,
I catch in the angle of that ascent,
in the justness of that event your pheasant nature,
and when dusk settles, the bushes creak and
snap in their natures with your creaking

and snapping nature . . .

even you risked all the way into the taking on of shape
and time. . . .

The poem wants to say that the coruscations of glory borne by leaf-speech and pheasant-flight and bush-snappings are nothing other than the blaze of the Sublime that, to be sure, is "beyond / tracings flesh can take" but that, by virtue of its immanence within all the things of earth, yet permits them to *come-to-presence*, finding its tongue in the poet's song (which becomes *our* song in those moments when we are most truly human). In short, the "you" being addressed in "Singing & Doubling Together" is simply the Wholly Other, the Incomparable, "the dearest freshness deep down things": it is none other than Being itself, "'that / which is to be praised'" and invested "with / our store of verve" ("Zero and Then Some," *Lake Effect Country*). And this aboriginal reality is addressed as "you," not because Ammons conceives it to be *a* being with personal attributes but rather, presumably, because he feels it to present itself with the same sort of graciousness that one encounters in the love of another person. He chooses not, in other words, to talk about "God" but, rather, to speak of that which approximates what Teilhard de Chardin called *le milieu divin*. Or, we might say that Ammons is a poet of what Stevens in a late poem ("Of Mere Being," *Opus Posthumous*) called "mere Being": we might say that he is a poet of that which, though not coextensive with all things, yet interpenetrates all things with the radiance of its diaphanous presence.

Although Harold Bloom's exuberant enthusiasm for Ammons's poetry, in its various expressions over many years, has no doubt been insufficiently modulated, he was surely right when, in *The Ringers in the Tower* (1971), he declared him to be "the central poet" of our generation, for this indeed is what he is. And he holds such a position in part because his special *pietas* speaks so deeply and so reassuringly to a malaise by which few reflective people of our period are untouched. It might be said to be simply an ennui of the human, a weariness of looking out upon a world that seems everywhere besmudged by ourselves, to have been shaped by some form of human intentionality—which leads in turn to a profound yearning to descry some "otherness" in reality that cannot be made subservient to the engines of our planning and our manipulation. But it will not suffice, of course, to find this otherness to be nothing more than the inert blankness of what Coleridge called "fixities and definites," for we seek (in Stevens's phrase) "a kind of total grandeur at the end," not a grandeur, as it were, overhead but *in* "the vulgate of experience," in "the actual landscape with its actual horns / Of baker and butcher blowing." And it is of just this that Ammons's poetry offers a presentment—as in the great final poem in *Lake Effect Country*, "Meeting Place":

> The water nearing the ledge leans down with
> grooved speed at the spill then,
> quickly groundless in air, bends
>
> its flat bottom plates up for the circular
> but crashes into irregularities of lower
> ledge, then breaks into the white
>
> bluffs of warped lace in free fall that
> breaking with acceleration against air
> unweave billowing string-maze
>
> floats: then the splintery regathering
> on the surface below where imbalances
> form new currents to wind the water

away: the wind acts in these shapes, too,
and in many more, as the falls also does in
many more, some actions haphazardly

unfolding, some central and accountably
essential: are they, those actions,
indifferent, nevertheless

ancestral: when I call out to them
as to flowing bones in my naked self, is my
address attribution's burden and abuse: of course

not, they're unchanged, unaffected: but have I
fouled their real nature for myself
by wrenching their

meaning, if any, to destinations of my own
forming: by the gladness in the recognition
as I lean into the swerves and become

multiple and dull in the mists' dreams, I know
instruction is underway, an
answering is calling me, bidding me rise, or is

giving me figures visible to summon
the deep-lying fathers from myself,
the spirits, feelings howling, appearing there.

CHAPTER NINE

James Wright's Lyricism

*M*ore than a decade having gone by since James Wright's death in 1980, at least some of his readers are doubtless conscious of their surprise at the persistency with which much of the poetry *lasts*. It is more frequently than not the case that the literary art that becomes immovably a part of the furniture of one's mind and spirit wins its place of settlement by reason of a pleasure it affords that is consequent upon the cogency with which, through the brilliant suasiveness of its syntax, it conducts a certain kind of argument. But this is a particular pleasure— offered, say, amongst the people of his generation, by a Richard Wilbur or an Anthony Hecht—that is rarely to be come by in Wright's poetry, so greatly did he yield to that poetics of the "deep image" that he was persuaded to embrace by his friend Robert Bly.

In the late 50s and 60s when Bly was laying out his program, he never revealed any real talent for theoretical formulation, and yet his various manifestoes in the journal he edited (successively called *The Fifties*, *The Sixties*, and *The Seventies*), though consistently marked by a windy sort of vagueness, proved remarkably successful in giving many young American poets of the time a sense of deliverance from the hegemony of that traditionalist formalism which had become, under the influence of the New Criticism, the reigning orthodoxy. He wanted poems "in which everything is said by image, and nothing by direct statement at all." "The poem," as he said, "*is* the images, images touching all the senses, uniting the world beneath and the world above."[1] But precision of definition regarding just what a "deep image" is was hard to come by. True, Bly apparently wanted to register an emphatic disapproval of the kind of Imagism classically instanced in William Carlos Williams's famous poem "The Red Wheelbarrow," which says simply:

so much depends
upon

a red wheel
barrow

glazed wi .h rain
water

beside the white
chickens.

Indeed, he declared the poetics of Imagism, as espoused at one or another point by figures such as Ezra Pound, Richard Aldington, H.D., and Williams to be an affair of nothing more than mere "picturism," which, as he felt, was calculated only to abort the true "poem in which the image is released from imprisonment among objects."[2] The deep image did not, in other words, posit a mimetic norm. But, beyond the proscription of any sort of linear discursiveness and syntactical order, this new poetic of the 60s was something highly nebulous and indeterminate, and Paul Breslin is surely right in suggesting that what its hermeticism comes down to in the end is little more than an attribution of "an inherent significance to a recurring symbolic vocabulary" and that learning to decipher the deep-image poem is "largely a matter of initiation into that vocabulary."[3]

Wright's poems, for example, are filled with ants, caterpillars, sparrows, finches, spiders, cicadas, roots, wings, stones, caves, bones, roots, darkness, the wind, and the moon. And it is with such an apparatus that deep-image poets—Bly and W. S. Merwin and Galway Kinnell and Charles Simic—have tended to work. But, of course, given their mistrust of the capacity of a rational poetic discourse to render, through regularity of meter, the rhythms of the collective unconscious, their procedure tends to be that of simply juxtaposing, say, stones and bones in the hope, as Cleanth Brooks remarked some years ago, that "the steel of the first will strike a spark from the flint of the second, and thus kindle the reader's imagination. But," as Brooks said, "my metaphor actually overstates the technique, for there is nothing in this poetry so violent as the striking of sparks. What is to happen is more nearly analogous to spontaneous combustion: the poet does no more than put one substance beside the other and leave the combustion to occur, or not to occur, in the reader's imagination"[4]—as when Galway Kinnell in *The Book of Nightmares* bids us

. . . to touch
the almost imaginary bones

under the face, to hear under the laughter
the wind crying across the black stones.[5]

And Wright's commitment to this *mystique* is clearly manifest, for example, in the kind of free-associational language employed in the Phi Beta Kappa poem that he read at the College of William and Mary in December 1969:

> The long body of his dream is the beginning of a dark
> Hair under an illiterate
> Girl's ear.
> (*AR*, 212)[6]

The first meeting between Wright and Bly did not occur, however, until the summer of 1958, by which time Wright's first collection of poems, *The Green Wall*, had already been issued by the Yale University Press in its Series of Younger Poets, and he had also then completed the manuscript of his second volume, *Saint Judas*, which was to be published by the Wesleyan University Press in 1959. He had happened to come on the first issue of *The Fifties*, which Bly had begun to edit from his farm in Minnesota, and, as he said in an interview with Peter Stitt in the spring of 1972,[7] by way of response he sent Bly a sixteen-page letter to which the reply was but a single sentence—"Come on out to the farm." And Wright's journeying for their first encounter into the western part of the state from Minneapolis (where he was then teaching at the University of Minnesota) marked the beginning of one of the great friendships of his life.

Now the frequently reiterated view that has become indeed the conventional judgment says that it was under Bly's influence that Wright forsook the meterical regularities and rhymes and quasi-metaphysical intensities of the kind of *poème bien fait* to the pattern of which much of the work in *The Green Wall* and *Saint Judas* had been cut, and thus a radical change in the general tonality of his work is declared to have been signalized by his book of 1963, *The Branch Will Not Break*. But this is an assessment that, though carrying a modicum of truth, does in some measure over-dramatize the sort of development that this phase of his career underwent. He had, after all, studied under John Crowe Ransom during his undergraduate years at Kenyon College, and, though he ultimately took a conventional Ph.D. in English at the University of Washington, writing his dissertation on "The Comic Imagination of Charles Dickens," he began his graduate studies in Seattle by enrolling in the M.A. program in creative writing, in the course of which he worked intensively under the direction of Theodore Roethke, who supervised those students in the program whose principal interest was in poetry. So, having been deeply touched by such mentors as these, it was altogether natural that the young poet of *The Green Wall* and *Saint Judas* should have evidenced so highly self-conscious a craftsmanship and so serious an attachment to traditional forms as he did.

Yet already a poem such as "At the Executed Murderer's Grave" in *Saint Judas*, as one looks at it from the perspective of his later years, appears to presage Wright's movement toward the "surrealism" of the deep image. At the grave of an executed Ohio rapist and murderer, George Doty, he reflects on how, when "the princes of the sea come down / To lay away their robes, to judge the earth / And its dead, and we dead stand undefended everywhere, / . . . My sneaking crimes"—and *yours! hypocrite lecteur! mon semblable! mon frère!*—will be found inseparably entangled with Doty's. His language, though rhymed and metrically ordered, is rough-cast and craggy, and then the final strophe says:

> Doty, the rapist and the murderer,
> Sleeps in a ditch of fire, and cannot hear;
> And where, in earth or hell's unholy peace,
> Men's suicides will stop, God knows, not I.
> Angels and pebbles mock me under trees.
> Earth is a door I cannot even face.
> Order be damned, I do not want to die,
> Even to keep Belaire, Ohio, safe.
> The hackles on my neck are fear, not grief.
> (Open, dungeon! Open, roof of the ground!)
> I hear the last sea in the Ohio grass,
> Heaving a tide of gray disastrousness.
> Wrinkles of winter ditch the rotted face
> Of Doty, killer, imbecile, and thief:
> Dirt of my flesh, defeated, underground.
>
> (*AR*, 84)

In lines such as these Wright is beginning to forswear any sort of expositional discourse, is beginning to abandon logical connectives between images, and to rely simply on images themselves for the conveyance of his meanings. Or, again, it is a similar bravura, in an even extremer form, that one notices in "The Quail" in *The Green Wall*, where he says:

> The blue dusk bore feathers beyond our eyes,
> Dissolved all wings as you, your hair dissolved,
> Your frame of bone blown hollow as a house

Beside the path, were borne away from me
Farther than birds for whom I did not care,
Commingled with the dark complaining air.
(*AR*, 32)

And there is much else in this mode in his first books. But, of course, by the time he issued *The Branch Will Not Break*, as a result of his tutelage under poets such as Juan Ramón Jiménez and Jorge Guillén and Pablo Neruda and César Vallejo and Georg Trakl and through the influence of Bly, this tendency had been greatly radicalized, though he was surely not without justification in resisting the suggestion (as he did in an interview for the *Southern Humanities Review* in 1970)[8] that there is an absolute break between the idioms of *The Green Wall* and *Saint Judas* and the books that followed.

What it may be most important to remark, however, is that, for all Wright's commitment to the poetics of the deep image, his immense compassion for the poor and the unlucky and the disprized and his obsession with certain aspects of the American landscape could never allow him to elect any sort of enclosure within the infinite subjectivity of his own inwardness or to regard the external world as a mere assemblage of stimuli for poetic reverie. In the Seventh of the *Duino Elegies*, Rilke says: "*Nirgends, Geliebte, wird Welt sein als innen*"—"Nowhere, beloved, will be world but within." And this, in a way, is what the poetry of W. S. Merwin and Galway Kinnell and Mark Strand and Robert Bly is saying, that the locus of the real is to be found not in the realm of men and beasts and mountains and stars but in that invisible world of the soul's inwardness into which it is the poet's vocation to gather the things and creatures of the visible world. Wright, however, in his best moments is preserved from that solipsism courted by the deep-image poets in their fealty to what Hegel in his *Aesthetik* denominated "absolute inwardness"—and what saves him is simply the sanity of a tough, commonsensical intelligence and the deep impress upon his sensibility of certain American places and human types to which he was so anchored as never to have been able to desert them merely for the sake of descending into the depths of the psyche.

The opening passage of "At the Executed Murderer's Grave" says:

My name is James A. Wright, and I was born
Twenty-five miles from this infected grave,
In Martins Ferry, Ohio, where one slave
To Hazel-Atlas Glass became my father.
He tried to teach me kindness. I return
Only in memory now, aloof, unhurried,

To dead Ohio, where I might lie buried,
Had I not run away before my time.
(*AR*, 82)

And that region of southern Ohio which is separated from West Virginia
by the Ohio River had so deeply formed his sense of the world that the
meditations recorded by the poetry rarely veer away from it for long.
Indeed, this valley in which he grew up in the 1930s and early 40s, with
its grimy factories and polluted air and water and with its landscape fearfully bruised and blasted by rampant strip mining, appears to have become for him the very definition of hell itself:

. . . the river at Wheeling, West Virginia,
Has only two shores:
The one in hell, the other
In Bridgeport, Ohio.

And nobody would commit suicide, only
To find beyond death
Bridgeport, Ohio.
(*AR*, 173)

"My rotted Ohio, / It was only a little while ago / That I learned the
meaning of your name. / The Winnebago gave you your name, Ohio, /
And Ohio means beautiful river" (*AR*, 211). But today, as he reminds us
in "Three Sentences for a Dead Swan" (*Shall We Gather at the River*, 1968),
the Ohio River is, like William Carlos Williams's "filthy Passaic," a thing
of slops and slime "that is no tomb to / Rise from the dead / From" (*AR*,
164). So he does not find it at all surprising that "the good men who lived
along that shore" in Martins Ferry, sensing that the Ohio River was
dying, should (under the auspices of the WPA) have chosen to dig a
swimming pool for their families—which gives him the anecdote recounted in the beautiful poem, "The Old WPA Swimming Pool in Martins Ferry, Ohio" (*Two Citizens*, 1973):

Uncle Sherman,
Uncle Willie, Uncle Emerson, and my father
Helped dig that hole in the ground.

I had seen by that time two or three
Holes in the ground,
And you know what they were.

But this one was not the usual, cheap
Economics, it was not the solitary

Scar on a poor man's face, that respectable
Hole in the ground you used to be able to buy
After you died for seventy-five dollars and
Your wages tached for six months by the Heslop
Brothers.
. . . .
No, this hole was filled with water,
And suddenly I flung myself into the water.
All I had on was a jockstrap my brother stole
From a miserable football team.

Oh never mind, Jesus Christ, my father
And my uncles dug a hole in the ground,
No grave for once. It is going to be hard
For you to believe; when I rose from that water,

A little girl who belonged to somebody else,
A face thin and haunted appeared
Over my left shoulder, and whispered, Take care now,
Be patient, and live.
                    (*AR*, 236–37)

So the poetry is to be found over and again sometimes sadly sighing and sometimes ferociously declaring that Ohio is a "dead place," and it presents a variety of people—waifs and outcasts of one sort or another—who in diverse ways have been twisted and broken by the desolation of this midwestern backwater. But, among the large gallery of portraits it presents, there are many which are devoted to those who front the surrounding deadness with a quiet heroism and an unshakable decency and generosity of spirit. In, for example, the moving "prose piece" included in *To a Blossoming Pear Tree* (1977), "The Flying Eagles of Troop 62," Wright remembers his Scoutmaster back in Martins Ferry, Ralph Neal, who

. . . knew all about the pain of the aching stones in our twelve-year-old groins, the lava swollen half-way between our peckers and our nuts that were still green and sour as half-ripe apples two full months before the football season began. . . .

I think Ralph Neal loved us for our scrawniness, our acne, our fear; but mostly for his knowledge of what would probably become of us. He was not a fool. He knew he would never himself get out of that slime hole of a river valley, and maybe he didn't want to. . . .

Some of us wanted to get out, and some of us wanted to and didn't. . . .

When I think of Ralph Neal's name, I feel some kind of ice breaking open in me. . . . I feel a rush of long fondness for that good man
Ralph Neal, that good man who knew us dreadful and utterly vul-
nerable little bastards better than we knew ourselves, who took care
of us better than we took care of ourselves, and who loved us, I
reckon, because he knew damned well what would become of most
of us, and it sure did, and he knew it, and he loved us anyway. The
very name of America often makes me sick, and yet Ralph Neal was
an American.

(AR, 289–90)

Or, again, in the poem "Paul" in *Two Citizens*, Wright recalls the days
of his boyhood in Martins Ferry:

> Plenty of times
> I ran around in the streets in that small
> Place. I didn't know what in hell
> Was happening to me.
>
> I had a pretty good idea
> It was hell.
> (*AR*, 237)

And he speaks of a day when he was picked up on those streets by a man
named Paul, who was driving a "cracked truck." Paul said, "Come on, /
Get in, and we drove down to Brookside." He remembers the affectionate
concern that Paul expressed when he got "a speck of coal" in his eye, and
he says:

> You were making less than twenty dollars a week.
> You drove that cracked truck down to Brookside
>   lovelier and friendlier
> Than Alcaeus loving Sappho.
>
> You wouldn't even know what I'm talking about.
>
> I wouldn't even know what you're talking about.
>
> By God, I know this much:
> When a fine young man is true to his true love
> And can face out a fine deep shock on his jaw
> (That scar so low off, that true scar of love),
> And when a man can stand up in the middle of America
> (That brutal and savage place whom I still love),

· 232 ·

Never mind your harangues about religion.
Anybody could pick me up out of the street
Is good to me, I would like to be good

To you, too, good man.
(AR, 238)

And the steadfast gentleness and selfless beneficence of his father are
elegized over and over again:

My father toiled fifty years
At Hazel-Atlas Glass,
Caught among girders that smash the kneecaps
Of dumb honyaks.
Did he shudder with hatred in the cold shadow
of grease?
Maybe. But my brother and I do know
He came home as quiet as the evening.
(AR, 162)

Although these and numerous other figures are gratefully remembered
as having been amongst those who graced his "native country" of southern Ohio, he, even at the end of his life—in the poem "A Flower Passage"
in the posthumous volume *This Journey* (1982)—was marveling "That for
some hidden reason nobody raped / To death" in Martins Ferry "The still
totally unbelievable spring beauty" (AR, 355) that Maytime brought each
year.

So asperities abound when Ohio is in view, for it makes Wright think

. . . of Polacks nursing long beers in Tiltonsville,
And gray faces of Negroes in the blast furnace at Benwood,
And the ruptured night watchman of Wheeling Steel,
Dreaming of heroes.

Its men are so enervated by their hard, dehumanizing labor as cogs of
the modern industrial machine that they

are ashamed to go home.
Their women cluck like starved pullets,
Dying for love.
(AR, 121)

In the logic of his symbolism Ohio stands, in short, as a *figura* of all those
bright promises held forth by the American Dream which have been broken, and thus he faces it with a fierce kind of reproachfulness and wrath.

But crabbedness and acerbity do not by any means define the predominating tone and spirit of Wright's poetry, as we will be reminded, for example, by a beautiful poem in *The Branch Will Not Break*, "Today I Was Happy, So I Made This Poem":

> As the plump squirrel scampers
> Across the roof of the corncrib,
> The moon suddenly stands up in the darkness,
> And I see that it is impossible to die.
> Each moment of time is a mountain.
> An eagle rejoices in the oak trees of heaven,
> Crying
> *This is what I wanted.*
>   (*AR*, 141)

Or one will think of another poem in the same volume, "Lying in a Hammock at William Duffy's Farm in Pine Island, Minnesota"—to which one ought perhaps to bring some recollection of Hawthorne's story "The Artist of the Beautiful," which concerns a young man, Owen Warland, who, in a difficult moment of his life, falls into the habit of chasing butterflies "through the woods and fields, and along the banks of streams. . . . There was something truly mysterious in the intentness with which he contemplated these living playthings, as they sported on the breeze." And his sober, industrious neighbors were not pleased. "He wasted the sunshine, as people said." This is the great line that, when summoned up in memory, will enable us properly to read Wright's poem:

> Over my head, I see the bronze butterfly,
> Asleep on the black trunk,
> Blowing like a leaf in green shadow.
> Down the ravine behind the empty house,
> The cowbells follow one another
> Into the distances of the afternoon.
> To my right,
> In a field of sunlight between two pines,
> The droppings of last year's horses
> Blaze up into golden stones.
> I lean back, as the evening darkens and comes on.
> A chicken hawk floats over, looking for home.
> I have wasted my life.
>   (*AR*, 122)

Now some commentators on this poem have expressed a sense of shock at the suddenness with which a tranquil bucolic reverie is interrupted by what appears to be the harshest kind of self-accusation—"I have wasted my life"—which is felt to have no organic relation to all that precedes it. But the mistake being made is that of failing to notice the playful irony with which the poet is speaking in the final line. To be sure, he is speaking confessionally, but not in a spirit of self-reproach. Like William Blake, he is saying: "Damn braces, bless relaxes." He is suggesting that there is a certain ultimate dimension in the life of the human spirit in which strenuousness is of no avail, that true sanity of mind is not won by grabbing at this and that—and he is confessing that *he* has chosen to "waste" his life (sometimes in a hammock), in something like the way in which Hawthorne's Owen Warland "wastes the sunshine." He is confessing his having chosen to submit himself to such an exigent discipline as is exacted by a truly intransitive attentiveness before the things and creatures of earth—butterflies asleep on a tree, cowbells following one another into the distances of the afternoon, the droppings of last year's horses blazed up into golden stones, or a chicken hawk floating over as it looks for home.

In Wright's own sense of the course taken by his development it was, as he felt, to the Austrian poet Georg Trakl more than to anyone else that he was most deeply indebted for his introduction to the discipline of opening one's eyes, of being silent and listening and waiting patiently "for the inward bodies of things to emerge, for the inward voices to whisper."[9] By the early 60s *The Branch Will Not Break* made it clearly evident that his meditations were increasingly being guided by such a discipline, and nowhere in that volume to more brilliant effect than in the great poem "A Blessing":

Just off the highway to Rochester, Minnesota,
Twilight bounds softly forth on the grass.
And the eyes of those two Indian ponies
Darken with kindness.
They have come gladly out of the willows
To welcome my friend and me.
We step over the barbed wire into the pasture
Where they have been grazing all day, alone.
They ripple tensely, they can hardly contain their happiness
That we have come.
They bow shyly as wet swans. They love each other.
There is no loneliness like theirs.
At home once more,
They begin munching the young tufts of spring in the darkness.
I should like to hold the slenderer one in my arms,

For she has walked over to me
And nuzzled my left hand.
She is black and white,
Her mane falls wild on her forehead,
And the light breeze moves me to caress her long ear
That is delicate as the skin over a girl's wrist.
Suddenly I realize
That if I stepped out of my body I would break
Into blossom.
(*AR*, 143)

It is difficult to specify what makes this poem so deeply affecting: it may be the utter surprise we are made to feel at the strange way in which, beginning as it does, it ends where it does. The opening phrase is ever so casual and matter-of-fact—"Just off the highway to Rochester, Minnesota." But, then, immediately, the independent clause that follows plunges us into a world of wonder and enchantment, where "Twilight bounds softly forth on the grass." And the spell that is instantly cast is no doubt consequent upon the radicality with which the poem jettisons anything resembling a subject-object dualism. As the speaker and his friend step over the barbed wire and enter the pasture, the purity of attention that they bestow upon those two Indian ponies is so unmenacing that the ponies, despite their shyness, walk over to them, as if bidden unto a relationship of complete reciprocity. The speaker finds "the slenderer one" nuzzling his left hand. He caresses her long ear—"delicate as the skin over a girl's wrist"—and, suddenly, he knows that, were he to step out of his body, he would "break / Into blossom": in this moment in which the frontier line between nature and the human order is wholly transcended the spirit of the visitor literally *flowers*, and the poem itself becomes, as James E. B. Breslin so aptly observes, "a corridor . . . that opens a passageway between self and world."[10]

This lambent, gentle lyricism—so characteristically expressed in a poem such as "A Blessing"—is very much to the fore in Wright's late work, in *To a Blossoming Pear Tree* and *This Journey,* but it is also shaping many of the poems in *Shall We Gather at the River* (1968). And, there, in a poem such as "Brush Fire" (as, indeed, in many others), one cannot but remark how reminiscent his accent is of his greatly esteemed early mentor, Theodore Roethke, particularly in his devotion to what Roethke called "the small things" of the world:

In this field,
Where the small animals ran from a brush fire,
It is a voice

In burned weeds, saying
I love you.
Still, when I go there,
I find only two gray stones,
And, lying between them,
A dead bird the color of slate.
It lies askew in its wings,
Its throat bent back as if at the height of some joy too great
To bear to give.
And the lights are going out
In a farmhouse, evening
Stands, in a gray frock, silent, at the far side
Of a raccoon's grave.
   (*AR*, 164–65)

But in one important particular the general perspective of the poet of *Shall We Gather at the River* differs very considerably from that of Roethke, for Roethke's "minimalism," his responsiveness to "littles," to weeds and worms and moles and snails, tends to shut out of his poetry the hard, tough, concrete social realities that belong to the common experience of the daily round—whereas these are things that are never lost sight of in Wright's book of 1968, which makes us feel that he was constantly impelled to test "the visionary gleam" (as Wordsworth spoke of it) against the intractable circumstances of our life together in the workaday world. So, for example, in one of the finest poems in this volume, "Before a Cashier's Window in a Department Store," the speaker recounts his experience of the humiliation to which he was reduced in the credit office of a Minneapolis department store by his inability to clear up an indebtedness:

The beautiful cashier's white face has risen once more
Behind a young manager's shoulder.
They whisper together, and stare
Straight into my face.
I feel like grabbing a stray child
Or a skinny old woman
And driving into a cellar, crouching
Under a stone bridge, praying myself sick,
Till the troops pass.

Why should he care? He goes.
I slump deeper.
In my frayed coat, I am pinned down

By debt. He nods,
Commending my flesh to the pity of the daws of God.

(*AR*, 156)

Or, again, a similar experience is spoken of in the poem "In Terror of Hospital Bills":

I still have some money
To eat with, alone
And frightened, knowing how soon
I will waken a poor man.

It snows freely and freely hardens
On the lawns of my hope, my secret
Hounded and flayed. I wonder
What words to beg money with.
. . . .

Soon I am sure to become so hungry
I will have to leap barefoot through gas-fire veils of shame,
I will have to stalk timid strangers
On the whorehouse corners.
. . . .

I will learn to scent the police,
And sit or go blind, stay mute, be taken for dead
For your sake, oh my secret,
My life.

(*AR*, 151)

In an interview with Michael André in 1972, Wright was asked if such poems had been "taken from life," and he said:

The one in the drunk tank ["Inscription for the Tank"] and "In Terror of Hospital Bills," yes, that's right. I didn't have enough money to pay a hospital bill, and it's very frightening. And the one about not being able to pay my bill at, what the Hell's the name of that department store in Minneapolis? Of course, I got out of that very easily, but I realized after their fish eye that there were a lot of people who weren't going to go back as a professor at a university. As Huck Finn's father said, "He was a professor at a college." There are plenty of people who can't do that, and I just got a flash of that, in the moment. And it's no goddam joke, to have people look at you like that.[11]

Now it is the admission of this kind of gritty reality into poems such as "The Minneapolis Poem" and "Gambling in Stateline, Nevada" and

"The Poor Washed Up by Chicago Winter" and "Willy Lyons" and "The River Down Home" that gives a special power to *Shall We Gather at the River*, particularly by reason of the degree to which this strain feeds and wins incorporation into a lyricism that, though not unaware of what is stained and broken and scurvy in the human actuality, can yet take wing—as in the concluding strophe of "The Minneapolis Poem":

> I want to be lifted up
> By some great white bird unknown to the police,
> And soar for a thousand miles and be carefully hidden
> Modest and golden as one last corn grain,
> Stored with the secrets of the wheat and the mysterious lives
> of the unnamed poor.
>   (*AR*, 149)

In 1971 Wright published his *Collected Poems,* which won for him the Pulitzer Prize for Poetry in the following year. Earlier garlands had come his way—the Eunice Tietjens Memorial Prize in 1955; a *Kenyon Review* fellowship in 1958; grants from the National Instiute of Arts and Letter (1959), the Rockefeller Foundation (1969), and the Ingram Merrill Foundation (1969); and the Brandeis University Creative Arts Citation in Poetry in 1971. But the Pulitzer Prize was the first really major award, and one suspects that the jury was prompted to confer it not only by reason of what had been Wright's manifestly central role in the experimental movement in American poetry during the 60s but also because of the impressive achievement represented by the thirty-one "New Poems" in his book of 1971. In one of these poems ("Many of Our Waters: Variations on a Poem by a Black Child") he says:

> The kind of poetry I want to write is
>   The poetry of a grown man.
> The young poets of New York come to me with
> Their mangled figures of speech,
> But they have little pity
> For the pure clear word.
>
> I know something about the pure clear word,
> Though I am not yet a grown man.
>   (*AR*, 212)

It was indeed "the pure clear word" of which by this stage in his career Wright was beginning unmistakably to be in full command. Here, for example, is one of the most poignant of the "New Poems"—"Small Frogs

Killed on the Highway"—and it puts us in view of a central motif in the late poetry:

> Still,
> I would leap too
> Into the light,
> If I had the chance.
> It is everything, the wet green stalk of the field
> On the other side of the road.
> They crouch there, too, faltering in terror
> And take strange wing. Many
> Of the dead never moved, but many
> Of the dead are alive forever in the split second
> Auto headlights more sudden
> Than their drivers know.
> The drivers burrow backward into dank pools
> Where nothing begets
> Nothing.
>
> Across the road, tadpoles are dancing
> On the quarter thumbnail
> Of the moon. They can't see,
> Not yet.
>
> (AR, 196)

Now, as it became increasingly evident in the poems of his last years, "light" was for Wright an image of the Sublime: he thought of it as a *figura* of Glory, of that which eye hath not seen nor ear heard and of which the tongue can stammer only brokenly but which, in its splendor, overwhelms the heart. So great is its power of allurement that it is no wonder that, when little frogs on a highway at night see light, they leap at it. But, of course, the pity of it is that they do not realize that the light they are facing comes from the headlights of oncoming automobiles by which, being in their path, they are overrun. Yet, as the poet says, were I a frog, "I would leap too."

Theodore Roethke wanted to exclaim: "To have the whole air! / The light, the full sun. . . ." And one imagines Wright as having also wanted to exclaim: "Oh, the light! the light!" In, for example, "A Letter to Franz Wright," one of the prose poems addressed to his son, he speaks of having visited with his second wife, Annie, "a place in Tuscany in late autumn" that could be reached only by a very circuitous journey. Midway, they "finally found the sign" which they needed—*San Gimignano*. Then they "drove up, and up, and around, and up, and around, and up again, till we found ourselves picking our way in semi-darkness. . . . It was almost like being in Ohio, and I felt a momentary convulsion of home-sickness":

> Then we emerged on a town square, not a very large one as piaz-zas go, and checked in at a hotel over in the corner. The town seemed pleasant enough. We were road-weary and hungry. We stepped a few doors down the street to a trattoria for a small late meal, and went back to bed.
> The next morning Annie rose first, opened the curtained doors to bright sunlight, and went out on the balcony. I thought I heard her gasp. When she came back into the room again, she looked a little pale, and said, "I don't believe it."
> San Gimignano is poised hundreds of feet in the air. The city is comparatively small, and it is perfectly formed. We felt ourselves strange in that presence, that city glittering there in the lurid Tuscan morning, like a perfectly cut little brilliant sparkling on the pinnacle of a stalagmite.

> > (AR, 268)

Oh, the light! the light!

Another prose poem with an Italian setting, "The Turtle Overnight," speaks of Wright's experience one evening of watching an old turtle tak-ing "a pleasant bath in his natural altogether":

> When it began to rain, he appeared in his accustomed place and emerged from his accustomed place and emerged from his shell as far as he could reach—feet, legs, tail, head. He seemed to enjoy the rain, the sweet-tasting rain that blew all the way across lake water to him from the mountains, the Alto Adige. . . . All the legendary faces of broken old age disappeared from my mind, the thickened muscles under the chins, the nostrils brutal with hatred, the mur-dering eyes. He filled my mind with a sweet-tasting mountain rain, his youthfulness, his modesty as he washed himself all alone, his religious face.

Then the next morning Wright from his window watches the old turtle lying in the grass below, as he lifts his face toward the sun. "It is a raising of eyebrows toward the light, an almost imperceptible turning of the chin, an ancient pleasure, an eagerness." But after a time the turtle leaves, and Wright cannot descry even the merest "footprint in the empty grass. So much air left, so much sunlight, and still he is gone" (AR, 323–

24). Thus the poem ends, with something like a sigh of wonderment at the turtle's departure. Yet, while he lingered in the grass, he, as he lifted his face upward, made a perfect example of docile and reverent acceptance of the grace and glory that indwell the world.

Or, again, in "The Journey," one of the most beautiful poems in *This Journey,* Wright says:

> Many men
> Have searched all over Tuscany and never found
> What I found there, the heart of the light
> Itself shelled and leaved, balancing
> On filaments themselves falling.
>
> (*AR*, 338)

And recurrently in the late poems he is disclosing in various ways how ineluctably he was drawn to that *mysterium tremendum et fascinans* which was for him imaged forth in light.[12] So committed was he to the deep image that Wright's poetry is, of course, rarely touched by systematic ideas of any sort, and thus the kind of stupor into which he can be quickly thrown by his intoxication with the Sublime is never conceptualized in terms that would allow its formal explication. No doubt this mystical strain in his sensibility requires to be thought of as a type of "natural supernaturalism," but his reticence makes it difficult with any real precision to take the measure of just what his religious vision entailed—and yet one often feels that Wright *wanted* to say something approximating the word of the seventeenth-century poet and mystic Thomas Traherne, that "Eternity . . . [is] manifest in the light of the day." Indeed, it would appear that the unconfessed assumption underlying much of the late poetry is formulable in the terms of Traherne's *Centuries:*

> Your enjoyment of the World is never right, till you so esteem it, that everything in it, is more your treasure than a King's exchequer full of Gold and Silver.[13]

> Your enjoyment of the world is never right, till every morning you awake in Heaven; see yourself in your Father's Palace; and look upon the skies, the earth, and the air as Celestial Joys: having such a reverend esteem of all, as if you were among the Angels.[14]

> Yet further, you never enjoy the world aright, till you so love the beauty of enjoying it, that you are covetous and earnest to persuade others to enjoy it. . . . The world is a mirror of infinite beauty, yet no man sees it. It is a Temple of Majesty, yet no man regards it. It is

a region of Light and Peace, did not men disquiet it. It is the Paradise of God.[15]

The riches of the Light are the Works of God which are the portion and inheritance of His sons, to be seen and enjoyed in Heaven and Earth, the Sea, and all that is therein: the Light and the Day, great and fathomless in use and excellency, true, necessary, freely given.[16]

In the last decade of his life Wright fell deeply in love with Italy, and, of the many meditations prompted by his various Italian experiences that his poetry presents, the one needing at this point to be thought of is that recorded in the marvelous poem in *Two Citizens*, "Bologna: A Poem about Gold." He is recalling the hours in Bologna he spent gazing at Raphael's *St. Cecilia*. It appears, however, that his attention was chiefly captivated not by St. Cecilia, for it strikes him that, in Raphael's rendering, she is one who simply stands "in the center of a blank wall," "Smirking" and "Adoring / Herself." No, it is Mary Magdalene, positioned at the far right of Raphael's canvas, by whom he was most deeply stirred. She, he says, "the lowly and richest of all women eyes / Me the beholder, with a knowing sympathy." She is, of course, said to have been a prostitute, but St. Luke's Gospel tells us that, though her sins were many, they were forgiven, "for she loved much" (Luke 7:47). And she became one of Jesus's most steadfast followers. She was among the last to leave the Cross at the place called Golgotha (Matt. 27:55–56), and, after Pilate handed over the lifeless body of Jesus to Joseph and fine linen had been secured wherewith to wrap it up, she was present when the crucified Christ was deposited in the sepulcher (Mark 16:47). She was among those who first conveyed to the apostles the news of the empty tomb (Luke 24:10), and she was the first to behold the risen Christ (Mark 16:9), by whom she was enjoined to make known to his followers the event of the resurrection (John 20:17). So she was, indeed, though "lowly . . . [yet] richest of all women," and Wright says:

> Oh,
> She may look sorry to Cecilia
> And
> The right-hand saint on the tree,
> But
> She didn't look sorry to Raphael,
> And
> I bet she didn't look sorry to Jesus,
> And

> She doesn't look sorry to me.
> (Who would?)
> She doesn't look sorry to me.
>
> (*AR*, 248)

Indeed, as he stands in the old church in which Raphael's great canvas hangs, he is moved to address an apostrophe to his beloved Horace: "Give me this time, my first and severe / Italian, a poem about gold, / . . . And the heavy wine . . . , / The glass that so many have drunk from." In the idiom of the poem, Mary Magdalene was, of course, herself "gold," pure gold, and she kept a great "love / For the golden body of the earth." But the poem is also about the "White wine of Bologna" whose actual color is golden, and in this church it is natural for a man of Protestant background, forgetting that Catholics traditionally received only the eucharistic wafer at the communion rail, to think of the chalices filled with the golden wine of Bologna "that so many have drunk from" over generations. (It is a pardonable mistake of one whose nurture in southern Ohio was Baptist!) And, moreover, quite apart from its use in the *Missa Fidelium*, his own private enheartening by the great local wine is for him a foremost fact of his time in the city:

> I have brought my bottle back home every day
> To the cool cave, and come forth
> Golden on the left corner
> Of a cathedral's wing. . . .
>
> (*AR*, 247)

So it makes a splendid kind of sense for Wright to conclude this poem about gold, about how much Mary "looks like only the heavy deep gold," by exclaiming:

> Mary in Bologna, sunlight I gathered all morning
> And pressed in my hands all afternoon
> And drank all day with my golden-breasted
>
> Love in my arms.
>
> (*AR*, 248)

Gold was Mary Magdalene, gold is the wine of Bologna which may be used not only as one species of the Christian sacrament but also as a catalyst of erotic communion ("with my golden-breasted / Love"), gold is the sunlight that is the medium of theophany—which is, in a way, for the poem to assert the essential coinherence of the sacred and the profane. And it is such a vision of the unsunderable unity of nature, humanity, and God which informs and underlies the poems in Wright's last books, *To a Blossoming Pear Tree* and *This Journey.*

Among the "New Poems" included in the *Collected Poems* of 1971 there is one entitled "A Secret Gratitude," in the course of which Wright says:

> Man's heart is the rotten yolk of a blacksnake egg
> Corroding, as it is just born, in a pile of dead
> Horse dung.
> I have no use for the human creature.
> He subtly extracts pain awake in his own kind.
> I am born one, out of an accidental hump of chemistry.
> I have no use.
>   (*AR*, 191)

But the kind of sour, black sentimentality expressed in these lines, though it frequently disfigures his earlier work, rarely appears in the final books, which are relatively untouched by that strain of loosely self-indulgent malevolence that we remark particularly in *Shall We Gather at the River* and *Two Citizens*. In an essay on Thomas Hardy's *Far From the Madding Crowd*, Wright says of Hardy's protagonist Gabriel Oak: ". . . we find Oak a man of deep and serene feeling. He is always surrounded by things which fill him with inexorable affection, and with which, at last, he becomes miraculously identified: sheep, dogs, plants, trees."[17] And so it tends to be with the poet of *To a Blossoming Pear Tree* and *This Journey*. True, the world sometimes appears to him to be a very imperfect place— and yet, often when least expected, he finds things strangely suffused with *light*. In, for example, "Beautiful Ohio," the final poem of *Blossoming Pear*, he recalls how, as a boy, he would sit on a railroad tie above a sewer main, but, whereas at an earlier time the remembrance of what this great pipe disgorged into the Ohio River would have occasioned a savage indictment of an industrial society's pollution of its natural environment, he now considers the noisome discharge of that sewer main to have shone with "the speed of light," since its way of quickening the river revealed something of what is primitively marvelous in that ceaseless flux that feeds and sustains the essential dynamism of the world. Indeed, as he thinks of the 16,500 people "more or less" who dwelt in his home-town, Martins Ferry, and, as he thinks of how that sewer pipe was lit up with radiance, he says:

> And the light caught there
> The solid speed of their lives
> In the instant of that waterfall.

> I know what we call it
> Most of the time.
> But I have my own song for it,
> And sometimes, even today,
> I call it beauty.
>
> (*AR*, 318)

Or, again, the glory wherewith the world is charged flames out for Wright in his late phase in even the merest insect. In "To the Cicada" (*This Journey*) he remembers how on an Ohio field at twilight he listened to cicadas singing:

> Still, now, I hear you, singing,
> A lightness beginning among the dark crevices,
> In the underbark of the locust, beyond me,
> The other edge of the field.
> A lightness,
> You begin tuning up for your time,
> Twilight, that belongs to you, deeper and cooler beyond
> The barbed wire of this field, even beyond
> The Ohio River twenty-five miles away,
> Where the Holy Rollers rage all afternoon
> And all evening among the mud cracks,
> . . . .
> But you, lightness,
> Light flesh singing lightly,
> Trembling in perfect balance on the underbark,
> The locust tree of the southeast, you, friendly
> To whatever sings in me as it climbs and holds on
> Among the damp brambles:
>
> You, lightness,
> How were you born in this place, this heavy stone
> Plummeting into the stars?
> . . . .
> You, lightness, kindlier than my human body,
> Yet somehow friendly to the music in my body. . . .
>
> (*AR*, 341)

But *nell' ultima parte del cammin di sua vita* Wright swayed and vibrated not merely with cicadas and spiders and lightning bugs and moor birds and turtles, for ever so much more frequently than in his earlier years he was often finding his human neighbors also to be vessels and conduits of grace. One will think in this connection of the beautiful prose poem "The

Silent Angel" in *To a Blossoming Pear Tree*, which speaks of his having on one occasion taken a bus out of Verona on which no sooner than he was seated he looked over his left shoulder and saw a man "standing in one of the pink marble arches at the base of the great Roman Arena":

> He smiled at me, a gesture of the utmost sweetness, such as a human face can rarely manage to shine with, even a beloved face that loves you in return.
>
> He seemed dressed like a musician, as well he might have been, emerging for a moment into the sunlight from one of the secluded and cool rehearsal chambers of the upper tiers of the Arena.
>
> As the bus driver powered his motor and drew us slowly around the great public square, the Piazza Bra, the man in the half-golden rose shadow of the Arena kept his gaze on my face. He waved goodbye to me, his knowing eyes never leaving me as long as he could still see any of me at all, though how long that was I don't precisely know.
>
> He raised his hand at the last moment to wave me out of Verona as kindly as he could. . . .
>
> The musician had not played me a single tune, he had not sung me a single song. He just waved me as gently as he could on the way out, the way that is my own, the lost way.
>
> I suppose I asked for it. And he did his best, I suppose. He owns that heavenly city no more than I do. He may be fallen, as I am. But from a greater height, unless I miss my guess.
>
> (*AR*, 309–10)

It is in the experience of his late years precisely such evidences as he comes by in the nameless Veronese musician of the neighbor's capacity for graciousness that lead Wright toward the kind of engagement recorded in the deeply affecting poem "To a Blossoming Pear Tree." He is contemplating the splendid self-sufficiency of this blooming tree that, as it stands "without trembling," appears "unburdened / By anything but . . . [its] beautiful natural blossoms," and the very nonchalance of its self-containment prompts him to feel that it is quite "beyond my reach":

> How I envy you.
> For if you could only listen,
> I would tell you something,
> Something human.
> (*AR*, 316)

And the story he would tell concerns an encounter he had had years earlier, when an old homosexual, ashamed and hopeless, paused on a

Minneapolis street and stroked his face, declaring in his desperation that he would "pay . . . anything." "Both terrified, / We slunk away, / Each in his own way dodging / The cruel darts of the cold":

> . . . He was so near death
> He was willing to take
> Any love he could get,
> Even at the risk
> Of some mocking policeman
> Or some cute young wiseacre
> Smashing his dentures,
> Perhaps leading him on
> To a dark place and there
> Kicking him in his dead groin
> Just for the fun of it.
> (*AR*, 317)

This young tree, of course, could not "possibly / Worry or bother or care / About the ashamed, hopeless / Old man," for it knows nothing of the terrors and desolateness that win tenancy within the human heart, but, says Wright, "the dark / Blood in my body drags me / Down with my brother." One's neighbor, in other words, whoever he or she may be, makes an unignorable claim on one's sympathy and understanding to disregard which is for one's own selfhood to be diminished.

It needs to be remarked, however, that, despite what appears to be implied by "To a Blossoming Pear Tree," Wright does not at all intend to posit any sort of absolute disjunction between the human order and the natural world. A pear tree may not be able to "listen" to a story of "something human," but this is not to say that there is no point of union or contact between nature and the human spirit—which is indeed what "A Blessing" and "Brush Fire" and "Milkweed" and numerous other poems want very much to insist upon. One thinks, for example, of the late prose poem "A Reply to Matthew Arnold," whose epigraph is drawn from Arnold's early sonnet "In Harmony with Nature"—"'In harmony with Nature?' Restless fool. . . . Nature and man can never be fast friends." To which Wright wants to say that, notwithstanding Arnold's word of denigration, he is himself just such a fool. The poem speaks of the occasion on which, as he was preparing to leave the Italian coast town of Fano after a happy visit of five days, he brought a "wild chive flower down from a hill pasture" and, in the manner of a farewell salute, offered it to the Adriatic—as a "fast friend":

I am not about to claim that the sea does not care.
It has its own way of receiving seeds, and today the
sea may as well have a flowering one, with a poppy
to float above it, and the Venetian navy underneath.
Goodbye to the living place, and all I ask it to do is
to stay alive.
              (*AR*, 331)

True, many think of the sea as a place of turbulence and perishing, as
in the words of Melville's Ishmael) "a fiend to its own off-spring; worse
than the Persian host who murdered his own guests; sparing not the
creatures which itself hath spawned. Like a savage tigress that tossing in
the jungle overlays her own cubs," says Ahab's young probationer, "so
the sea dashes even the mightiest whales against the rocks, and leaves
them there side by side with the split wrecks of ships. No mercy, no
power but its own controls it." And so a familiar kind of verdict goes. But
though there is, to be sure, "the Venetian navy underneath," Wright, as
he bids good-by to the Adriatic, recognizing all the while its capability
for smashing life, chooses not "to claim that the sea does not care." "It
has its own way of receiving seeds," and it "may as well have a flowering
one, with a poppy to float above it." He wants to speak only in the terms
of affection, without any abeyance of the sympathy with which he regularly approaches the things of nature.

Now it is such a *pietas* toward the world at hand that almost uninter-
mittently informs Wright's late poems. Everywhere there is "light," and,
because things "shine," he himself shines. In "Lightning Bugs Asleep in
the Afternoon" (*This Journey*) he remarks these "fluttering jewels," "this
little circle of insects / Common as soot, clustering on dim stone, / Together with their warm secrets." And then he says:

I think I am going to leave them folded
And sleeping in their slight gray wings.
I think I am going to climb back down
And open my eyes and shine.
              (*AR*, 342)

Or, again in the prose poem "The Secret of Light" (*To a Blossoming Pear
Tree*), as he sits "alone in a little park near the Palazzo Scaligere in Verona,
glimpsing the mists of early autumn as they shift and fade among the
pines and city battlements on the hills above the river Adige," he turns
his face toward this beloved river and thinks: "It is all right with me to
know that my life is only one life. I feel like the light of the river Adige"

(*AR*, 302–3). And in the beautiful closing poem in *This Journey*, "A Winter Daybreak above Vence," at dawn he looks down at the valley below, as he hears "the startled squawk / Of a rooster" and "The gumming snarl of some grouchy dog." The "night still hangs on," but the break of day is slowly coming, so that here and there things below begin to take form. He hears "a bucket rattle or something, tinny, / No other stirring behind the dim face / Of the goatherd's house," and he imagines that the herds-man's "goats are still sleeping, dreaming. . . ." But then, after a time, all of a sudden he finds himself "On top of the sunlight":

> I turn, and somehow
> Impossibly hovering in the air over everything,
> The Mediterranean, nearer to the moon
> Than this mountain is,
> Shines. A voice clearly
> Tells me to snap out of it. Galway
> Mutters out of the house and up the stone stairs
> To start the motor. The moon and the stars
> Suddenly flicker out, and the whole mountain
> Appears, pale as a shell.
>
> Look, the sea has not fallen and broken
> Our heads. How can I feel so warm
> Here in the dead center of January? I can
> Scarcely believe it, and yet I have to, this is
> The only life I have. I get up from the stone.
> My body mumbles something unseemly
> And follows me. Now we are all sitting here strangely
> On top of the sunlight.
> (*AR*, 376)

To be on "top of the sunlight" is, in short, to be where one is when, having measured the excellence of all things, one wants, in the manner of St. Francis of Assisi, to call all creatures by the name of brother and to declare (with Thomas Traherne) that one is "pleased with all that God hath done."[18] And it is something like such a declaration that is implicitly being made by this poet who, as he matured, increasingly found the world, often in even the unlikeliest places, suffused with "light."

True, anger and despondency and despair frequently enter Wright's poetry, particularly in its earlier phase, and he sometimes appears to have lost the Good Place, but he wins through time and again to that point of vantage from which he can discern that what is ultimately called for is a resounding affirmation that ours is a dispensation "immeasurably good." There was never, of course, anything of the dandy in Wright: as he said in the closing poem of *Two Citizens*, ". . . I ain't much. / The one tongue I can write in / Is my Ohioan." So his lyricism was never a thing of suave, easy mellifluousness: in, for example, the poem "Among Sun-flowers" in *This Journey*, he says simply: "Any creature would be a fool to take the sun lightly," and the song he wants to sing is regularly rendered in such a plain-spoken parlance. But so capably does it carry its freight of naked feeling that for the young in the 1960s and 70s he spoke more persuasively and movingly than did perhaps any other American poet of the time, and what asks now for happy acknowledgment is the perdur-ing strength of his legacy.

CHAPTER TEN

Howard Nemerov's Broken Music

*F*or more than forty years the late Howard Nemerov has been a major presence in American poetry, and, following the appearance in 1947 of *The Image and the Law,* the first collection of his poems, he produced an immense body of work (not to speak of his novels and the volumes of his essays and criticism). His *Collected Poems* of 1977 brought together in more than five hundred pages an enormous harvest from nine previous books, and in the years thereafter before his death in July 1991 he issued *Sentences* (1980), *Inside the Onion* (1984), and *War Stories: Poems about Long Ago and Now* (1987). But, though he was laden with honors—election to membership in the National Institute of Arts and Letters in 1965, the National Book Award in poetry and the Pulitzer Prize for poetry in 1978, the Bollingen Prize for poetry in 1981, election as U.S. Poet Laureate in 1988, and numerous other laurels—one's impression is that the kind of large celebrity that gathered about Stevens and Frost and Warren did somehow escape him. Undoubtedly, a part of the explanation is to be found in the modest, reasonable, witty, lucid, temperate kind of intelligence that belongs to the persona consistently projected by his verse. Although intensity of passion is often just beneath the surface of his speech, the pitch of the voice is never raised, and he had no traffic with the various fashionable *frissons* of the age. So he has not appeared to be a focal strategist of the predominating sensibilities of the recent past, in the manner of an Allen Ginsberg or an Adrienne Rich or a John Ashbery.

Perhaps the more decisive reason for his never having laid claim to a larger *éclat* has to do with a certain ambivalence that is deeply a part of his general outlook and that is beautifully expressed in one of the great poems of his career, the title poem of *The Blue Swallows* (1967). The poet is standing on a bridge, looking downward at the millstream beneath, and he notices how

> Seven blue swallows divide the air
> In shapes invisible and evanescent,
> Kaleidoscopic beyond the mind's
> Or memory's power to keep them there.

And the swallows' tails appear to be "as nibs / Dipped in invisible ink, writing . . ." But no sooner is he struck by this elegant conceit than he scourges himself with lacerating reproaches:

> Poor mind, what would you have them write?
> Some cabalistic history
> Whose authorship you might ascribe
> To God? to Nature? Ah, poor ghost,
> You've capitalized your Self enough.
> That villainous William of Occam
> Cut out the feet from under that dream
> Some seven centuries ago.
> It's taken that long for the mind
> To waken, yawn and stretch, to see
> With opened eyes emptied of speech
> The real world where the spelling mind
> Imposes with its grammar book
> Unreal relations on the blue
> Swallows. Perhaps when you will have
> Fully awakened, I shall show you
> A new thing: even the water
> Flowing away beneath those birds
> Will fail to reflect their flying forms,
> And the eyes that see become as stones
> Whence never tears shall fall gain.

> O swallows, swallows, poems are not
> The point. Finding again the world,
> That is the point, where loveliness
> Adorns intelligible things
> Because the mind's eye lit the sun.

Now one suspects that at some point during his student years at Harvard College Nemerov had a course in philosophy in which he discovered the medieval English Franciscan William of Occam and that somehow Occam's "razor" as it is called, the principle that entities are not to be multiplied except as may be necessary (*Entia non multiplicanda præter necessitatem*), got immovably lodged in the deeper recesses of this young American's mind. For, when Nemerov is overtaken by a contemplative or philosophical mood, he is to be found over and again adumbrating the old nominalist doctrine that only particulars are to be accorded any kind of truly ontological priority and that nothing else can be thought to exist *extra mentem*. And thus in "The Blue Swallows" we are confronted with the paradox of an extraordinarily beautiful lyric repudiating its own lyrical meditation, as it insists that "the spelling mind / Imposes with its grammar book / Unreal relations on the blue / Swallows." What is real, as the poem wants anxiously to assert against itself, is not the "spindrift web" of "nibs / Dipped in invisible ink," but simply the actual particulars, the "flying forms," of these seven blue swallows whose presence, quite surpassing the mimetic power of poetic art, can be justly remarked only by "opened eyes emptied of speech."

But, then, the concluding strophe presents us with a strange oxymoron:

> O swallows, swallows, poems are not
> The point. Finding again the world,
> That is the point, where loveliness
> Adorns intelligible things
> Because the mind's eye lit the sun.

Till now, the poem has indeed wanted to say, "Finding again the world / That is the point." Yet in the final lines it turns around and tells us that "loveliness / Adorns intelligible things / Because the mind's eye lit the sun." Up to this point the voice to which we have been listening has appeared to be guided at once by a kind of nominalism and by something like Santayana's "materialism." The nominalism lines itself up behind such a dictum as William Carlos Williams's famous utterance in *Paterson*—"no ideas but in things." And Nemerov appears to think of "things," in the absolute specificity of their actual existence, as enshrouded within the impenetrable hiddenness and ineffability that belong to what Santayana denominated as "matter." But, curiously, the final lines of "The Blue Swallows," in suggesting that the loveliness of "intelligible things" is consequent upon "the mind's eye," seem to be embracing a kind of primitive Kantianism that sees the world, in so far as we have a world, as a product of the constructive imagination.

David Perkins, in a thoughtful and sensitive review of Nemerov's *Collected Poems* (*Poetry* Magazine in the autumn of 1978), expressed, though admiring of sundry local felicities, some frustration at the difficulty of identifying any prevailing "point of view." In his concluding paragraph he spoke of how "the greatest poets of our century thought they had something important to say," of how Eliot and Pound and Stevens

> sought, tested, and imparted a comprehensive and profound truth on the basis of which life, they hoped, could be enjoyed or endured or redeemed. Eliot's troubled Christianity, Yeats's *Vision*, Stevens's imagination, Pound's commitment to ideals of perfected intellectual sincerity and unity with nature are hopelessly inadequate labels, but at least remind us that we could say what these poets proposed. That Nemerov has no such truth to tell limits the excitement and impact of his poetry.

It is a severe judgment, no doubt excessively so, for Nemerov was by no means without a special point of view, and his poetry is far from being devoid of avowal: yet it is such a judgment that others also have rendered, perhaps because the particular ambivalence at the heart of "The Blue Swallows" does so frequently mark his testimony. But his indecisiveness, his irresolution, with respect to the question as to whether the real sovereignty belongs to "the spelling mind" or to the aboriginal reality of the world itself deserves to be thought of as a sign of the integrity and candor with which he carried forward his central project of pondering the relation between the self and the not-self, between the restless eye and the things it perceives.

From certain perspectives the world may be considered to be our own creation, and such design as is to be found may appear consequent upon our own rage for order. Or, again, viewed differently, all that which has preceded us and which stands over against us and which can in no way be thought to belong to the apparatus of *la présence humaine* surely deserves to be accorded pride of place. But, then, as Stevens gently suggests in his essay "The Noble Rider and the Sound of Words" (*The Necessary Angel*), "from one of the many points of view from which it is possible" to consider this matter, what we may be struck by "is an interdependence of the imagination and reality as equals."[1] And if Stevens, who reflected on this issue more obsessively than any other poet of the modern period, could not finally come down resoundingly on the side of either reality or imagination, perhaps Nemerov ought not to be too closely bargained with because of the difficulty he had in adjudicating the ancient claims of philosophical realism and idealism.

Yet, despite his frequent attraction to the kind of epistemology and metaphysics proposed by philosophical idealism, Nemerov's predominating sympathy is for the sober-mindedness of realism, and in the great poem "The Loon's Cry" (*Mirrors and Windows*, 1958) he acknowledges that he has "fallen from / The symboled world, where I in earlier days / Found mysteries of meaning, form, and fate / Signed on the sky." And the sort of ethic and poetic by which he wanted most to be guided were for him, as he indicates in "Vermeer" (*The Next Room of the Dream*, 1962), most wonderfully exemplified in the seventeenth-century Dutch master:

> Taking what is, and seeing it as it is,
> Pretending to no heroic stances or gestures,
> Keeping it simple; being in love with light
> And the marvelous things that light is able to do,
> How beautiful! a modesty which is
> Seductive extremely, the care for daily things.
> . . . .
> If I could say to you, and make it stick,
> A girl in a red hat, a woman in blue
> Reading a letter, a lady weighing gold . . .
> If I could say this to you so you saw,
> And knew, and agreed that this was how it was
> In a lost city across the sea of years,
> I think we should be for one moment happy
> In the great reckoning of those little rooms
> Where the weight of life has been lifted and made light,
> Or standing invisible on the shore opposed,
> Watching the water in the foreground dream
> Reflectively, taking a view of Delft
> As it was, under a wide and darkening sky.

In Nemerov's book *Reflexions on Poetry & Poetics* (1972), the essay "Attentiveness and Obedience" says that, "having a dominantly aural imagination, I not so much look at nature as I listen to what it says. This is a mystery, at least in the sense that I cannot explain it—why should a phrase come to you out of the ground and seem to be exactly right? But the mystery appears to me as a poet's proper relation with things, a relation in which language, that accumulated wisdom and folly in which the living and the dead speak simultaneously, is a full partner and not merely a stenographer."[2] And then he cites "A Spell before Winter" (*The Next Room of the Dream*) as a poem (about the late autumn in Vermont) in which, as he says, he "tried to say something of this more or less directly":

> After the red leaf and the gold have gone,
> Brought down by the wind, then by hammering rain
> Bruised and discolored, when October's flame

Goes blue to guttering in the cusp, this land
Sinks deeper into silence, darker into shade.
There is a knowledge in the look of things,
The old hills hunch before the north wind blows.

Now I can see certain simplicities
In the darkening rust and tarnish of the time,
And say over the certain simplicities,
The running water and the standing stone,
The yellow haze of the willow and the black
Smoke of the elm, the silver, silent light
Where suddenly, readying toward nightfall,
The sumac's candelabrum darkly flames.
And I speak to you now with the land's voice,
It is the cold, wild land that says to you
A knowledge glimmers in the sleep of things:
The old hills hunch before the north wind blows.

"To see certain simplicities and to say over the certain simplicities—
they are in a sense," as Nemerov reminds us, "the same thing. . . ." And
what he had in mind was Heidegger's notation in *On the Way to Language*
that *to say* descends from the Old Norse word meaning "to show," "to let
this or that be seen." Which brings us close to one major premise of his
ars poetica, for he very much wanted to be carefully heedful of and to
"listen" to all the circumstances of nature and history by which he found
himself surrounded and to "show" them. Indeed, as the poem "Sight-
seers" *(The Blue Swallows)* indicates, he conceived it to be a sort of blasphemous *trahison* to wander through the world with a little black box
aimed

> at all
> Remarkable things:
> *Click,* the Vatican,
> *Click,* the Sphinx,
> *Click,* in the Badlands. . . .

And, in the face of such heedlessness, things sometimes dream

> Of looking alive,
> Of being released
> To the ripple and flash
> Of a fiery world
> Where the dragonfly
> Glitters and goes

> And the gold sun sinks
> In the oil black film
> Of a pool, forever
> Evanescent, but
> No: reflexion
> Has intervened, and
> Again, in the box
> The dark will won
> That knows no now,
> In the mind bowed down
> Among the shadows
> Of shadowy things,
> Itself a shadow
> Less sure than they.

The careful heedfulness, the vigilant advertence, and a purity of intransitive attention are, of course, what lie behind so exquisite a poem as "The Junction, on a Warm Afternoon" *(The Next Room of the Dream)*. The poet is standing in some rural district at a railroad crossing, when a slow freight train rises into view, rounds the bend, and passes on, as the crew courteously acknowledge the greetings of the handful of spectators who are gathered at the junction:

> Out of the small domestic jungle,
> The roadside scribble of wire and stick
> Left over from last fall as we come
> Into spring again, a slow freight
> Incongruously rises into view.
> The tall boxcars, rounding the bend,
> Rattle their chains, and from the high
> Cab of the engine, from the caboose,
> The old men in caps and spectacles,
> Gentle old men, some smoking pipes,
> Nod with a distant courtesy,
> Kindly and yet remote, their minds
> On other things.
>   Sunlight is warm
> And grateful. The old railroad men
> Are growing obsolete with the great
> Engines whose demands they meet,
> And yet they do not fail in their
> Courtly consideration of the stranger
> Standing in sunlight while the freight

Passes slowly along the line
To disappear among small trees,
Leaving empty the long, shining rails
That curve, divide, vanish, and remain.

If for a moment the action in this scene could be frozen just as the people standing at the junction are waving at the train and the crew are saluting them, it would be such a scene, enveloped in silences, as an Edward Hopper might have rendered. What is presented is simply a marvelously accurate sensory image that, precisely by dint of being untouched by any kind of *paysage moralisé*, has a wonderfully profound resonance for every reader who knows something of the American landscape.

Or one thinks of another great poem in *The Blue Swallows*, "The Mud Turtle," which, again, splendidly exemplifies Nemerov's genius for empathy. It invites us to contemplate an old turtle emerging from water and dragging itself over a stubbled field till it finally reaches a hilltop and a garden where it rests for an hour:

His lordly darkness decked in filth
Bearded with weed like a lady's favor,
He is a black planet, another world
Never till now appearing, even now
Not quite believably old and big,
Set in the summer morning's midst
A gloomy gemstone to the sun opposed.
Our measures of him do not matter,
He would be huge at any size;
And neither does the number of his years,
The time he comes from doesn't count.

Some mischievous boys begin to tease him with sticks, and, "when they turn him on his back / To see the belly heroically yellow,"

He throws himself fiercely to his feet,
Brings down the whole weight of his shell,
Spreads out his claws and digs himself in
Immovably, invulnerably,
But for the front foot on the left,
Red-budded, with the toes torn off.
So over he goes again, and shows
us where a swollen leech is fastened
Softly between plastron and shell.
Nobody wants to go close enough

To burn it loose; he can't be helped
Either, there is no help for him
As he makes it to his feet again
And drags away to the meadow's edge.
We see the tall grass open and wave
Around him, it closes, he is gone
Over the hill toward another water,
Bearing his hard and chambered hurt
Down, down, down, beneath the water,
Beneath the earth beneath. He takes
A secret wound out of the world.

It is, one feels, an absolutely perfect poem, in part because it never deviates from its object. And the sympathy, the tenderness, with which it presents this scarred old reptile taking its "secret wound out of the world" will remind us of that similar feat of compassionate imagination which is performed in Elizabeth Bishop's great poem "The Fish" (*North & South*), or in her moving prose poem "Giant Snail" (*The Complete Poems*).

But though Nemerov, as in "The Mud Turtle," is recurrently—in, say, the title poem in *The Salt Garden*, or in "Painting a Mountain Stream" and "Trees" in *Mirrors and Windows*, or in "Wintering" in *Inside the Onion*, or in much else—bent on "finding again the world," he wants us never to forget what he reminds us of in "The Companions" (*The Blue Swallows*), that it is "the deep folly of man / To think that things can squeak at him more than things can." And whenever or wherever he descries any forgetfulness of the world's radical alterity, his tone immediately becomes harshly ironic and polemical. One thinks, for example, of "Elegy for a Nature Poet" (*The Next Room of the Dream*) in which he is recalling one who in October, his favorite season, caught in his last walk a catarrh that he "let go uncared for," so rapt was he in his contemplation of Nature, and we are told how his friends, as they mourned his death, "thought of his imprudence, and how Nature, / Whom he'd done so much for, had finally turned / Against her creature":

His gift was daily his delight, he peeled
The landscape back to show it was a story;
Any old bird or burning bush revealed
At his hands just another allegory.

Nothing too great, nothing too trivial
For him; from mountain range or humble vermin

He could extract the hidden parable—
If need be, crack the stone to get the sermon.

And now, poor man, he's gone. Without his name
The field reverts to wilderness again,
The rocks are silent, woods don't seem the same;
Demoralized small birds will fly insane.

Rude Nature, whom he loved to idealize
And would have wed, pretends she never heard
His voice at all, as, taken by surprise
At last, he goes to her without a word.

And it is such a figure as the Nature Poet who prompts Nemerov to probe over and again the false habits of mind that precipitate us into the kind of pathos that this poem wants to remark.

Of all the miscalculations engendered by forgetfulness of the world's alterity that with which Nemerov is perhaps most impatient is the assumption that the ideas and categories and postulates wherewith we order experience are connatural with the world itself and may therefore be carelessly reified into objective actuality. But, as "The View from Pisgah" (*The Next Room of the Dream*) suggests, this is but "to alphabet the void." So elusive indeed is the world that even our sciences are in the end reduced to a kind of stutter and stammer, for

Below the ten thousand billionth of a centimeter
Length ceases to exist. Beyond three billion light years
The nebulae would have to exceed the speed of light
In order to be, which is impossible: no universe.
The long and short of it seems to be that thought
Can make itself unthinkable, and that measurement
Of reach enough and scrupulosity will find its home
In the incommensurable.

("The First Day," *The Blue Swallows*)

So it is no wonder that the speaker in "Beyond the Pleasure Principle" (*The Blue Swallows*) arrives at the point of realizing that "Our human thought arose at first in myth / And going far enough became a myth once more," since even our scientific discourse must finally be something analogic and metaphoric.

True, Nemerov (as in "One Way" [*The Blue Swallows*]) did on occasion contemplate the possibility that ours is "a world / Whose being is both thought / And thing, where neither thing / Nor thought will do alone /

Till either answers other; / Two lovers in the night / Each sighing other's name / Whose alien syllables / Become synonymous / For all their mortal night / And their embodied day." It is with such a dream—of "world / and spirit wed"—that the beautiful poem in *Mirrors and Windows* called "Writing" opens. The poet is thinking of how "when skaters curve / all day across the lake, scoring their white / records in ice," it is as if they were inscribing on the frozen lake a kind of memento or something like a happy rejoinder to its unvoiced salutation:

> Miraculous. It is as though the world
> were a great writing. Having said so much,
> let us allow there is more to the world
> than writing. . . .
> Not only must the skaters soon go home;
> also the hard inscription of their skates
> is scored across the open water, which long
> remembers nothing, neither wind nor wake.

Which is for the poem to say, no, the inevitable mysteriousness of things makes the moment of wedding between world and spirit inevitably and recalcitrantly very fleeting indeed.

Now it was Nemerov's continuing reflections on all these knotty questions concerning the relation between self and world (or imagination and reality) that often tended to interrupt and break the music to which the rhapsode within him was forever struggling to give voice. He was a sort of *philosophe manqué* who could never quite let go of those perennial issues bearing on the terms within which we are to understand how mind make contact (if it ever does) with reality, and thus his discourse is to be found over and again plunging into the thorniest bramble bushes of epistemology and metaphysics—to a far greater degree indeed than is the case (apart from Wallace Stevens) with any other major modern poet using the English tongue since Wordsworth and Coleridge. In this mode his writing is never touched by any sort of maladroitness and is marked by the urbane elegance that he regularly commanded. There are those, of course, who snappishly ask why he must always be bothering about the *hubris* of "the spelling mind," particularly when it did so manifestly not prove a temptation for himself, but his special penchant in this range of things must at last simply be accepted as a part of his signature. And, even when he remains captive to this besetting preoccupation, the greatness of his talent is often absolutely unignorable—as in "The Breaking of Rainbows," one of the most arresting poems in *The Blue Swallows* and one of the finest triumphs of his career. It speaks about oil spilling down a little stream beneath a bridge, and it wants to be taken as an allegory:

Oil is spilling down the little stream
Below the bridge. Heavy and slow as blood,
Or with an idiot's driveling contempt:
The spectral film unfolding, spreading forth
Prismatically in a breaking of rainbows,
Reflective radiance, marble evanescence,
It shadows the secret moves the water makes,
Creeping upstream again, then prowling down,
Sometimes asleep in the dull corners, combed
As the deep grass is combed in the stream's abandon,
And sometimes tearing open silently
Its seamless fabric in momentary shapes
Unlikened and nameless as the shapes of sky
That open with the drift of cloud, and close,
High in the lonely mountains, silently.
The curve and glitter of it as it goes
The maze of its pursuit, reflect the water
In agony under the alien, brilliant skin
It struggles to throw off and finally does
Throw off, on its frivolous purgatorial fall
Down to the sea and away, dancing and singing
Perpetual intercession for this filth—
Leaping and dancing and singing, forgiving everything.

Here, it will be natural for the contemporary reader who comes to the poem without any awareness of Nemerov's central interests to take this remarkable lyric as a meditation on the kind of ecological tragedy by which we are now everywhere surrounded, and it is in such a context that the poem clearly places itself. The oil spilling down the stream, "with an idiot's driveling contempt" and without any regard at all for this little freshet's "agony under the alien, brilliant skin," is an image of all those pollutants wherewith the people of our age, in their zeal for commerce and industrial enterprise, have recklessly befouled and devastated the things of earth. But to those who are familiar with Nemerov's deepest concerns it will be immediately apparent that to read the poem in such terms is to miss what the poem most basically intends to remark. And this surely bears on his sense of how relentlessly all our projects for arranging and organizing and regulating reality—all the well-driven machines of our philosophy and science and engineering—are calculated to impose a "heavy" and an "alien" design on the "seamless fabric" of the world. Yet that this stream, after it has thrown off "the alien . . . skin," should nevertheless dance and sing intercession for the "filth" that would defile it, "forgiving everything," attests to the strange beneficence in things to which some choose to allude metaphorically by the term God. So it is that the lesson of this gentle pedagogue goes in "The Breaking of Rainbows."

But, when Nemerov does break loose from his philosophical engrossments, he allows us the clearest view of his true genius, as he simply thrusts us into the marvelous plenitude presented by all the things and creatures of this world. In *this* mode his poetry puts us in mind of the beautiful passage in "Maestria," his moving tribute to Ezra Pound (*New and Selected Poems*, 1960), in which he speaks of what abides after one has inspected "the rusting, controversial wheels / Of the abandoned machinery":

> There remains
> A singular lucidity and sweetness, a way
> Of relating the light and the shade,
> The light spilling from fountains, the shade
> Shaken among the leaves.

And it is indeed "a singular lucidity and sweetness" by which we will be struck in an immense variety of the lyrics that manage to win some independence from his special philosophical interests.

The title poem, for example, of *The Salt Garden* (1955), presents a fine case in point of the deeply satisfying reflectiveness with which Nemerov handles the ordinary stuff of our daily round. In approaching this poem one should perhaps have it in mind that he was reared in New York City, educated at Harvard where he took his baccalaureate degree in 1941, and then, after spending the war years as a fighting pilot in the Royal Canadian Air Force and the Eighth U.S. Army Air Force, returned to the States in 1945, shortly after which he briefly held an appointment in English at Hamilton College in Clinton, New York, before joining in 1948 the faculty of Bennington College in Vermont, where he remained for eighteen years. He himself acknowledged that, in taking up residence in Vermont, he was a "city boy who came late to the country; [and thus] 'nature,' whatever that is, had a powerful effect for being an effect so long delayed." So here he is in "The Salt Garden," a few years after settling into rural Vermont, contemplating as a transplanted New Yorker the "good house" in which he and his wife and their child dwell and contemplating the

> ground whereon
> With an amateur's toil
> Both lawn and garden have been won

From a difficult, shallow soil
That, now inland, was once the shore
And once, maybe, the ocean floor.
Much patience, and some sweat,
Have made the garden green,
And even green the lawn.

And, as the poet sits by his wife on this late afternoon, he thinks "that
here our life / Might be a long and happy one." But, then, the complacent
satisfaction with which he contemplates "Turnip and bean and violet / In
a decent order set" suddenly vanishes, as he watches the flowers and
vegetation and all the work he and his wife have done "bend in the salt
wind." This wind dispels the momentary sense of security because it
causes him to remember the distant ocean, and in relation to the world
without end of those briny deeps he is at once reminded that no eternal-
ity can be expected for any "work of the hand."

The next morning he rises at dawn and sees a "great gull come from
the mist / To stand upon the lawn." And, as he watches the "fierce austerity" with which the bird shakes "his savage wing," he thinks of "the
wild sea lanes" by which this creature has wandered and "the wild
waters" where it sleeps. So it occurs to him that this gull is

> like a merchant prince
> Come to some poor province,
> Who, looking all about, discerns
> No spice, no treasure house,
> Nothing that can be made
> Delightful to his haughty trade,
> And so spreads out his sail,
> Leaving to savage men
> Their miserable regimen;
> So did he rise, making a gale
> About him by his wings,
> And fought his huge freight into air
> And vanished seaward with a cry. . . .

Then the poem concludes:

> When he was gone
> I turned back to the house
> And thought of wife, of child,
> And of my garden and my lawn
> Serene in the wet dawn;
> And thought that image of the wild

Wave where it beats the air
Had come, brutal, mysterious,
To teach the tenant gardener,
Green fellow of this paradise,
Where his salt dream lies.

So it is that the poet is reminded, in ways that make us think at once of Yeats and Frost, that the land, even that little demesne which we redeem from wildness and disorder, is not ours, that we are but tenants on the land, and that, however efficacious our tenancy may be in the reclamation of what "was once the shore / And once, maybe, the ocean floor," the fruits of our labor are so impermanent as to require us to put to ourselves the question that the speaker in Nemerov's poem must face— namely, "what can man keep?"

The same sort of gently ironic wisdom shaping the title poem of *The Salt Garden* is met in another great poem in that volume, "The Pond," and it, too, particularly by reason of the richness of the narrative, will put us in mind of Frost and of his deep responsiveness to the heartrending mishaps that are often a part of rural life. We are taken into a neighborhood where, at the end of a long meadow, "the road runs / High on a bank, making a kind of wall," and where the rains of one October gradually built up a "pond some hundred yards across / And deep maybe to the height of a man's thigh / At the deepest place." "By Christmastime the pond was frozen solid," and children

skated all the darkening afternoons
Until the sun burnt level on the ice,
And built their fires all along the shore
To warm their hands and feet, and skated nights
Under the full moon or the dark. . . .

So things went until the day on which the newspapers carried a headline that said: " 'Pond Claims First Victim.' " A little boy had been "Skating in darkness all alone, away / From the firelight—the others heard his cry / But he was gone before they found the place. . . ." Even then, however,

the skating didn't stop
Despite the funeral and motherly gloom
And editorials; what happened was
The pond took the boy's name of Christopher,
And this was voted properly in meeting
For a memorial and would be so

On the next map, when the next map was drawn:
Christopher Pond: if the pond should still be there.

By Eastertide the pond was again free of ice and slowly warmed into life:

> grackle, starling and flicker
> Settled to stay; and the sparrowhawk would stand
> In the height of noon, a stillness on beating wings,
> While close over the water swallows would trace
> A music nearly visible in air,
> Snapping at newborn flies.

"By day the birds, and then the frogs at night, / Kept up a music there, part requiem, / Part hunting-song," till "day by day, in the heat of June, the green / World raised itself to natural arrogance, / And the air sang with summer soon to come."

Then, by the time the sullen days of August had come, "under the massy heat / Of the sun," the pond was slowly drying up. Indeed, it was no longer a pond

> But a swamp, a marsh, with here and there a stretch
> Of open water, even that half spread
> With lily pads and the rich flesh of lilies.
> And elsewhere life was choking on itself
> As though, in spite of all the feeding there,
> Death could not keep the pace and had to let
> Life curb itself. . . .

"So, Christopher," the narrator thinks, as the pond begins to disappear,

> All that your body and your given name
> Could do in accidental consecrations
> Against nature, returns to nature now,
> And so, Christopher, goodbye.

But the poem is not yet ready to end merely by remarking the transiency of nature and its indifference to all our "consecrations." For, as the narrator is reminded by a dragonfly, the cyclicism that dominates the history of nature ordains in strange ways that death and renewal endlessly succeed each other. His eye falls on a dragonfly that has settled on a stem— which makes him think

> that this winged animal of light,
> Before it could delight the eye, had been

In a small way a dragon of the deep,
A killer and meat-eater on the floor
Beneath the April surface of the pond;
And that it rose and cast its kind in May
As though putting away costume and mask
In the bitter play, and taking a lighter part.
And thinking so, I saw with a new eye
How nothing given us to keep is lost
Till we are lost, and immortality
Is ours until we have no use for it
And live anonymous in nature's name
Though named in human memory and art.

So now at last the poem can conclude, as the speaker says:

Not consolation, Christopher, though rain
Fill up the pond again and keep your name
Bright as the glittering water in the spring;
Not consolation, but our acquiescence.
And I made this song for a memorial
Of yourself, boy, and the dragonfly together.

Yet the ending of the poem brings us to no real point of closure, since it is at last unclear as to whether the final reality we face is simply the anonymity to which we are fated "in nature's name" or whether "human memory and art" offer some proximate "consolation"—though it would *seem* that the "acquiescence" to which we are bidden entails a very stern sort of stoicism. The concluding lines resist any clean translation at a discursive level. But at least they propel us onward to many of Nemerov's later poems that offer further disclosures of his genius for reading the *liber naturae*—to "Trees" and "The Loon's Cry" in *Mirrors and Windows*, to "The Crossing" and "Late Butterflies" in *Gnomes & Occasions*, to "The Dependencies" and "Walking down Westgate in the Fall" and "Nature Morte" in *The Western Approaches* (1975), to "The Dying Garden" and "By Al Lebowitz's Pool" in *Sentences*, to "A Sprig of Dill" and "This Present Past" in *Inside the Onion*, and to many, many others.

To conceive Nemerov to be most principally a poet of nature would be, however, very greatly to underestimate his range, for he brought within the circle of his attention perhaps a wider variety of subjects than any other American poet has scanned since Auden, and Willard Spiegelman in a fine essay (in his book *The Didactic Muse*) has remarked "the . . . courteous intelligence" with which he addressed himself to "suburbs, football, black holes, waiting rooms, pockets, Christmas shopping, Bach cello suites,"[3] and dozens of other topics thrust up by the quotidian material of American life. But, in taking the measure of how considerably his work surpasses the genre of nature poetry, what one needs particularly to have in view are the many remarkable poems that deal sacramentally with persons or personal relationships—as (to use the language of the Anglican Catechism) "outward and visible signs of [an] inward and spiritual grace" or of the hope for such grace.

In this connection one will think, for example, of such a lovely poem as "The Sweeper of Ways" in *The Blue Swallows*—which, along with "A Negro Cemetery Next to a White One" in the same volume, presents (excepting, of course, the work of Afro-American writers) a well-nigh unique instance among poets of Nemerov's generation of any attention at all being paid to the humanity and experience of black people. It invites us to contemplate "a small mild Negro man with a broom / [who] Sweeps up the leaves that fall along the paths." In a brief and firmly reticent essay on the poem (*Reflexions on Poetry & Poetics*) Nemerov says only that he encountered this man "at a college"—which could have been Bennington College to whose faculty he was attached from 1948 to 1966. But, given the period in which the poem was written, one suspects (particularly since there is not much of a black populace in rural Vermont) that he more probably encountered this man on the campus of Hollins College in Virginia, where he served as Writer-in-Residence during the academic year 1962–63. This "small mild Negro man with a broom"

> carries his head to one side, looking down
> At his leaves, at his broom like a windy beard
> Curled with the sweeping habit. Over him
> High haughty trees, the hickory and ash,
> Dispense their more leaves easily, or else
> The district wind, hunting hypocrisy,
> Tears at the summer's wall and throws down leaves
> To witness of a truth naked and cold.
>
> Hopeless it looks, on these harsh, hastening days
> Before the end, to finish all those leaves
> Against time. But the broom goes back and forth
> With a tree's patience, as though naturally
> Erasers would speak the language of pencils.
> A thousand thoughts fall on the same blank page,
> Though the wind blows them back, they go where he
> Directs them, to the archives where disorder
> Blazes and a pale smoke becomes the sky.
> The ways I walk are splendidly free of leaves.

We meet, we smile good morning, say the weather
Whatever. On a rainy day there'll be
A few leaves stuck like emblems on the walk;
These too he brooms at till they come unstuck.
Masters, we carry our white faces by
In silent prayer, Don't hate me, on a wave-
length which his broom's antennae perfectly
Pick up, we know ourselves so many thoughts
Considered by a careful, kindly mind
Which can do nothing, and is doing that.

The job performed by this man is, of course, a menial one, and, as Nemerov suggests in his essay on the poem, given the autumn setting with leaves constantly drifting downward, it might indeed be taken as a kind of "parody of one of the labors of Hercules: cleaning up leaves that continue to fall from a vast treasury overhead." But, nevertheless, the humble workman drives his broom across the many pathways that criss-cross this college campus "With a tree's patience." The servility of his status offers him little else in which to take pride apart from the fidelity and efficiency with which he performs an inglorious function—and thus the ways the speaker walks "are splendidly free of leaves." The station this nameless hireling occupies in the world reflects a long history of his kind being excluded from the promises of American life, and about that he "can do nothing, and is doing that": he is simply sweeping the side-walks over which he holds custodianship. So the poem wants to express admiration for the quiet dignity of the "small mild" man. But in this there is no easy sentimentality, for the Sweeper directs the bristles of his broom across the footpaths of his campus as if these bristles were like "Erasers [that] would speak the language of pencils"—and, as a result, "A thou-sand thoughts fall on the . . . blank page." Moreover, among these thoughts are thoughts that bring uneasiness to the speaker. He and the Sweeper exchange a smile of good morning, and, as they do so, the poet hopes that, with the white face of the "Masters," no ill-will toward him-self will be harbored by this "careful, kindly" man, since he, too, "can do nothing"—or next to nothing—by way of rectifying centuries of wrong-doing.

Or, again, for another and quite different example of the kind of rev-erent carefulness with which Nemerov faces into the human commu-nion, we may turn to "September, the First Day of School," one of the finest poems in *Gnomes & Occasions* (1973). Here, in six beautifully crafted stanzas, he speaks of an experience than which perhaps none could be more universal—namely, the pain of being separated from one's child on the morning of his or her first day at school:

My child and I hold hands on the way to school,
And when I leave him at the first-grade door
He cries a little but is brave; he does
Let go. My selfish tears remind me how
I cried before that door a life ago.
I may have had a hard time letting go.

Each fall the children must endure together
What every child also endures alone:
Learning the alphabet, the integers,
Three dozen bits and pieces of a stuff
So arbitrary, so peremptory,
That worlds invisible and visible

Bow down before it, as in Joseph's dream
The sheaves bowed down and then the stars bowed down
Before the dreaming of a little boy.
That dream got him such hatred of his brothers
As cost the greater part of life to mend,
And yet great kindness came of it in the end.

As the poet watches his little boy leave him to pass through the doors of his school, he thinks of the many disciplines, some of them apparently authoritarian and arbitrary, to which his son will be required to submit, but he anticipates all the incalculable ways in which this necessary *paideia* will so enrich the interior life of the lad as perhaps even to give rise in him to visions before which the world will bow down, as was the case with Joseph. Joseph, of course, in the Old Testament narrative was the great-grandson of Abraham, the legendary patriarch of the Jewish people, and so greatly adored was he by his father, Jacob, that he was given a coat of many colors which enabled him to be recognized a long way off. This angered his brothers, and their anger was intensified by the dreams the boy kept reporting himself to have had which, in his account of them, seemed to indicate that he expected to become greater than they. Indeed, after he reported having dreamt that the sun and the moon and all the stars bowed down to him, on a certain day when their father had sent them out to feed his flocks on the plains of Shechem, they sold Joseph to Ishmaelite traders for twenty pieces of silver. And in turn these Ishmaelites sold him to an officer of the Pharaoh, king of Egypt, where, after undergoing much hardship, Joseph at last won such preferment under the Pharaoh as to become lord of all Egypt and thus to be able to rescue his brothers from the scourge of a great famine that befell the land of Canaan. In short, despite the years of tribulation prepared for Joseph by his dreams, "great kindness came of it in the end." And the father hopes that so too may it be with his son.

Yes, as the father reflects to himself,

> A school is where they grind the grain of thought,
> And grind the children who must mind the thought.
> It may be those two grindings are but one,
> As from the alphabet come Shakespeare's Plays,
> As from the integers comes Euler's Law,
> As from the whole, inseparably, the lives,
>
> The shrunken lives that have not been set free
> By law or by poetic phantasy.
> But may they be. My child has disappeared
> Behind the schoolroom door. And should I live
> To see his coming forth, a life away,
> I know my hope, but do not know its form
>
> Nor hope to know it. May the fathers he finds
> Among his teachers have a care of him
> More than his father could. How that will look
> I do not know, I do not need to know.
> Even our tears belong to ritual.
> But may great kindness come of it in the end.

The poet hopes, of course, that the dreams of his own son may not entail such a cost as did Joseph's which required "the greater part of life to mend." But he wants his child's mind and spirit to be "set free / By law or by poetic phantasy." He knows that it is futile to try to anticipate just how the formative process will proceed from stage to stage: "How that will look / I do not know, I do not need to know." But he prays that those to whom he is entrusting the lad will "have a care of him" and that "great kindness [may] come of it in the end." And thus he gently bestows a blessing on his little boy as he disappears "Behind the schoolroom door." It is all spoken with a tenderness that wrenches the heart.

Nemerov was, of course, a luminously clever man of many moods and inclinations, and often his great gift was invested in a mordant kind of satire. In "Boom!" (*New and Selected Poems*), for example, he ridicules the bumptious little Presbyterian clergyman who was Dwight Eisenhower's pastor during his years in the White House and who on one occasion announced that American affluence had "provided the leisure, the en-

ergy, and the means for a level of human and spiritual values never before reached." Or "Santa Claus" (*The Next Room of the Dream*) presents
a jeremiad directed at the travesty of religious sentiment that is exemplified by the rituals centered on "this overstuffed confidence man, / . . .
who climbs at night / Down chimneys, into dreams, with this world's
goods":

> Played at the better stores by bums, for money,
> This annual savior of the economy
> Speaks in the parables of the dollar sign:
> Suffer the little children to come to Him.

Or, again, "Grace to Be Said at the Supermarket" (*The Blue Swallows*)
invites us to consider how this "God of ours, the Great Geometer," in
"compressing the little lambs in orderly cubes / Making the roast a decent cylinder, / Fairing the tin ellipsoid of a ham, / Getting the luncheon
meat anonymous / In squares and oblongs with the edges beveled," confers "aesthetic distance / Upon our appetites, and on the bloody / Mess
of our birthright, our unseemly need." So the doxology says, "Praise
Him. . . .":

> Through Him the brutes
> Enter the pure Euclidean kingdom of number,
> Free of their bulging and blood-swollen lives
> They come to us holy, in cellophane
> Transparencies, in the mystical body
>
> That we may look unflinchingly on death
> As the greatest good, like a philosopher should.

And there is an enormous lot of poems in this general vein. To cite but
one more example, consider "Thirtieth Anniversary Report of the Class
of '41" (*Gnomes & Occasions*):

> We who survived the war and took to wife
> And sired the kids and made the decent living,
> And piecemeal furnished forth the finished life
> Not by grand theft so much as petty thieving—
>
> Who had the routine middle-aged affair
> And made our beds and had to lie in them
> This way or that because the beds were there,
> And turned our bile and choler in for phlegm—
>
> Who saw grandparents, parents, to the vault
> And wives and selves grow wrinkled, grey and fat

And children through their acne and revolt
And told the analyst about all that—

Are done with it. What is there to discuss?
There's nothing left for us to say of us.

It is a strangely arch and icily constrained declaration, and, for the sake of keeping the brittleness of tone he has chosen, Nemerov does not hesitate even greatly to misrepresent his own character.

In one of the most penetrating observations of his poetic manner that has ever been made, Robert Boyers has suggested in his essay "Howard Nemerov's True Voice of Feeling" (in Boyers' volume, *Excursions: Selected Literary Essays*), that he deserves to be regarded as

> a poet of bad conscience, a poet trained in irony and *double entendre* whose instinct . . . [was] to banish them and attain to transparence, to a vision clear and unmistakably right, though tainted still by memory and artifice. It is a project that comes bursting forth here and there in Nemerov's volumes, tumbling with delight into the domain of nature's careless embrace, the compulsive irony and slightly malevolent twinkle of the inveterate poseur suspended if not entirely banished.[4]

And surely here Boyers has hold of something essential. Nemerov's American generation in poetry (Richard Wilbur, Anthony Hecht, Howard Moss, William Meredith, *et al.*) was, of course, early on deeply formed by that modernist poetic which found its normative canon in Donne, Marvell, Dryden, Pope, Hopkins, and in such twentieth-century guides as Yeats, Pound, Eliot, and Ransom. And though he in his late poetry, like many of his immediate contemporaries, steadily moved toward simpler and more direct modes of expression, the poet of *The Image and the Law* and *Guide to the Ruins* and *The Salt Garden* was one who had been taught by his masters to seek through irony and paradox and metaphor what Eliot termed an "alliance of levity and seriousness" whereby, as he laid it down, "the seriousness is intensified." It was, indeed, this whole way of thinking about literary enterprise that originally defined Nemerov's poetic conscience. But his instinct was, as Boyers says, "to . . . attain to transparence," and this is what he managed to do in the great poems—in "The Salt Garden," "The Pond," "The Loon's Cry," "Trees," "To Lu Chi," "The Junction, on a Warm Afternoon," "Vermeer," "The Breaking of Rainbows," "The Mud Turtle," "The Beekeeper Speaks," "The Blue Swallows," and a vast number of others. The music that we hear in such poems, however, is often interrupted and broken by the puns and jokes and schemes of irony and self-irony to which he had

recourse in much of his work, and his penchant for this kind of idiom
needs to be thought of as having been at once a part of what his historical
moment in some measure committed his special talent to and also a part
of the burden that this side of his talent entailed.

But when he was least distracted by "the stormy crows" he sometimes
heard inside his head ("Brainstorm," *Mirrors and Windows*), he knew with
utmost clarity what his true course should be, as the marvelous poem
"Lion & Honeycomb" (*The Next Room of the Dream*) makes apparent:

> He didn't want to do it with skill,
> He'd had enough of skill. If he never saw
> Another villanelle, it would be too soon;
> And the same went for sonnets. If it had been
> Hard work learning to rime, it would be much
> Harder learning not to. The time came
> He had to ask himself, what did he want?
> What did he want when he began
> That idiot fiddling with the sounds of things?
>
> He asked himself, poor moron, because he had
> Nobody else to ask. The others went right on
> Talking about form, talking about myth
> And the (so help us) need for a modern idiom;
> The verseballs among them kept counting syllables.
>
> So there he was, this forty-year-old teen-ager
> Dreaming preposterous mergers and divisions
> Of vowels like water, consonants like rock
> (While everybody kept discussing values
> And the need for values), for words that would
> Enter the silence and be there as a light.
> So much coffee and so many cigarettes
> Gone down the drain, gone up in smoke,
> Just for the sake of getting something right
> Once in a while, something that could stand
> On its own flat feet to keep out windy time
> And the worm, something that might simply be,
> Not as the monument in the smoky rain
> Grimly endures, but that would be
> Only a moment's inviolable presence,
> The moment before disaster, before the storm,
> In its peculiar silence, an integer
> Fixed in the middle of the fall of things,

> Perfected and casual as to a child's eye
> Soap bubbles are, and skipping stones.

And in those poems in which Nemerov managed to be obedient to his deepest instincts—of which, happily, there are scores and scores—what we are given is, indeed, "a moment's inviolable presence," something "Perfected and casual as to a child's eye / Soap bubbles are, and skipping stones." It is one of the great legacies in American poetry of our period.

NOTES

1. Introduction

1. George Steiner, *Real Presences* (London: Faber and Faber, 1989), p. 132.
2. Henry G. Bugbee, Jr., *The Inward Morning: A Philosophical Exploration in Journal Form* (New York: Harper and Row [Harper Colophon Books], 1976), pp. 167–68.
3. Ibid., pp. 168–69.
4. H. D. Lewis, *Morals and Revelation* (London: Allen and Unwin, 1951), p. 212.
5. Ernest de Selincourt, ed., *The Poetical Works of William Wordsworth*, 2d ed., Vol. 2 (London: Oxford University Press, 1952), p. 438.
6. Philip Wheelwright, *Metaphor and Reality* (Bloomington: Indiana University Press, 1962), p. 167.
7. Philip Wheelwright, *The Burning Fountain: A Study in the Language of Symbolism* (Bloomington: Indiana University Press, 1954), p. 122.
8. Steiner, *Real Presences*, p. 121.
9. Jacques Maritain, "The Frontiers of Poetry," in *Art and Scholasticism*, trans. J. F. Scanlan (New York: Charles Scribner's Sons, 1943), p. 91. See also Maritain's *Creative Intuition in Art and Poetry*, Bollingen Series 35, vol. 1 (New York: Pantheon Books, 1953), chap. 4.
10. Hugh McCarron, *Realization: A Philosophy of Poetry* (London: Sheed and Ward, 1937), p. 35.
11. Lewis, *Morals and Revelation*, p. 241. See also Wallace Stevens, "About One of Marianne Moore's Poems," in *The Necessary Angel: Essays on Reality and the Imagination* (New York: Vintage Books, 1965), for Stevens' commentary on Lewis's essay.
12. M. Chaning-Pearce, *The Terrible Crystal* (New York: Oxford University Press, 1941), p. 143.
13. Bugbee, *The Inward Morning*, p. 164.
14. See Mai-Mai Sze, *The Tao of Painting*, 2 vols., Bollingen Series 49 (New York: Pantheon Books, 1956). Vol. 1 is devoted to Miss Sze's account of how Chinese painting is related to *Tao* and to *Ch'i* ("heavenly inspiration") and to her interpretation of "the four treasures" (brush, ink, inkstone, and parchment). Vol. 2 consists of her translation of *The Mustard Seed Garden Manual*.
15. Steiner, *Real Presences*, p. 140.

16. Martin Heidegger, "On the Essence of Truth," in *Existence and Being*, trans. R. F. C. Hull et al. (Chicago: Henry Regnery Co., 1949), p. 333.
17. Martin Heidegger, *Discourse on Thinking*, trans. John M. Anderson and E. Hans Freund (New York: Harper and Row, 1966), pp. 54–55.
18. Martin Heidegger, *Holzwege* (Frankfurt-am-Main: Vittorio Klostermann, 1950), p. 303.
19. Ibid., p. 45.
20. George Santayana, *Three Philosophical Poets: Lucretius, Dante, and Goethe* (Cambridge: Harvard University Press, 1945), pp. v–vi.
21. Tony Tanner, *The Reign of Wonder: Naivety and Reality in American Literature* (Cambridge: Cambridge University Press, 1965), p. 349.

2. Stevens' Route—Transcendence Downward

1. *The Collected Poems of Wallace Stevens* (New York: Alfred A. Knopf, 1954), p. 464; hereafter cited as *CP* in the text.
2. Wallace Stevens, *Opus Posthumous*, ed. Milton J. Bates (New York: Alfred A. Knopf, 1989), p. 260; hereafter cited as *OP* in the text.
3. Julian Huxley, *Religion without Revelation* (London: Max Parrish, 1957), p. 58.
4. See Milton J. Bates, "Major Man and Overman: Wallace Stevens' Use of Nietzsche," *Southern Review* 15, no. 4 (1979): 811–39.
5. S. T. Coleridge, *Biographia Literaria*, ed. J. Shawcross, vol. 1 (London: Oxford University Press, 1907), chap. 13, p. 202.
6. Wallace Stevens, *The Necessary Angel: Essays on Reality and the Imagination* (New York: Alfred A. Knopf, 1951), p. 61; hereafter cited as *NA* in the text.
7. This remark of Stevens appeared on the wrapper of *The Man with the Blue Guitar and Other Poems* (New York: Alfred A. Knopf, 1937). The statement of which it was a part appears in *Opus Posthumous*, p. 233.
8. Simone Weil, *Gravity and Grace*, trans. Arthur Wills (New York: G. P. Putnam's Sons, 1952), p. 78.
9. A. Alvarez, *The Shaping Spirit: Studies in Modern English and American Poets* (London: Chatto and Windus, 1958), p. 132.
10. Joseph N. Riddel, *The Clairvoyant Eye: The Poetry and Poetics of Wallace Stevens* (Baton Rouge: Louisiana State University Press, 1965), p. 168.
11. *Letters of Wallace Stevens*, ed. Holly Stevens (New York: Alfred A. Knopf, 1970), pp. 426–27; hereafter cited as *L* in the text.
12. Lucy Beckett, *Wallace Stevens* (London: Cambridge University Press, 1974), p. 118.
13. *The Poems of Gerard Manley Hopkins*, ed. W. H. Gardner and N. H. Mackenzie, 4th ed. (London: Oxford University Press, 1967), p. 90.
14. Ibid., p. 70.
15. See Coleridge, *Biographia Literaria*, p. 202.
16. See Harold Bloom, *Wallace Stevens: The Poems of Our Climate* (Ithaca: Cornell University Press, 1977), pp. 204–8.

17. A. J. Ayer, *Language, Truth and Logic*, rev. ed. (London: Victor Gollancz, 1946), pp. 42–43.
18. *The Poems of Gerard Manley Hopkins*, p. 66.
19. Randall Jarrell, *Poetry and the Age* (New York: Alfred A. Knopf, 1953), p. 144.
20. Martin Heidegger, *Being and Time*, trans. John Macquarrie and Edward Robinson (New York: Harper and Row, 1962), p. 236.
21. See Martin Heidegger, *Basic Writings*, ed. David Farrell Krell (New York: Harper and Row, 1977), p. 221: "Man is not the lord of beings. Man is the shepherd of Being" ("Letter on Humanism").
22. H. D. Lewis, "Revelation and Art," in *Morals and Revelation* (London: Allen and Unwin, 1951), p. 212.
23. See Heidegger, *Basic Writings*, p. 210: " 'Being'—that is not God and not a cosmic ground" ("Letter on Humanism").
24. *The Collected Poems of Dylan Thomas* (New York: New Directions, 1953), p. 10.
25. Teilhard de Chardin, *Hymn of the Universe*, trans. Simon Bartholomew (New York: Harper and Row, 1965), pp. 83, 28.
26. See Amos N. Wilder, *The New Voice: Religion, Literature, Hermeneutics* (New York: Herder and Herder, 1969), p. 236: "If we are to find grace it is to be found in the world and not overhead."
27. As he was looking toward the preparation of *The Collected Poems*, Stevens proposed in a letter (27 April 1954) to Alfred Knopf that the volume be entitled *The Whole of Harmonium* (L, 831). Knopf raised objections, however, and the formulation finally settled on was *The Collected Poems of Wallace Stevens*—"a machine-made title if there ever was one," said Stevens (L, 834).
28. Frank Kermode, "Dwelling Poetically in Connecticut," in *Wallace Stevens: A Celebration*, ed. Frank Doggett and Robert Buttel (Princeton: Princeton University Press, 1980), p. 268.

3. W. H. Auden's Way: Toward the City— From the "Suburb of Dissent"

1. R. P. Blackmur, *Anni Mirabiles, 1921–1925: Reason in the Madness of Letters* (Washington, D.C.: Library of Congress, 1956), p. 37.
2. Rainer Maria Rilke, *Briefe aus Muzot, 1921–1926* (Leipzig: Insel-Verlag, 1938), p. 334.
3. Rainer Maria Rilke, *Tagebücher aus der Frühzeit* (Leipzig: Insel-Verlag, 1942), p. 140.
4. The phrase is Michael Hamburger's: see his *The Truth of Poetry* (New York: Harcourt Brace Jovanovich, 1969), p. 102.
5. Wallace Stevens, *The Necessary Angel: Essays on Reality and the Imagination* (New York: Alfred A. Knopf, 1951), p. 173.
6. Ibid., p. 31.
7. Wallace Stevens, "Adagia," in *Opus Posthumous*, ed. Milton J. Bates (New York: Alfred A. Knopf, 1989), p. 189.

8. Wallace Stevens, "Angel Surrounded by Paysans," in *The Collected Poems* (New York: Alfred A. Knopf, 1954), p. 496.

9. Stevens, "Adagia," p. 195.

10. Stevens, *The Necessary Angel*, p. 31.

11. Wallace Stevens, "Questions Are Remarks," in *The Collected Poems of Wallace Stevens*, p. 463.

12. W. H. Auden, "Squares and Oblongs," in *Poets at Work*, ed. C. D. Abbott (New York: Harcourt, Brace and Co., 1948), p. 177.

13. W. H. Auden, "Mimesis and Allegory," in *English Institute Annual, 1940*, ed. Rudolf Kirk (New York: Columbia University Press, 1941), p. 17.

14. T. S. Eliot, "Tradition and the Individual Talent," in *Selected Essays: 1917–1932* (New York: Harcourt, Brace and Co., 1932), p. 10.

15. T. S. Eliot, *The Use of Poetry and the Use of Criticism* (London: Faber and Faber, 1933), p. 111.

16. Stephen Spender, *World within World* (London: Hamish Hamilton, 1951), p. 51.

17. See T. E. Hulme, "Romanticism and Classicism," in *Speculations*, ed. Herbert Read, 2d ed. (London: Kegan Paul, Trench, Trubner and Co., 1936).

18. Ibid., p. 135.

19. W. H. Auden, "Introduction," in *The Complete Poems of Cavafy*, trans. Rae Dalven (New York: Harcourt, Brace and World, 1961), p. ix.

20. W. H. Auden, "The Sea and the Mirror," in *The Collected Poems*, ed. Edward Mendelson (New York: Random House, 1976), p. 335.

21. W. H. Auden, "For the Time Being: A Christmas Oratorio," in *The Collected Poems*, p. 307.

22. Auden, "Squares and Oblongs," p. 179.

23. W. H. Auden, "In Memory of W. B. Yeats," in *The Collected Poems*, p. 197.

24. Auden, "Squares and Oblongs," p. 170.

25. Ibid., p. 171.

26. Ibid., p. 179.

27. W. H. Auden, "New Year Letter," in *The Collected Poems*, p. 162.

28. See W. H. Auden, "Making, Knowing and Judging," in *The Dyer's Hand* (New York: Random House, 1962), pp. 57–58.

29. Auden, "Squares and Oblongs," p. 173.

30. W. H. Auden, "Cav & Pag," in *The Dyer's Hand*, p. 482.

31. See Susanne Langer, *Feeling and Form* (New York: Charles Scribner's Sons, 1953).

32. W. H. Auden, "The Poet of the Encirclement" (a review of T. S. Eliot's *A Choice of Kipling's Verse*), *New Republic* 109, no. 17 (25 October 1943): 579.

33. Auden, "The Sea and the Mirror," p. 313.

34. Ibid., p. 339.

35. W. H. Auden, "The Virgin & the Dynamo," in *The Dyer's Hand*, p. 71.

36. W. H. Auden, "Art and Psychology," in *The Arts Today*, ed. Geoffrey Grigson (London: John Lane, 1935), p. 18.

37. See Auden, "Making, Knowing and Judging," pp. 54–60.

38. Cecil Day Lewis, *A Hope for Poetry* (Oxford: Basil Blackwell, 1934), p. 46.
39. Edward Mendelson, ed., *The English Auden: Poems, Essays, and Dramatic Writings, 1927–1939* (New York: Random House, 1977), p. 39.
40. W. H. Auden and Louis MacNeice, *Letters from Iceland* (London: Faber and Faber, 1937), p. 258.
41. John Hollander, "Auden at Sixty," *Atlantic Monthly* 220, no. 1 (July 1967): 84.
42. Ibid.
43. *New Year Letter*—published in 1941 (London: Faber and Faber; New York: Random House [under the title *The Double Man*])—is dated "January 1, 1940" and was, therefore, written in Auden's thirty-third year (the date of his birth having been 21 February 1907).
44. See B. C. Bloomfield and Edward Mendelson, *W. H. Auden—A Bibliography, 1924–1969,* (Charlottesville: University Press of Virginia, 1972), p. 51.
45. Ibid.
46. See Philip Larkin, "What's Become of Wystan?" *Spectator,* no. 6890 (15 July 1960): 104–5.
47. Stephen Spender, "The Life of Literature," *Partisan Review* 15, no. 11 (November 1948): 1207.
48. Barbara Everett, *Auden* (Edinburgh: Oliver and Boyd, 1964), p. 25.
49. W. H. Auden, "A Literary Transference," *Southern Review* 6, no. 1 (Summer, 1940): 83.
50. Stephen Spender, "W. H. Auden and His Poetry," *Atlantic Monthly* 192, no. 1 (July 1953): 75.
51. Geoffrey Grigson, "Auden as a Monster," in *New Verse,* nos. 26–27 (November 1937): 15.
52. "Editor's Introduction," in *The Portable Greek Reader,* ed. W. H. Auden (New York: Viking Press, 1948), p. 20.
53. W. H. Auden, "Air Port," in *Nones* (New York: Random House, 1951), p. 23.
54. *The Poems of Gerard Manley Hopkins,* ed. W. H. Gardner and N. H. Mackenzie, 4th ed. (New York: Oxford University Press, 1967), p. 100.
55. William F. Lynch, S. J., *Christ and Apollo: The Dimensions of the Literary Imagination* (New York: Sheed and Ward, 1960), p. 94.
56. Justin Replogle, *Auden's Poetry* (Seattle: University of Washington Press, 1969), p. 170.
57. Christopher Fry, "Comedy," in *The New Orpheus: Essays toward a Christian Poetic,* ed. Nathan A. Scott, Jr. (New York: Sheed and Ward, 1964), p. 287.
58. François Duchene, *The Case of the Helmeted Airman: A Study of W. H. Auden's Poetry* (London: Chatto and Windus, 1972), p. 176.
59. See Richard M. Ohmann, "Auden's Sacred Awe," *Commonweal* 78 (31 May 1963): 279–81.
60. Sören Kierkegaard, *The Present Age,* trans. Alexander Dru and Walter Lowrie (New York: Oxford University Press, 1940), p. 17.
61. Ibid., p. 41.
62. Ibid., p. 16.
63. Ibid., p. 33.

64. Jacques Ellul, *The Technological Society*, trans. John Wilkinson (New York: Alfred A. Knopf, 1964), p. 138.
65. W. H. Auden, "Criticism in a Mass Society," in *The Intent of the Critic*, ed. Donald A. Stauffer (Princeton: Princeton University Press, 1941), p. 129.
66. Ibid., p. 127.
67. W. H. Auden, "Yeats as an Example," *Kenyon Review* 10, no. 2 (Spring 1948): 191.
68. W. H. Auden, "Introduction," in *Poets of the English Language*, ed. W. H. Auden and Norman Holmes Pearson, vol. 5 (New York: Viking Press, 1950), p. xxv.
69. Hannah Arendt, *The Human Condition* (Chicago: University of Chicago Press, 1958). The quotations that follow are from the "Collector's Edition" (5th impression), 1969.
70. See Richard Johnson, *Man's Place: An Essay on Auden* (Ithaca: Cornell University Press, 1973), pp. 213–16 and pp. 224–25. Note that Auden's *Forewords and Afterwords* (New York: Random House), published in spring 1973, a few months before his death, is dedicated to Hannah Arendt.
71. W. H. Auden, "Thinking What We Are Doing," *Encounter* 12, no. 6 (June 1959): 72.
72. Arendt, *The Human Condition*, p. 28.
73. Ibid., p. 40.
74. Ibid., p. 64.
75. Ibid., p. 41.
76. Ibid., p. 38.
77. Karl Jaspers, *Man in the Modern Age*, trans. Eden and Cedar Paul (Garden City, N.Y.: Doubleday Anchor Books, 1957), p. 50.
78. Arendt, *The Human Condition*, p. 69.
79. W. H. Auden, "Thinking What We Are Doing," p. 76.
80. W. H. Auden, *The Enchafèd Flood, or The Romantic Iconography of the Sea* (New York: Random House, 1950), p. 27.
81. Auden, *The Dyer's Hand*, p. 80.
82. Ibid., p. 84.
83. Charles Williams, *He Came Down from Heaven* (London: Faber and Faber, 1940), p. 96.
84. See Daniel Bell, *The End of Ideology* (New York: Collier Books, 1961).
85. W. H. Auden, *The Dyer's Hand*, p. 87.
86. Lionel Trilling, *The Liberal Imagination* (New York: Viking Press, 1950), p. 100.
87. Duchene, *The Case of the Helmeted Airman*, p. 165.
88. The phrase is Gerald Graff's: see his *Poetic Statement and Critical Dogma* (Evanston: Northwestern University Press, 1970), chap. 6.
89. The concluding figure in the sentence draws on Auden's "The Garrison" (in *Epistle to a Godson*). And, in this sentence, a portion of what precedes the concluding figure represents a raiding of a fine passage in Irving Howe's essay "The City in Literature," in which, after having brilliantly reviewed the kind of animus toward the city carried by much of modern literature, he asks

finally what it is, indeed, that we may be expected to do in the *Just* City—to which he answers: "Take our Sunday baths. . . ." See his *The Critical Point* (New York: Horizon Press, 1973), p. 58.

90. See Lionel Trilling, *Sincerity and Authenticity* (Cambridge: Harvard University Press, 1972), chap. 2.

91. Ibid., p. 39.

92. Hollander, "Auden at Sixty," p. 87.

4. *Theodore Roethke's Doxology*

1. Philip Wheelwright, *The Burning Fountain: A Study in the Language of Symbolism* (Bloomington: Indiana University Press, 1954), p. 81.

2. Ibid., p. 78.

3. Ibid., p. 82. Wheelwright is quoting from Edward Bullough, " 'Psychic Distance' as a Factor in Art and an Aesthetic Principle," *British Journal of Psychology* 5 (June 1912): 87ff.

4. Wheelwright, *The Burning Fountain*, p. 78.

5. Ibid., p. 88. Wheelwright is here paraphrasing Goethe.

6. See Martin Heidegger, *Gelassenheit* (Pfullingen: Gunther Neske Verlag, 1959); the English version, trans. John M. Anderson and E. Hans Freund, bears the title *Discourse on Thinking* (New York: Harper and Row, 1966).

7. Conrad Bonifazi, *A Theology of Things* (Philadelphia: J. B. Lippincott Co., 1967), p. 165.

8. Edmund Husserl, *Ideas*, trans. W. R. Boyce Gibson (New York: Macmillan Co., 1931), p. 88.

9. See Husserl, *Ideas*, passim; see also his *Cartesian Meditations*, trans. Dorion Cairns (The Hague: Martinus Nijhoff, 1960), sec. 14, pp. 31–33.

10. Martin Buber, *I and Thou*, trans. Ronald Gregor Smith (Edinburgh: T. and T. Clark, 1937), p. 7.

11. Rainer Maria Rilke, "Of One Who Listened to the Stones," in *Stories of God*, trans. M. D. Herter Norton and Nora Purtscher-Wydenbruch (New York: W. W. Norton and Co., 1932), pp. 115–21.

12. Theodore Roethke, "Comment," in "The Poet and His Critics: A Symposium," ed. Anthony Ostroff, *New World Writing*, vol. 19 (Philadelphia: J. B. Lippincott Co., 1961), p. 214.

13. See Martin Heidegger, "On the Essence of Truth," in *Existence and Being*, trans. Douglas Scott et al. (Chicago: Henry Regnery Co., 1949), pp. 319–51.

14. Allan Seager, *The Glass House: The Life of Theodore Roethke* (New York: McGraw-Hill, 1968), p. 21.

15. See Kenneth Burke, "The Vegetal Radicalism of Theodore Roethke," in *Sewanee Review* 58, no. 1 (January-March 1950): 68–108.

16. Ibid., 97–98.

17. Seager, *The Glass House*, p. 13.

18. Christopher Smart, *A Song to David*, stanza 77, which supplied Roethke with

the title for the opening poem ("Where Knock Is Open Wide") in *Praise to the End!* See *The Collected Poems of Theodore Roethke* (Garden City, N.Y.: Doubleday and Co., 1966), p. 71.

19. John Ciardi, "Theodore Roethke: A Passion and a Maker," *Saturday Review* 46 (31 August 1963): 13.

20. Jean Piaget, *Judgment and Reasoning in the Child* (Paterson, N.J.: Littlefield, Adams and Co., 1964), p. 4.

21. Theodore Roethke, "Open Letter," in *On the Poet and His Craft: Selected Prose of Theodore Roethke,* ed. Ralph J. Mills, Jr. (Seattle: University of Washington Press, 1965), p. 41.

22. Ibid.

23. Ibid., p. 42.

24. Carl G. Jung, *Psyche and Symbol* (New York: Doubleday, 1958), p. 131.

25. Theodore Roethke, "On 'Identity,'" in *On the Poet and His Craft,* pp. 24–25. This paper was originally presented at Northwestern University as part of a panel discussion devoted to the theme of "Identity."

26. Wallace Stevens, "Tea at the Palaz of Hoon," in *The Collected Poems of Wallace Stevens* (New York: Alfred A. Knopf, 1955), p. 65.

27. William F. Lynch, S. J., *Christ and Apollo: The Dimensions of the Literary Imagination* (New York: Sheed and Ward, 1960), p. 11.

28. Ibid., p. 8.

29. Roethke makes us feel, indeed, that he foresaw his being taxed with pantheistic leanings—and wanted to shield himself from the charge—when he denies (in his Northwestern statement, "On 'Identity' ") that his "soul" was ever "absorbed in God": "No, God for me still remains someone to be confronted, to be dueled with." (p. 26).

30. Denis Donoghue, *Connoisseurs of Chaos: Ideas of Order in Modern American Poetry,* 2d ed. (New York: Columbia University Press, 1984), p. 241.

31. Tony Tanner, *The Reign of Wonder: Naivety and Reality in American Literature* (Cambridge: Cambridge University Press, 1965), p. 355.

32. Quoted in *Emerson: An Organic Anthology,* ed. Stephen Whicher (Cambridge, Mass.: Riverside Press, 1960), p. 492.

33. Tanner, *The Reign of Wonder,* p. 337.

34. See Martin Buber, *The Knowledge of Man,* trans. Maurice Friedman and Ronald Gregor Smith (New York: Harper and Row, 1965), pp. 72–88, 71.

35. William Butler Yeats, "The Everlasting Voices," in *The Collected Poems of W. B. Yeats* (New York: Macmillan Co., 1951), p. 53.

36. William Butler Yeats, "Politics," in *The Collected Poems,* p. 337.

37. Donoghue, *Connoisseurs of Chaos,* p. 223.

38. See Theodore Roethke, "The Renewal," in *The Collected Poems,* p. 135: "I know I love, yet know not where I am; / I paw the dark, the shifting midnight air."

39. Roethke, "Open Letter," p. 40.

40. Roethke held a professorship in the Department of English at the University of Washington (Seattle) from 1948 until his death in 1963, and the explanation offered by his friend and colleague Robert Heilman (then chairman of the department) in January 1959 to the vice-president of the university as to why

Roethke frequently required "leaves" for illness gives a sufficient statement of his difficulty: "Roethke has a nervous ailment of the 'manic-depressive' type. Periodically he goes into a 'high' or 'low' state in which he is incapable of teaching. It is in such periods that he has been on sick leave." Professor Heilman's letter—a moving document—is quoted in full in Allan Seager's *The Glass House*, pp. 253–56.

WORKS BY THEODORE ROETHKE

Open House. New York: Alfred A. Knopf, 1941.

The Lost Son and Other Poems. Garden City, N.Y.: Doubleday and Co., 1948.

Praise to the End! Garden City, N.Y.: Doubleday and Co., 1951.

The Waking: Poems, 1933–1953. Garden City, N.Y.: Doubleday and Co., 1953.

Words for the Wind: The Collected Verse of Theodore Roethke. Garden City, N.Y.: Doubleday and Co., 1958.

I Am! Says the Lamb. Garden City, N.Y.: Doubleday and Co., 1961.

Sequence, Sometimes Metaphysical. Iowa City: Stone Wall Press, 1963.

The Far Field. Garden City, N.Y.: Doubleday and Co., 1964.

The Collected Poems of Theodore Roethke. Garden City, N.Y.: Doubleday and Co., 1966.

Ralph J. Mills, Jr., ed., *On the Poet and His Craft: Selected Prose of Theodore Roethke*. Seattle: University of Washington Press, 1965.

Ralph J. Mills, Jr., ed., *Selected Letters of Theodore Roethke*. Seattle: University of Washington Press, 1968.

5. Elizabeth Bishop—Poet without Myth

1. Basil Willey, *The Seventeenth Century Background*, 4th impression (London: Chatto and Windus, 1949), p. 293.
2. See John Locke, *An Essay Concerning Human Understanding*, ed. Peter H. Nidditch (Oxford: Clarendon Press, 1975), bk. 2, chap. 11, sect. 2, pp. 156–57.
3. Basil Willey, *The Seventeenth Century Background*, p. 297.
4. Ibid., pp. 298–99.
5. Ibid., p. 305.
6. John Bayley, *The Characters of Love* (New York: Basic Books, 1960), p. 267.
7. In "An Interview with Elizabeth Bishop" (*Shenandoah* 17, no. 2 [Winter 1966]: 11), Ashley Brown asked Bishop, "Do you think it necessary for a poet to have a 'myth'—Christian or otherwise—to sustain his work?" She answered: "It all depends—some poets do, some don't. . . . The question, I must admit, doesn't interest me a great deal. I'm not interested in big-scale work as such. Something needn't be large to be good."
8. See Jan B. Gordon, "Days and Distances: The Cartographic Imagination of Elizabeth Bishop," *Salmagundi*, nos. 22–23 (Spring-Summer 1973): 301.
9. Elizabeth Bishop, "Laureate's Words of Acceptance," *World Literature Today* 51, no. 1 (Winter 1977): 11.

10. John Ashbery, "Second Presentation of Elizabeth Bishop," *World Literature Today* 51, no. 1 (Winter 1977): 11.
11. Elizabeth Bishop, "In the Village," in *Questions of Travel* (New York: Farrar, Straus and Giroux, 1965), p. 77.
12. Elizabeth Bishop, "At the Fishhouses," in *The Complete Poems: 1927–1979* (New York: Farrar, Straus and Giroux, 1983), p. 66; hereafter cited in the text as *CP*.
13. Quoted in Anne Stevenson, *Elizabeth Bishop* (New York: Twayne Publishers, 1966), p. 66
14. David Kalstone, "All Eye," *Partisan Review* 38, no. 2 (1970); 312.
15. Wallace Stevens, "Notes toward a Supreme Fiction," in *The Collected Poems* (New York: Alfred A. Knopf, 1955), p. 383.
16. Quoted in "Poets," *Time* 89, no. 22 (2 June 1967); 68.
17. Alain Robbe-Grillet, *For a New Novel: Essays on Fiction*, trans. Richard Howard (New York: Grove Press, 1965), p. 58.
18. Louis L. Martz, *The Poetry of Meditation* (New Haven: Yale University Press, 1954), p. 27.
19. St. Francis de Sales, *Introduction to the Devout Life*, trans. John K. Ryan (Garden City, N.Y.: Doubleday and Co., 1955), p. 88.
20. See "An Interview with Elizabeth Bishop," 9.
21. Ibid., p. 11.
22. S. T. Coleridge, "On Poesy or Art," in *Biographia Literaria*, ed. J. Shawcross, vol. 2 (London: Oxford University Press, 1907), p. 258.
23. Ibid., p. 259.
24. Willard Spiegelman, "Elizabeth Bishop's 'Natural Heroism,' " *Centennial Review* 22, no. 1 (Winter 1978): 35.
25. Wallace Stevens, "From Miscellaneous Notebooks," in *Opus Posthumous*, ed. Milton J. Bates (New York: Alfred A. Knopf, 1989), p. 204.
26. Dylan Thomas, Prefatory "Note," in *The Collected Poems* (New York: New Directions, 1953), p. xiii.
27. Robert Mazzocco, "A Poet of Landscape," in *New York Review of Books* 9, no. 6 (12 October 1967): 6.

6. Robert Penn Warren's Career in Poetry: Taking Counsel of the Heart Alone

1. "Robert Penn Warren: An Interview," in *Robert Penn Warren: A Vision Earned*, ed. Marshall Walker (New York: Harper and Row, 1979), p. 225.
2. A good deal of this kind of excess has, of course, been pared away in the revised version of *Brother to Dragons*, published in 1979. But the results of poets undertaking to "improve" already published work often proves something poorer than the original. Indeed, Warren himself did express misgivings about John Crowe Ransom's efforts in this direction. And, in the case of his own book of 1953, the 1979 version, though there are many points gaining force through its leaner rhetoric, it does too frequently obscure the logic of his thought and weaken the momentum in his narrative, as Richard Chris-

man cogently argues in his essay in *Robert Penn Warren's Brother to Dragons: A Discussion*, ed. James A. Grimshaw, Jr. (Baton Rouge: Louisiana State University Press, 1983).

3. Jefferson's silence is confirmed as thoroughly as no doubt it can be by careful historical scholarship in Boynton Merrill's *Jefferson's Nephews: A Frontier Tragedy* (Princeton: Princeton University Press, 1976): "No evidence has been discovered . . . that Jefferson ever wrote or spoke a word directly concerning this crime, or that it changed his life or attitudes." Warren's rehearsal of the story in his 1953 text differs in several small details from Merrill's authoritative reconstruction. But in the preface to the 1953 version of *Brother to Dragons*, though he had declared it to have been his intention to stay "within the outlines of [the] record," he had insisted that he had been "trying to write a poem and not a history, and therefore . . . [had not had any] compunction about tampering with facts." Nevertheless, in his 1979 text he takes advantage of Merrill's work in certain particulars. He corrects the spelling of the elder brother's name, changing it from "Lilburn" to "Lilburne," as he also corrects the spelling of Lilburne's wife's name, changing it from "Laetitia" to "Letitia." Or, again, Merrill having shown that Lilburne Lewis's father was not a physician and deserved only the title of his rank in the Revolutionary Army, he is spoken of in the 1979 text not as Dr. Lewis but as Colonel Lewis. And other small corrections of a similar sort are also made.

4. "Robert Penn Warren: An Interview," p. 255.

5. Peter Stitt, *The World's Hieroglyphic Beauty* (Athens: University of Georgia Press, 1985), pp. 241–58.

6. Calvin Bedient, *In the Heart's Last Kingdom: Robert Penn Warren's Major Poetry* (Cambridge: Harvard University Press, 1984), p. 3. and p. 12.

7. See Harold Bloom's "Introduction" (pp. 1–11) and his essay "Sunset Hawk: Warren's Poetry and Tradition" (pp. 195–210), in *Robert Penn Warren*, ed. Harold Bloom (New York and New Haven: Chelsea House, 1986).

8. Paul Mariani, *A Usable Past: Essays on Modern and Contemporary Poetry* (Amherst: University of Massachusetts Press), p. 166.

9. Stitt, *The World's Hieroglyphic Beauty*, p. 216 and p. 258.

7. The Poetry of Richard Wilbur: "The Splendor of Mere Being"

1. Richard Wilbur, "On My Own Work," in *Responses: Prose Pieces, 1953–1976* (New York: Harcourt Brace Jovanovich, 1976), p. 125.

2. Richard Wilbur, "The House of Poe," in *The Recognition of Edgar Allan Poe*, ed. Eric W. Carlson (Ann Arbor: University of Michigan Press, 1966), p. 277.

3. Quoted in Wilbur, "Edgar Allan Poe," in *Responses*, p. 46.

4. Ibid., pp. 63–64.

5. Charles Williams, *The Figure of Beatrice: A Study in Dante* (London: Faber and Faber, 1943), p. 44.

6. Jonathan Edwards, "Notes on the Mind," in *The Works of President Edwards*, ed. Serano E. Dwight, vol. 1 (New York, 1829), p. 676.

7. Perry Miller, *Jonathan Edwards* (New York: William Sloane Associates, 1949), p. xii.

8. Irving Howe, *The American Newness: Culture and Politics in the Age of Emerson* (Cambridge: Harvard University Press, 1986), pp. 69–70.

9. Theodore Holmes, "A Prophet without Prophecy," *Poetry* 100, no. 1 (April 1962): 38.

10. Randall Jarrell, *Poetry and the Age* (New York: Vintage Books, 1955), pp. 227 and 229.

11. Holmes, "A Prophet without Prophecy," p. 38.

12. See *New Republic* 174, no. 23 (5 June 1976): 21.

13. Robert Duncan, "Towards an Open Universe," in *Poets on Poetry*, ed. Howard Nemerov (New York: Basic Books, 1966), p. 139.

14. Richard Wilbur, "The Art of Poetry," *Paris Review* 19, no. 72 (Winter 1977): 83.

8. *The Poetry of A. R. Ammons*

1. See Delmore Schwartz, "The Fiction Chronicle: The Wrongs of Innocence and Experience," *Partisan Review* 19, no. 3 (May-June 1952): 359: "Reality (hear! hear!) is not mocked . . . as long as such a book [*Invisible Man*] can be written."

9. *James Wright's Lyricism*

1. Robert Bly, "The Work of Robert Creeley," *Fifties* 2 (1959): 14.

2. Robert Bly, "A Wrong Turning in American Poetry," *Choice* 3 (1963): 40, 47.

3. Paul Breslin, *The Psycho-Political Muse: American Poetry since the Fifties* (Chicago: University of Chicago Press, 1987), p. 120.

4. Cleanth Brooks, "Poetry since *The Waste Land*," *Southern Review* 1, n.s. (Summer 1965): 499.

5. Galway Kinnell, *The Book of Nightmares* (Boston: Houghton Mifflin, 1971), p. 52.

6. All quotations from Wright's poetry are from *Above the River: The Complete Poems* (New York: Farrar, Straus and Giroux and University Press of New England, 1990); hereafter cited in the text *AR*.

7. "Interview with James Wright," in Peter Stitt, *The World's Hieroglyphic Beauty* (Athens: University of Georgia Press, 1985), p. 203. This interview—"The Art of Poetry XIX: James Wright"—first appeared in the *Paris Review* 16 (Summer 1975): 34–61.

8. "Something to Be Said for the Light: A Conversation with William Heyen and Jerome Mazzaro," *Southern Humanities Review* 6 (1972): 134–53.

9. James Wright, "A Note on Trakl," in *Collected Prose*, ed. Anne Wright (Ann Arbor: University of Michigan Press, 1983), pp. 83–84.

10. James E. B. Breslin, *From Modern to Contemporary: American Poetry, 1945–1965* (Chicago: University of Chicago Press, 1984), p. 206.

11. James Wright, "An Interview with Michael André," in *Collected Prose*, pp. 145–46.

12. Hank Lazer thoughtfully discusses the role of light in Wright's "uncertain natural theophany" in his essay ""The Heart of Light' " (*Virginia Quarterly Review* 59, no. 4 [Autumn 1983]: 711–24.

13. Thomas Traherne, *Centuries* (New York: Harper and Brothers, 1960), p. 13.

14. Ibid., p. 14.

15. Ibid., p. 15.

16. Ibid., p. 17.

17. Wright, *Collected Prose*, p. 27.

18. "Dumnesse," *The Poetical Works of Thomas Traherne*, ed. Gladys I. Wade (London, P. J. and A. E. Dobell, 1932), p. 24.

10. *Howard Nemerov's Broken Music*

1. Wallace Stevens, *The Necessary Angel* (New York: Vintage Books, 1965), p. 27.

2. Howard Nemerov, *Reflexions on Poetry & Poetics* (New Brunswick: Rutgers University Press, 1972), p. 166.

3. Willard Spiegelman, *The Didactic Muse: Scenes of Instruction in Contemporary American Poetry* (Princeton: Princeton University Press, 1989), p. 36.

4. Robert Boyers, *Excursions: Selected Literary Essays* (Port Washington, N.Y.: Kennikat Press, 1977), p. 222.

BIBLIOGRAPHICAL NOTES AND
ACKNOWLEDGMENTS

I want first of all to say that I am deeply grateful to four friends and colleagues at the University of Virginia—David Levin, J. C. Levenson, and Robert and Francesca Langbaum—for their counsel in relation to one or another phase of this book and for the affirmation of my endeavors that they have generously offered over many years. But, of course, as authors commonly declare in this connection, these friends bear no responsibility for such errors and misconstructions as may be found here.

•

Certain chapters of this book have previously appeared in journals to whose editors I am grateful for the readiness with which they acceded to the reissuance of essays that they originally published. The chapter on Elizabeth Bishop first appeared in the *Virginia Quarterly Review* (60, no. 2 [Spring 1984]) and is here published by permission of the editor, Staige D. Blackford. The essay on A. R. Ammons first appeared in the *Southern Review* (24, no. 4, n.s. [Autumn 1988]), as did the essay on James Wright (27, no. 2, n.s. [Spring 1991]), and both are published here with the permission of the editors. The essay on Richard Wilbur first appeared in *Christianity and Literature* (39, no. 1 [Autumn 1989]) and is published here with the permission of the editor, Robert Snyder. And the essay on Robert Penn Warren first appeared in the *Centennial Review* (33, no. 2 [Spring 1989]) and is published here by permission of the managing editor, Cheryllee Finney.

The chapter on Wallace Stevens originally appeared in my book *The Poetics of Belief,* and it is reissued here with the permission of the publisher, the University of North Carolina Press (copyright © 1985).

The chapter on Theodore Roethke first appeared in my book *The Wild Prayer of Longing: Poetry and the Sacred,* and it is reissued here with the permission of the publisher, the Yale University Press (copyright © 1971).

The essay on W. H. Auden first appeared in my book *The Poetry of Civic*

Virtue (copyright © 1976, Fortress Press), and it is reissued here by permission of Augsburg Fortress.

·

Margaret Nemerov has granted me permission to quote passages from volumes of Howard Nemerov's poetry published by the University of Chicago Press. Edward Mendelson, on behalf of the Estate of W. H. Auden (which holds the copyrights for his work), has granted me permission to quote passages from his poetry. Mary E. Ryan, the permissions manager of W. W. Norton and Co., has granted me permission to quote passages from A. R. Ammons's *Briefings, Collected Poems: 1951–1971, Lake Effect Country, The Snow Poems, Sphere,* and *Tape for the Turn of the Year.* Wesleyan University Press, by permission of the University Press of New England and Farrar, Straus and Giroux, has consented to my quoting passages from James Wright's *Above the River: The Complete Poems* (copyright © 1990 by Anne Wright). And for these permissions I am most deeply grateful, since in each case all fees were waived—which represents a quite remarkable generosity in a period when, more and more, publishing houses are outrageously exacting huge sums of money from working scholars who need in critical studies to quote passages from volumes of poetry which they have issued, and this kind of inhospitality I have suffered at the hands of many firms.

·

Quotations from the following poems of Theodore Roethke (from *The Collected Poems of Theodore Roethke*) are used by permission of Doubleday, a division of Bantam Doubleday Dell Publishing Group, Inc.: "Root Cellar," copyright © 1943 by Modern Poetry Association, Inc.; "Meditations of an Old Woman," copyright © 1958 by Theodore Roethke; "The Light Comes Brighter," copyright © 1938 by Theodore Roethke; "Cuttings (Later)," copyright © 1948 by Theodore Roethke; "Weed Puller," copyright © 1946 by Editorial Publications, Inc.; "The Minimal," copyright © 1942 by Theodore Roethke; "Transplanting," copyright © 1948 by Theodore Roethke; "Old Florist," copyright © 1946 by Harper and Brothers; "Frau Bauman, Frau Schmidt and Frau Schwartze," copyright © 1952 by Theodore Roethke; "Where Knock Is Open Wide," copyright © 1950 by Theodore Roethke; "O Lull Me, Lull Me," copyright © 1951 by Theodore Roethke; "Bring the Day!," copyright © 1951 by Theodore Roethke; "The Lost Son," copyright © 1947 by Theodore Roethke; "A Field of Light," copyright © 1948 by *The Tiger's Eye;* "Words for the Wind," copyright © 1955 by Theodore Roethke; "I Knew a Woman," copyright © 1954 by Theodore Roethke; "The Partner," copyright © 1952 by Theodore

Roethke; "The Wraith," copyright © 1953 by Theodore Roethke; "The Sensualists," copyright © by Theodore Roethke; "First Meditation," copyright © 1955 by Theodore Roethke; "The Abyss," copyright © 1963 by Beatrice Roethke, Administratrix of the Estate of Theodore Roethke; "The Shape of the Fire," copyright © 1947 by Theodore Roethke.

Quoted passages from *Collected Poems* by Wallace Stevens (copyright © 1954 by Wallace Stevens) and from *Opus Posthumous* by Wallace Stevens (copyright © 1957 by Elsie Stevens and Holly Stevens) are reprinted by permission of Alfred A. Knopf, Inc.

Excerpts from *The Complete Poems: 1927–1979* by Elizabeth Bishop (copyright © 1979, 1983 by Alice Helen Methfessel) are reprinted by permission of Farrar, Straus and Giroux, Inc.

Excerpts from *Above the River* by James Wright (copyright © 1990 by Anne Wright) are reprinted by permission of Farrar, Straus and Giroux, Inc.

An excerpt from "The Mind Reader" in *The Mind Reader and Other Poems* (copyright © 1976 by Richard Wilbur) is reprinted by permission of Harcourt Brace Jovanovich, Inc. An excerpt from "Lying" in Richard Wilbur's *New and Collected Poems* (copyright © 1988 by Richard Wilbur) is reprinted by permission of Harcourt Brace Jovanovich, Inc. "Praise in Summer" and an excerpt from "Objects" in Richard Wilbur's *The Beautiful Changes and Other Poems* (copyright © 1947 and renewed 1975 by Richard Wilbur) are reprinted by permission of Harcourt Brace Jovanovich, Inc. Excerpts from "A World without Objects Is a Sensible Emptiness" and "Giacometti" in Richard Wilbur's *Ceremony and Other Poems* (copyright © 1950 and renewed 1978 by Richard Wilbur) are reprinted by permission of Harcourt Brace Jovanovich, Inc. An excerpt from "Love Calls Us to the Things of This World" in Richard Wilbur's *Things of This World* (copyright © 1956 and renewed 1984 by Richard Wilbur) is reprinted by permission of Harcourt Brace Jovanovich, Inc. An excerpt from "All These Birds" in Richard Wilbur's *Things of This World* (copyright © 1955 and renewed 1983 by Richard Wilbur) is reprinted by permission of Harcourt Brace Jovanovich, Inc. This poem originally appeared in *The New Yorker*. An excerpt from "The Beacon" in Richard Wilbur's *Things of This World* (copyright © 1952 and renewed 1980 by Richard Wilbur) is reprinted by permission of Harcourt Brace Jovanovich, Inc. This poem originally appeared in *The New Yorker*. An excerpt from "Aspen and the Stream" in Richard Wilbur's *Advice to a Prophet and Other Poems* (copyright © 1961 and renewed 1989 by Richard Wilbur) is reprinted by permission of Harcourt Brace Jovanovich, Inc. This poem originally appeared in *The New Yorker*. An excerpt from "Walking to Sleep" in Richard Wilbur's *Walking to Sleep: New Poems and Translations* (copyright © 1967 by Richard Wilbur) is reprinted by permission of Harcourt Brace Jovanovich, Inc. An excerpt from "For Dudley" in Richard Wilbur's *Walking to Sleep: New Poems and Translations* (copyright © 1969 by Richard Wilbur) is reprinted by permission of Harcourt Brace Jovanovich, Inc.

Quotations from *Brother to Dragons* by Robert Penn Warren (copyright © 1953 by Robert Penn Warren) are reprinted by permission of Random House, Inc. Quotations from Robert Penn Warren's *Promises: Poems 1954–1956* (copyright © 1957 by Robert Penn Warren) are reprinted by permission of Random House, Inc. Quotations from Robert Penn Warren's *Being Here: Poetry 1977–1980* (copyright © 1978, 1979, 1980 by Robert Penn Warren) are reprinted by permission of Random House, Inc. Quotations from Robert Penn Warren's *New and Selected Poems: 1923–1975* (copyright © 1985 by Robert Penn Warren) are reprinted by permission of Random House, Inc.

Quotations from James Wright's *This Journey* (copyright © 1977, 1978, 1979, 1980, 1981, 1982 by Anne Wright, Executrix of the Estate of James Wright) are reprinted by permission of Random House, Inc.

INDEX

Addison, Joseph, 191
Albertus Magnus, 210
Aldington, Richard, 226
Alvarez, A., 16
Ammons, A. R., 169, 199–224
Anderson, Quentin, 174
André, Michael, 238
Arendt, Hannah, 69–74, 79, 80
Aristotle, 28
Arnold, Matthew, 112
Ashbery, John, 252
Athanasius, St., 173, 207
Auden, W. H., 8, 40–86, 108, 117, 119, 164, 185, 199, 268
Audubon, John James, 159
Ayer, A. J., 28

Bacon, Francis, 116
Barth, Karl, 49
Bates, Milton J., 14
Baudelaire, Charles, 49, 198
Bayley, John, 117
Bedient, Calvin, 163, 182
Bell, Daniel, 79
Bellow, Saul, 106
Bentham, Jeremy, 116
Berdyaev, Nicolas, 68
Bishop, Elizabeth, 116–35, 194, 260
Blackmur, R. P., 40
Blake, William, 10, 49, 114, 235
Bloom, Harold, 27, 156, 163, 174, 202, 223
Bly, Robert, 194, 225, 226, 227, 229
Boehme, Jakob, 29
Bonifazi, Conrad, 90
Borges, Jorge Luis, 198
Boyers, Robert, 274

Breslin, James E. B., 236
Brooks, Cleanth, 226
Browning, Elizabeth Barrett, 175
Buber, Martin, 74, 91, 107
Bugbee, Henry G., 2, 6
Burke, Kenneth, 95
Butler, Joseph, 203
Byron, George Gordon, Sixth Baron (Albè), 121

Cajetan, Tommaso de Vio, 210
Camus, Albert, 94
Carlyle, Thomas, 107
Chaning-Pearce, M., 6
Church, Henry, 17
Ciardi, John, 99
Clampitt, Amy, 8
Clark, Eleanor, 148
Clemens, Samuel Langhorne [pseud. Mark Twain], 106, 176
Cochrane, Charles Norris, 70
Cocteau, Jean, 55, 209
Coghill, Nevill, 82
Coleridge, Samuel Taylor, 3, 126, 145–47, 171, 223, 262
Comte, Auguste, 49
Conrad, Joseph, 117, 133
Crane, Hart, 8
Creeley, Robert, 194
Cummings, E. E., 8

Dante, 8, 174
Davies, Sir John, 109
Davison, Peter, 8
Dickinson, Emily, 40
Dionysius the Areopagite, 29, 173, 207
Donne, John, 122, 274

By NATHAN A. SCOTT, JR.

Rehearsals of Discomposure: Alienation and Reconciliation
in Modern Literature (1952)

Modern Literature and the Religious Frontier (1958)

Albert Camus (1962)

Reinhold Niebuhr (1963)

Samuel Beckett (1965)

The Broken Center: Studies in the Theological Horizon
of Modern Literature (1966)

Ernest Hemingway (1966)

Craters of the Spirit: Studies in the Modern Novel (1968)

Negative Capability: Studies in the New Literature and the Religious Situation (1969)

The Unquiet Vision: Mirrors of Man in Existentialism (1969)

Nathanael West (1971)

The Wild Prayer of Longing: Poetry and the Sacred (1971)

Three American Moralists—Mailer, Bellow, Trilling (1973)

The Poetry of Civic Virtue—Eliot, Malraux, Auden (1976)

Mirrors of Man in Existentialism (1978)

The Poetics of Belief: Studies in Coleridge, Arnold, Pater, Santayana,
Stevens, and Heidegger (1985)

EDITED BY NATHAN A. SCOTT, JR.

The Tragic Vision and the Christian Faith (1957)

The New Orpheus: Essays toward a Christian Poetic (1964)

The Climate of Faith in Modern Literature (1964)

Man in the Modern Theatre (1965)

Four Ways of Modern Poetry (1965)

Forms of Extremity in the Modern Novel (1965)

The Modern Vision of Death (1967)

Adversity and Grace: Studies in Recent American Literature (1968)

The Legacy of Reinhold Niebuhr (1975)

Nathan A. Scott, Jr., is William R. Kenan Professor Emeritus of Religious Studies and Professor Emeritus of English at the University of Virginia. Among his many books are *Samuel Beckett, The Broken Center, Negative Capability, The Wild Prayer of Longing, The Poetry of Civic Virtue,* and *The Poetics of Belief.* He is a Fellow of the American Academy of Arts and Sciences, and he holds honorary degrees from the University of Michigan, Brown, Northwestern, Wesleyan, Bates College, the University of the South, and numerous other institutions.

Designed by Laury A. Egan

Composed by Graphic Composition, Inc.,
in Palatino text and display

Printed on 50-lb. Glatfelter MV Eggshell
and bound in Holliston Aqualite
by The Maple Press Company

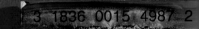